THE LELE OF THE KASAI

Old man sewing raffia skirt

The Lele of the Kasai

MARY DOUGLAS

Published for the
INTERNATIONAL AFRICAN INSTITUTE
by the
OXFORD UNIVERSITY PRESS
LONDON   IBADAN   ACCRA
1963

Oxford University Press, Amen House, London E.C.4

GLASGOW   NEW YORK   TORONTO   MELBOURNE   WELLINGTON
BOMBAY   CALCUTTA   MADRAS   KARACHI   LAHORE   DACCA
CAPE TOWN   SALISBURY   NAIROBI   IBADAN   ACCRA
KUALA LUMPUR   HONG KONG

PRINTED IN GREAT BRITAIN

CONTENTS

ILLUSTRATIONS

FIGURES

TABLES

ACKNOWLEDGEMENTS

I wish to thank the International African Institute for the Fellowship by which both my visits to the Lele were paid for and organized, particularly the secretary, Mrs. Wyatt for her personal part, and also the *Institut de Recherche Scientifique dans l'Afrique Centrale* for its further financial and practical support.

It is impossible for me to name all the people in Belgium and the Congo who gave me help and hospitality. I am specially grateful to the late Professor F. M. Olbrechts and also to his successor at the *Musée Royale de l'Afrique Centrale* at Tervuren, M. Louis Cahen and to M. J. P. Harroy who was then Secretary General of I.R.S.A.C. In the Congo itself I am grateful to the members of the Colonial Administration whose help was given with such courtesy and tact, particularly to M. Vandenbossche, at that time Curator of the *Musée de la Vie Indigène* at Léopoldville and to M. Georges Brausch on whose good advice I originally chose the Lele for my study and who let me draw generously on his experience. The Company office of the Huileries du Congo Belge and its Research Department jointly took over all responsibility for my communications and transport; the Sisters of St. Vincent de Paul at Brabanta energetically solved all my other practical problems and I thank all three for having kept an eye on my general well-being.

Mr. A. W. Excell of the Natural History Museum helped me to identify plants, M. A. J. Jobaerts of the Bushimaie Game Reserve helped me to identify animals of the Kasai region, and Professor Meeussen of Tervuren helped me to understand Lele grammar. I was specially lucky in the presence of my old friend and colleague, Professor J. Vansina in the adjoining territory, as his study of the Bushong threw light on the special character of Lele culture. I cannot thank individually the many Lele who gave me friendship and help, but Makum Elias stands out in my memory for his strong support and for the epic quality which livened his discussion of Lele ways. All their names have, of course, been changed.

Too many years have gone by since I started this study and I fear that without a Fellowship from the Leverhulme Research Awards Committee and a year's leave of absence from University College, London, it would still not be written. I am very grateful to both bodies.

In the intervening time several articles have appeared on the Lele and I thank the publishers of *Africa, Zaïre*, and the *Journal of the Royal Anthropological Institute* for permission to draw on the same material and also Professor Forde, Professor Bohannan and Dr. Middleton for permission to use material from symposia which they have edited. I would also like to thank those who have at different times read and criticized parts of the manuscript, amongst others, Professor Gluckman, Mr. Robin Horton, Dr. V. Turner, Mr. W. B. Fagg and Mr. Maurice Snowden. I also owe thanks to Miss Barbara Pym for her help in seeing the manuscript through the press.

There are two people to whom my personal debt is greatest of all. Professor Evans Pritchard first taught me anthropology and set a standard for fieldwork of humility, patience and honesty which I can no more reach than his technical standard though both have been an inspiration. After fieldwork I came to London and so incurred my second great debt. Professor Forde knows very well that the book would never have been finished but for his constant guidance and encouragement, but it is impossible for him to know the full extent of my gratitude for his teaching, detailed criticism and friendship.

INTRODUCTION

THIS is primarily a study of authority—or rather of its failure. Those who have had anything to do with Lele must have noticed the absence of anyone who could give orders with a reasonable hope of being obeyed. They are not aggressive individualists refusing the right of others to command. On the contrary, Lele manners are humorously modest rather than self-assertive. Authority is supposed to reside with the senior person present in any situation. In practice the senior receives deference, but not power. The lack of authority goes a long way to explain their poverty. By their own standards the Lele are poorer than their neighbours. Their soil is admittedly less fertile, but a lack of enthusiasm for cultivating it is also evident. Other projects engross them more than the creation of wealth. Second, therefore, this is a study in economic backwardness.

Any society makes its own adaptation of means and ends. To appreciate the Lele way of life we should consider the kind of society they might have had. They contrast with the Lundaized Chokwe and Ndembu to the south and east. These tribes also practise hand-cultivation in a somewhat similar forest-park environment. They have small villages founded on matrilineal kinship and grouped into little chiefdoms. The headman is the focus of village unity. His office is desired and the principle of selection for it is sufficiently uncertain to divide the village between rival aspirants. Social life is strenuously competitive as candidates for headmanship strive to attract adherents. It is certainly not an old man's world. Dr. Turner,[1] commenting on why Ndembu try to keep headmanship in the older generation, says that the general run of old men are mocked mercilessly and need the support of one of themselves in office.

All this is utterly alien to the Lele way of life. They never came under Lunda domination, probably having arrived in their area after Lunda expansion to the west had subsided. Their villages were larger, averaging 170 souls and many numbering over 400; in them village-wide institutions were emphasized at the expense

[1] 1959, p. 125.

of matrilineal kinship. Overt leadership was at a minimum and competition for office practically eliminated by unequivocal selection by seniority. The principle of seniority applied throughout their social system made in one sense an old man's world. It is unthinkable that old age should be ridiculed in such a culture.

To write of a culture as dominated by a single preoccupation is grossly to simplify. Lele institutions combined an infinite range of intentions. But if any one desire seemed paramount, it would be to secure dignity and well-being for old age. Tradition, order and stability for society at large are included with this, but some other things are not compatible. Lele would have needed a different philosophy for the all-out exploitation of their country.

It is easy to enumerate the ways in which they committed themselves to greater poverty than their neighbours. Their institutions were simply not directed to maximizing material wealth. In a sense, their low standard of life was the price of their unrealistic distribution of status, for in a primitive economy everything is weighted against the old. To try to invest the weakest section of the community with authority smacks of the quixotic—it could scarcely succeed. Therefore their society was without real authority, ridden with devious, hidden controls and vulnerable to external pressures for change.

The most important social unit of the Lele was the village. It was entirely autonomous. It did not fit like Chinese nesting boxes in a series of larger and smaller units. Compared with Chokwe villages it seems large, but taking it as the biggest social unit which Lele achieved, it is small indeed.

It looked small too. The sparse population (only four to the square mile) was gathered into numerous, compact, little settlements. The oblong raffia-frond houses were closely sited, often attached back to back, around an open square. Privacy within the family was partly sacrificed to the pleasure of living at close quarters, for a conversation in one hut could easily be joined by quiet voices from the next. If two men wanted to share a secret, they repaired to the middle of the square, the farthest point from eavesdroppers. The groupings of the houses did not correspond to kinship groupings. Men of the same age built near one another and away from their parents. They did not form 'age-villages' of the Nyakyusa type, but their age-quarters in a village had a similar role in diluting the intensity of kinship ties.

The corporate personality of the village was well to the fore in an elaborate organization of communal wives, communal children, communal sons-in-law and a communal treasury. Members of the village were recruited through the clan sections they belonged to, but the latter were important only for allocating wives and widows, and organizing blood-compensation. In village activities, individuals entered largely as individuals or as members of an age group, rather than as representatives of a clan.

Since marriage took place between villages and since women went to join their husbands, their matrilineal descendants started life dispersed through the various villages in which they had been born, but they eventually reassembled sooner or later. Everyone recognized the need to attract young men to maintain the size of the village and the balance of the generations. Though they did not talk, of course, in terms of a top-heavy age-pyramid, they were very explicit about the disadvantages of a village without enough young men. The various clan sections in a village tried to attract members from all quarters, wherever they had been born and however they were related. Not only fellow-clansmen but sons and grandchildren of the clan were warmly canvassed to stay and make their home together. This anxiety to recruit may explain why they soft-pedalled distinctions of descent within the clan. Anyone who joined was entitled to full parity of status, regardless of genealogical relationship. By his age and by nothing else a man found his correct position in his local clan section.

The deliberate playing down of specific matrilineal kinship laid up a store of difficulties, but it may have contributed to village unity, as well as to recruitment. Unilineal descent is one clear-cut way of allocating roles of authority and subordination. But, in so far as it attaches people together in groups, it detaches them from others. It is bound to import cleavages between descent groups. By not organizing their clan sections on genealogical principles, Lele obviated one cause of village fission. But, at the same time, they committed themselves to leaving roles within the clan section largely undefined. Add to this that the economy did not provide inducements with which seniors could attach junior clansmen to themselves. Seniors offered to young men rights over women and protection from sorcery, but with only one hand, as it were. With the other, the older generation kept the wives to themselves and threatened sorcery if their considerable privileges were not honoured. In this case privilege does not go with authority.

One side-effect of the rule of parity for all-comers was to check changes of residence after a certain age. Young men could be mobile because they increased the manpower wherever they went. But older men, by their seniority, displaced too much room in the status pattern to be welcome in a new village and they were correspondingly less valued as manpower. Other institutions combined to check tendencies to split the village and form new ones. The result was a group of adult men, committed to living together permanently and yet avoiding the most obvious way of regulating their possible conflicts—discrimination between descent lines. To this I attribute the great anxiety which was expressed whenever disputes threatened to flare up.

The productive side of the economy did not at all favour the older men. The Lele redressed the balance between the generations by the way they distributed the things they valued. Entry to cults was by fee and restricted to married men. As the age of marriage was late, this automatically reserved positions of esteem to older men and lined their pockets with the fees of new entrants. Polygyny created a scarcity of marriageable girls;[2] marriage fees were also high. So for the first step on the social ladder, marriage, a man had to go to his wealthy seniors and solicit their aid. Often a young man, receiving financial help, never touched the goods which were transferred in his name direct from one old man to another. And the same goes for every subsequent step, since wealth was thus drawn into the control of the older married men.

One may well ask why young men allowed their bachelorhood to be prolonged to middle age and accepted inferior cult status. In practice, the various institutions combined to make a framework from which an individual could hardly have broken out. They eagerly threw it over when the missions gave them an

[2] The ratio of the sexes was nearly equal. The doctor at Brabanta in charge of the Medical Census for 1949 calculated that there was only an 8 per cent excess of adult women.

opportunity. Until then they accepted the compensations which the system itself reserved for them. One was a life of freedom. In the old days, before they married, they were expected to do very little agricultural work, for their clan seniors had little control over them. Another compensation was the sharing of a communal wife. Another was the excitement of war between villages. Thus the low level of political integration was closely correlated with the general bias of their social system.

Although the older men had little direct power, it does not follow that the unmarried young men had power either, except the negative power of withdrawal. They could threaten to go away if their senior clansmen or fathers were too exigent or made things unpleasant with their complaints. The threat to leave the village was the last resort, the testing point at which the system of authority failed. But long before that point was reached it was anticipated by the undemanding behaviour of the older men. They never, or rarely, commanded so they were never, or rarely, defied. This is where polygyny appears as the essential, dominant institution. Older men were not well served by their junior relatives but, by reserving the marriageable girls for themselves, they were able to head large compounds, be served by female labour in the fields, beget many daughters and get some service for specified tasks by sons-in-law. The son-in-law was explicitly subordinate to the father-in-law—the one role of authority which was precisely defined without reference to age. By virtue of the shortage of wives, which polygyny created, men could get their sons-in-law to give the necessary help which they were not certain of getting from their own clansmen. In short, the principle of seniority was able to be applied right through the society, even to the upper age groups because the most important rights were rights over women acquired by parenthood and grandparenthood. Thus the delayed maturity of young men was the corollary of the delayed retirement of old men.

A high level of efficiency is not very likely where authority is weak. The environment of the Lele was poor but they exploited it with nothing like the steady application of certain close neighbours, the Pende of Gungu on the west or the Bushong on the east. They tended to work for a shorter period, to use less equipment and to aim at shorter-term results. Their soil was poor enough in all conscience and explained some of their poverty. But there is no denying that Lele were more interested in maintaining a certain distribution of prestige than in rewarding maximum efforts of production. Their social institutions were not consistent with the fullest possible exploitation of the environment. They were committed to hostility between generations in a village and hostility between villages, to ill-will and insecurity, enemies of sustained collaboration.

Without supposing that they consciously made these choices, I see them as falling into contradictions and conflicts in the course of attempting two difficult things. One is a large, compact, social unit—their village was larger than the needs of their type of economy would seem to warrant and larger than achieved by other tribes in similar circumstances.[3] The other is to protect a class which is at once vulnerable and important, the older men. These two objectives are probably related. A very small village could hardly maintain the number of cult and age associations and other complex institutions giving prestige to older members; and its inhabitants would be less amenable to this complicated method of directing wealth into the hands of the older men.

Any community has some kind of geriatric policy, even if only a negative one. Seniority, although it favours one age group, is basically egalitarian. Everyone has an equal stake in such a system, if only they live long enough to enjoy the postponed rewards. Lele consent is given implicitly at the earliest age at which a boy demands respect from his younger brother. Their stake increases with every year of waiting. The precedence of seniors is, therefore, one of the values implicit in the culture, subscribed to by all, unquestioned, in spite of the difficulties which it entails.

Sorcery beliefs complete and confirm the same picture from another angle. Since men past middle age could not easily change their village and so were penned together, as it were, indefinitely, sorcery suspicions could have made havoc with village peace. The special bias of their sorcery beliefs actually promoted the unity of the village by deepening suspicion of outsiders and provoking action against members who were unamenable to moral pressures. The general image of a sorcerer was an old man who was a skilled diviner. Consequently, diviners had a keen personal interest in diverting or checking indiscriminate accusations.

[3] See Chapter I, p. 28, for the comparative figures.

They tended to cite the dead, or unnamed enemies from other villages, thus boosting village solidarity at the expense of friendly external relations.

In spite of the restraining influence of diviners, an individual might attract such odium in his village that sorcery accusations would begin to pile up against him, each making the next more convincing. In the old days, the poison ordeal applied to the accused was the final arbiter, unlocking otherwise insoluble conflicts. Without this recourse, the Lele village could not deal with unassimilable characters: at any time they might emerge, men who threatened the harmony of the village, regularly pursuing other men's wives and falling below the approved standard of suavely controlled behaviour.

Men accused of sorcery in their own village were generally members of large clan sections where the confusingly undefined relationships were more disorganizing than in very small groups. They were often men who had pushed claims to authority too far. A number of well-aimed accusations could ruin them. Thus sorcery beliefs balanced the system of secret cults which purported to reserve power to the old men. Putting the whip into the hands of the young, sorcery beliefs gave the finishing touch to the negation of authority.

Suspicion and secrecy about their affairs made an intensive study of one single community the only course. Although I collected simple quantitative information from farther afield, the best case material comes from the village in which I lived the longest. In a culture of this kind, extensive surveys yield little that is trustworthy. Esotericism in cults, fear of attracting jealousy of neighbours, hostility against any outsider, were part of the culture. Furthermore, their central institutions had been all too recently suppressed. In 1948 the law against polyandry came into effect. In 1949, the Chief Perominenge having died, attempts to kill slaves at his funeral were checked. An anti-sorcery cult was being suppressed in 1953, at the time of my second visit, so it was clear that no dividends would come from a widening of the field of work. Fortunately each village drew much of its male population and its wives from abroad and there was frequent visiting between friendly villages. So I was able to check the general validity of my conclusions and to judge the extent to which the chosen village was typical or exceptional.

But its affairs opened such a wide window on Lele society at large that to understand what was happening in this one village we need a substantial book.

It is eight years since I last visited the Lele. This in itself would not justify departure from the usual practice of writing ethnography in the present tense. But in the last three years the Congo has changed so radically that it is very unlikely that things are still as I knew them. It is possible that the Lele villages, free from colonial restraint, have taken up their ancient antagonisms in more violent form. We know that they resorted again to the poison ordeal after Belgian administration had lapsed, and before the Congo became formally independent. It is very unlikely that the younger generation will have returned to its old straitjacket of the old society. But at present there is no means of knowing whether they have reverted direct to old customs, interrupted for only one generation—between 1933 and 1959—or whether new political interventions have changed their lives in a different direction. This is why I have preferred to use the past tense in this study.

Note on orthography

A soft Italian *c* instead of *tch* has been used in the spelling of Lele personal and clan names.

I

THE LELE ON THE MAP

Relation with other tribes

SUSPICIOUS, uncouth, warlike, the Lele struck Torday as
primitive compared with the Bushong. The artistry and charm
of Bushong villages contrasted with the fortified homes of the
Lele.

Here too we found enclosures, but instead of the leaf-walls which are
considered sufficient amongst the Bushongo, the separations were
palisades formed by solid stakes, driven into the ground. Such a wall
surrounded the whole village, and the single entrance was so arranged
that no more than one person was able to enter at a time.[1]

His companion gives a similar impression of a narrow, closed-
in way of life:

So little do the Bashilele wander beyond the immediate surroundings
of their own homes that very few of the inhabitants of any village are
acquainted with the track even to the next settlement of their own tribe:
and we found that often, even when carrying our loads to another
Bashilele village, the men would arm as if for war.[2]

In many villages they judged it wiser not to penetrate the
palisades; in others Lele accepted salt and knives, but were unwilling to carry their luggage to the next halt. Once the party
would have been stranded had not Torday won over the women
when the men refused to help. For lack of friendly informants
nearly everything that he wrote of the Lele was gleaned from
Bushong sources or confined to what he could observe with his
own eyes.[3]

His impression of the Lele as an outpost of Bushong culture,
independent and unruly, is accurate. Lele and Bushong and the
other members of the group of tribes known by outsiders as Kuba
reached their present territory some 250 years ago.[4] They

[1] 1925, p. 231.
[2] Simpson, 1911, p. 332.
[3] Torday and Joyce, 1910, pp. 16 and 46.
[4] Vansina, *Zaïre*, 1959.

9

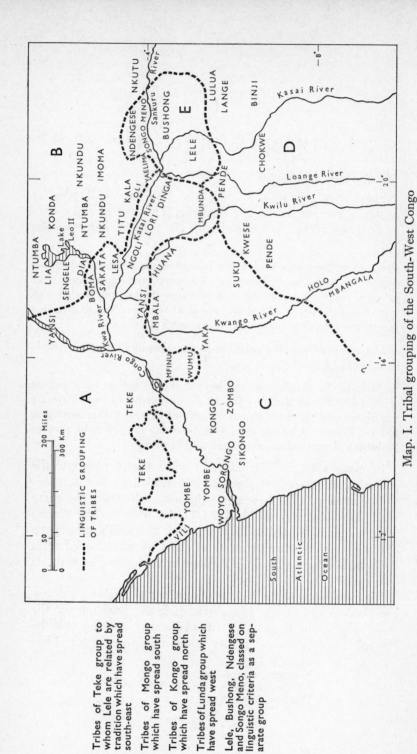

Map. I. Tribal grouping of the South-West Congo

A Tribes of Teke group to whom Lele are related by tradition which have spread south-east

B Tribes of Mongo group which have spread south

C Tribes of Kongo group which have spread north

D Tribes of Lunda group which have spread west

E Lele, Bushong, Ndengese and Songo Meno, classed on linguistic criteria as a separate group

LINGUISTIC GROUPING OF TRIBES

formed the van of a movement of peoples from the north-west (affiliated to the Teke of the République du Congo, formerly French Equatorial Africa) who thrust their way up the Kwa, Kwango, Kwilu and Kasai rivers. The Kuba are the eastern outliers of this movement, and the Lele stand on the southern-most point of their expansion.

To understand the relation of these tribes to other neighbours of the Lele we need a wider perspective of the history of this part of the Congo. Soon after the arrival of the Portuguese in Loanda in 1485, the wholesale export of slaves began to dominate the southern Congo. Petty chiefs and overlords became great emperors, with firearms and visible wealth from their commerce in ivory and slaves. Coastal tribes moved inland, pushing inland tribes farther back, and others undertook long migrations from their homes. The traditions of movement, meeting, fighting and retreating or conquering, give the impression of a vast upheaval, great distances covered and hardships endured. Pende escaping north-eastwards from Angola were met by invasions from the east, offshoots of the Lunda empire. Lunda descendants of the Mwata yamvo on the Lulua river came in the early seventeenth century to carve out new chiefdoms for themselves among the Mbangala, Pende, Holo and Suku tribes immediately south and west of the Lele territory, but they never gained suzerainty over the Kuba. If Professor Vansina is right in his historical calculations, Lele and other Kuba peoples were not in this area at the period of Lunda western expansion.

The Kuba group, to which the Lele belong, seems to have started from somewhere near Lake Tumba and Lake Leopold II, perhaps escaping slave raiders supplying the Stanleypool markets. It moved up the Kasai river, crossed it into the Sankuru-Kasai divide, fragments of the group going up the Loange. The present territory of the Lele was occupied by the descendants of one group which, after crossing the Kasai with them, quarrelled with the Bushong leaders, went south on the right bank, and then re-crossed the Kasai to the left bank, and moved north-wards again between the Kasai and Loange rivers. The other members of the original migration, without making this detour, had already settled along the farther banks of the Loange, and remain to this day known as Wongo.

The reversal of direction, from southwards to northwards,

accounts for the Lele current tradition that they came from the south, and for claims of other tribes to have met them near the sources of the Loange.[5] It is not certain what checked their southward movement. The first impetus of their migration had probably spent its force by the time they reached their present territory, which they found practically uninhabited except for a scattering of Pygmoid Chwa peoples. Lele occupation of their own territory from south to north shows the signs of a steady, peaceful expansion, not of a flight from foe or pest. It seems likely that they merely turned north because southwards they had reached the limits of hospitable territory. South of the sixth parallel forests give way to savannah, and the short dry season to one of four months. The vegetation and climate were therefore unfamiliar to people whose original home was near the equator. As Struyf[6] says of the movement of Teke tribes:

ayant traversé la grande forêt équatoriale, en venant du Haut-Fleuve, et en remontant le Kasai, ils s'étaient installés dans les forêts, occupant surtout les rives boisées du fleuve et des rivières . . . ils se sont arrêtés là où les rivières coulent dans les plaines . . .

At the end of their migration, Lele and the other Kuba tribes, having retained some of their own traditions and mingled them with those of their neighbours, now form a distinct cultural group, hardly more to be associated with the Teke than with the Mongo or other neighbours. Their languages have to be classed as a distinct linguistic group, which has taken much from its neighbours yet is not classifiable with other languages spoken around them.[7]

Most of the Lele are contained in the area between the Loange, and the great crook formed by the Kasai as it turns from northward to west, until it meets the Loange. Its other tributaries flow northward on the same incline. Lele naturally orientate themselves by the direction of these rivers, referring always to upstream and downstream for north and south. They also base symbolic orientations on them. Since they entered the territory

---

[5] According to Haveaux (1954), whose report Vansina criticizes as of doubtful validity, Mbunda and Pende met and repulsed the Lele; according to other accounts, Lele were met, but not defeated in battle: Struyf, 1931: 'Les Bashilele, cette grande race guerrière et indomptable'.

[6] 1931, p. 668.

[7] Bryan, 1959, p. 54.

from the south, upstream has all the prestige; downstream or north implies the relatively new inferior aspect. Just as we use an up-down scale of points for our social system, Lele use *tende*, the source of the river, in a sense divorced from the actual flow of the rivers. It can mean the headman's end of the village, the sleeping quarters of the hut, the head of the bed, the brim of a cup, the head of a man.

The Belgian Colonial Administration used the river system for the boundaries of its smaller administrative units, which it was careful to make conform as far as possible with ethnographic regions. As a result the administrative territory of Basongo contained the whole Lele tribe, with the exception of three over-spills, into the territories of Mweka, Idiofa and Oshwe. The few Lele villages in Mweka, living among the Kuba, can hardly be said to be in foreign territory, but the five villages in Oshwe, which crossed the Kasai in about 1909, suffered from frequent clashes with Basongo Meno and Nkutu there. Other Lele lived across the Loange, in the Secteur Bawongo of Idiofa district, with Dinga, Mbunda and Pende for neighbours.

Both these sizeable groups of Lele living outside Basongo territory enjoyed relative freedom from administrative control. Fugitives from justice in Basongo could find asylum there, and many old customs, such as ordeals which were suppressed in the main body of the tribe, were still practised across the rivers. Of the Lele living in Oshwe and Idiofa the Administrator in Basongo reported in 1943:

Ces quelques villages importants, quoique très peu éloignés de Basongo, échappent à son influence et jouissent d'une situation beau-coup plus indépendante par suite des distances qui les separent de l'administration territoriale dont ils dépendent. Il arrive notamment que des jeunes filles des villages du territoire de Basongo soient enlevées par un groupe des Bashilele résidant dans les villages étrangers au territoire. Une action directe n'est pas possible alors que cela se passe presque sous nos yeux. Il s'en suit nécessairement un long échange de correspondance qui s'échelonne sur de longs mois, sans qu'une décision definitive puisse etre prise . . .

The Lele were in the habit of trading with their neighbours. Although they exchanged raffia cloth with Nkutu for red cam-wood and meat, they feared and despised them. They would say that Nkutu neither washed, nor avoided their mothers-in-law, their women were badly dressed, and their cooking execrable. With the Dinga they traded raffia cloth, palm-rib benches and coffins, for fish. Wissman[8] admired the Dinga as the most dexterous navigators on the Kasai, but Lele merely despised them. Their word for slave was *ninga* (plural *badinga*), because Lele used to enslave Dinga children. They relished a legend about the first encounter of their ancestor with the Dinga, whose culture they allege was at that time at such a brutal level that they did not even know how to deliver their women in childbirth, but used to cut open the mother and throw away her corpse after having taken out the baby. The Lele, skilled even then in fertility ritual and medicine, were able to teach the Dinga some of these elementary arts of living.

Pende and Mbunda the Lele respected as skilled weavers of raffia cloth and workers of iron. They traded with them too, Lele raffia cloth for iron goods.

Lele were originally known as Wongo. The name of Lele was given to them by the aristocratic clan, called Tundu, whose religious supremacy they accepted when they settled down together in their present territory.[9] Although the ethnographic maps of Basongo sometimes show three groups, Lele to the right of the Loange, Wongo to the left, and Njembe to the south, all three are in fact branches of Lele. The term Wongo has two uses as Torday found.

Dans le village de Makasu les habitants disaient d'abord qu'ils étaient Bashilele; quand on leur demanda s'ils étaient Bakongo, ils repondirent: 'Certainement; nous sommes des Bashilele-Bakongo.' On leur demanda ensuite: 'Tous les Bakongo sont-ils des Bashilele?' et la reponse fut: 'Non,' mais à la question: 'Tous les Bashilele sont-ils des Bakongo?' ils répondirent: 'Certainement!'[10]

Sometimes Wongo is used with only local reference, meaning Lele on the left bank of the Loange, and at other times it has a purely social reference meaning all Lele who are not Tundu, that is, commoners as distinct from the aristocratic clan. A Tundu man will talk about 'Our Wongo' as of our subordinates.

[8] Wissman, pp. 28–29.
[9] Wautier, report on the Bashilele, AIMO, 1935. See chap. X, p. 199.
[10] p. 47.

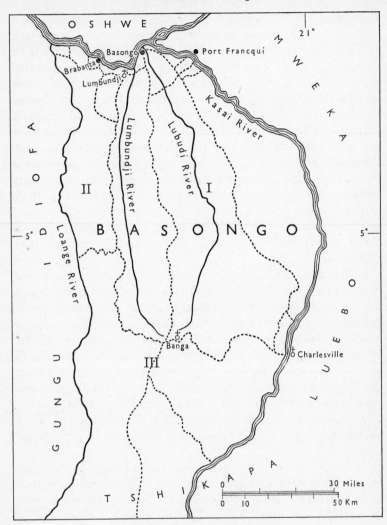

Map II. Basongo Territory 1948

I. Secteur Lumbundji-Kasai
(Lele   8,322)
(Chokwe 7,593)
(Others 2,604)

II. Secteur
Lumbundji-Loange
(Lele   9,728)
(Chokwe   544)
(Others   106)

III. Secteur du Sud
(Lele   8,197)
(Chokwe 1,980)
(Others   434)

Total 39,508

Population

To turn from the map of the south-west Congo to the map of the Territory of Basongo, and to the demographic records in Basongo, the Lele were sub-divided by the Belgian administration into three *Chefferies* or *Secteurs*. The first, which I refer to as the Eastern Lele, is separated from the second by the Lumbundji river, and the third, the Southern Lele, starts in the high land where the Lumbundji and Lubudi rivers take their source, and on the other side of which the tributaries of the Kasai flow towards the south. Lele are about equally distributed in these three areas. Including an additional 5,000 temporary immigrants working near Basongo, the total population in the whole territory of Basongo was about 44,000, of which the Lele only numbered 26,000. Allowing for the Lele living outside the Territory, the total number of Lele in all cannot have been more than 30,000.

In the east, the Lele were outnumbered by foreigners, one reason why I was content to study the Western Lele, but it was for practical reasons that I started fieldwork in the west, where communications were good enough to ensure supplies.

The existence of so many foreigners in Lele territory calls for comment. The large enclave of over 7,000 Chokwe in the eastern secteur had made its own peace with the Lele there before the Belgian administration was established. But the other tribesmen in the north, who had come as mechanics, clerks, drivers, cooks, depended on the Europeans for their protection. They would not have been tolerated by the Lele in pre-colonial times.

As late as 1960 any solitary Luba would be nervous of being found unprotected after dark, near a Lele village. Even individual Lele would be afraid for their lives, if caught in a strange forest in daylight by other Lele. The impression which Torday received of Lele as hostile and difficult was certainly matched fifty years later by the healthy respect in which foreign tribesmen held them.

I should not imply that by 1950 Lele were still entrenched in a spirit of isolation and defence. Breakdown and change had affected every department of their life. The map of their territory shows in the north Basongo, the administrative headquarters and Lumbunji, a mission station. Brabanta was a river trading station, with a wharf, and factory. These three European centres and their impact on Lele life will be described later.

Gourou has calculated that the 1948 population of 39,500 in the Territory of Basongo had a density of 2·6 to the square kilometre (6·5 to the sq. mile). Since we know that 8,000 of this population consisted of immigrant labourers, arrived since 1920, and that a further 10,000 were Chokwe who came late in the nineteenth century, this implies that before European advent the 26,000 Lele in the Territory lived at a density of only 1·6 to

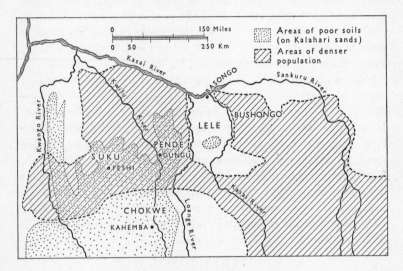

Map III. Kwango–Kasai–Sankuru

Density not congruent with soil fertility (Generalized from P. Gouru, *La Densité de la Population Rurale au Congo Belge*, A.R.S.C. 1955, p. 100).

the square kilometre (only 4 to sq. mile). This very low density can be accounted for to some extent by environmental conditions, but not entirely. The land between the Loange and the Kasai is the most easterly extension of the sterile soils of the Kwango plateau. Farther east on the other bank of the Kasai the soil is richer and more mineral deposits are found. But in much of Lele territory and east of the Lele to the Kwango river itself the soils derive from superior Kalahari, and are very poor and acid. They contain no heavy minerals, and little of any assimilable minerals, with the exception of some iron-ore found in the southern area. The soft rolling shape of the hills is due to their permeability. The sieve-like soils let the heavy showers wash out the useful elements. Hence the steppe-like vegetation, which would other-wise be surprising in so well-watered a land.[11]

The Kwango plateau has been called a human desert . . . it is one of the areas of extreme low density in the Congo. Yet there is only a very rough correlation of population density with the occurrence of these sterile soils, as the same map shows. We do not therefore assume that the Lele population had reached an optimum in relation to its resources such that an increase in population would reduce the *per capita* yield of their work. As some of their neighbours maintain a denser population on an equally poor soil, we need not be inhibited from asking some of the most interesting questions about a primitive economy. Low density is not necessarily the result only of a poor environment. It could be the result of inferior techniques applied with too little fervour to these same resources. The sparsity of population itself, by inhibiting specialization and large-scale collaboration, may also be responsible for a low level of output. Too often these questions cannot be raised, for lack of comparative material. In this part of the Congo we are able to compare the density of the Lele with four other neighbouring tribes, and say something in each case about the quality of the soil.

Table 1. *Comparison of population densities* [12]

Territ.:	Feshi		Kahemba	Gungu	Basongo	Mweka
Tribe:	Suku	Mbala	Chokwe	Pende	Lele	Bushongo
Pop. to sq. km.	3·9		2·6	14·35	2·6	3–4[13]

According to Gourou's map, above, the Lele have somewhat less of the Kalahari sands in their district, and the Bushongo have none at all, but they have lower populations than the Suku, while the Pende,[14] full in the region of Kalahari sands, have much the

[11] Nicolai, 1952.

[12] Nicolai, 1952.

[13] This figure excludes the foreign immigrants in Mweka territory, and purports to be a figure of Bushong density, Gourou, 1955.

[14] Professor Biebuyck suggests from personal observation that the Pende of Gungu have fertile soil in their river valleys which the map above ignores, and which would go some way to explain their greater density.

Map IV. Distribution of continuous forest in south-west of Kasai province (after Nicolai and Jacques, La Transformation du Paysage Congolais par le Chemin de Fer, 1954, p. 112)

highest population. Social explanations combine with environmental ones in accounting for the failure of the Lele to exploit their region more fully. At this stage it is necessary to establish differences in the environments of the Lele and of the tribe with whom they can be most easily compared, the Bushong. Of these two, the Lele have the less fertile, more permeable soils and a less well-forested surface.

3

When they first viewed Lele country from the banks of the Loange, Torday and Simpson described it as 'great rolling downs, on which scarcely a tree was visible'.[15] The map shows that the Lele are on the eastern border of a great stretch of savannah, while the Bushong are in an area of more continuous forest.

Climate

This part of the Congo has two short dry seasons, one, a mere pause in the rains in February, the other, the three months from mid-May to mid-August. Much of the annual rainfall (1,400 to 1,600 mm., or 40 to 60 inches) comes in heavy downpours, 80–100 mm. falling in a few hours, and pouring off the surface in violent streams. Lele stop all work, hunting or play in these showers; all take shelter except those who run out to dig channels in the sandy soil, to guide the rivulets away from their hut walls.

Table 2. Monthly rainfall 1930–39
(measured at Port Francqui)

Jan.	Feb.	Mar.	Apr.	May	Jun.	July	Aug.	Sep.	Oct.	Nov.	Dec.	Annual
123	117	132	156	93	17	14	51	150	201	207	236	1,497mm.

A. Vandenplas, Bulletin Agric. du C.B. 1943 *Vol. XXXIV*

One might expect them to welcome the short dry season as a relief. On the contrary, they dread the months of June, July and August as a dangerous period in which special ritual precautions are necessary. All weak things, women, children, young animals, are thought to be vulnerable, and likely to die in this season. It is a kind of limited close season for hunters, in which they are not supposed to take or eat the young of any animal or bird. At other times a man has no scruple about beating his wife, but boys are taught never to strike a woman in the dry season, lest she crumple up and collapse. Coughing and pulmonary diseases, which account for the majority of deaths in the Congo, are certainly rife, for the air is full of irritants, and this is the season of epidemics.

Paradoxically, this time, which the Lele regarded as unhealthily hot and unpleasant, was welcomed by the Europeans as *la saison froide* which they preferred to the hot, unpleasant wet season.

In the wet season, not only is the earth nearer to the sun and

[15] Simpson, 1911, p. 287.

radiant heat at a maximum, but the atmosphere is clearer. Its absorptive and diffusive powers for radiation are then at their greatest. At the same time, a dense cloud bank acts as a blanket to keep in the radiant heat from the earth. To those Europeans who know these things, it is natural that this should be recognized as the hot season, and the winter months of mid-May to mid-August as the cold season.

Yet, in practice it appears that neither season is so very much hotter or colder than the other. The average monthly temperatures vary by only one degree, so that instead of being 26° C. in the north of the region and 25° C. in the south, as it is all through the wet season, in the three months of the dry season the average temperature is 25° C. in the north, and 24° C. in the south.

If the daily variations in temperature were greater in the dry season, then the change from the heat of the day to the cold nights would explain the vulnerability of the natives to bronchial troubles at this time. But, again, in practice the diurnal variation is not much affected by the seasons, except in the south of Lele country (south of 5° S. Lat.), where the rocky and more exposed land warms up and cools off more quickly. In the north the forest exerts a moderating influence, so that the daily variation oscillates only between 10° and 14° C.

It is of the sun that the Lele complain in the dry season, and certainly the amount of direct insolation is greatest at this time of year.[16] They are used to living most of the year in a clear atmosphere, under a thick bank of cloud. When the cloud disappears they suffer from the effects of the direct sun, and even more from the dust and impurities in the atmosphere brought by the dry season, whereas the European's satisfaction at its arrival is accounted for, not by temperature so much as by relief from humidity.

The more satisfactorily we explain the differences between European and Lele attitudes to the dry season, the more interesting it is to find that the Bushong, on the other bank of the river, side with the Europeans and welcome the dry season as relatively cool and pleasant.

There are some slight differences of climate within Lele country, and between the Lele and the Bushong regions, which are worth examining. Less of Bushong country and more of Lele

[16] Vandenplas, 1948, p. 315.

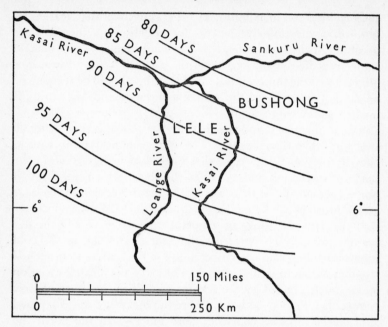

Map V. Average length of dry season (after F. Bultot, Saisòns et Périodes Sèches au Congo Belge, 1954)

country is situated in the areas of a dry season of ninety days. The effects of drought are naturally cumulative. For two or three weeks after the rain has stopped, the atmosphere is still moist, heavy mists wreathe the hills, and the grass is still soaked with dew. These effects gradually disappear, and the land begins to dry out. In the north of Bushong country this season lasts a mere eighty days, and in the south of Lele country it is ninety-five days, to wit, a fortnight longer.

This extra period of drought, and the relative lack of vegetable cover on the Lele side of the Kasai, explain why the Lele complained more of the dry season. It is important to allow for these environmental differences, since they aggravate the disadvantage of the Lele time-table by which they did their heaviest chores in the dry season.

Pattern of settlement

The village was by far the most important social group. We

shall see that preoccupation with its stability and size was a constant theme of their culture. Villages were built compactly in the grassland but never very far from the forest whose resources they exploited. The rectangular huts of palm rib and thatch were placed in a rough rectangle, often in double rows, around an open space used for dancing. Before the Belgian administration made it secure from attack, the whole village was surrounded by a stout palisade. A married man built a hut for each of his wives and put a high fence round the huts. A stranger to the village, faced by these high enclosures, would feel that he was entering a maze. Men did not build near their own parents or clansmen, but with their age-mates, so the layout of the village did not give any clue as to the links of kinship between members. Outside the village were the groves of raffia palms, plaited for shade and for the convenience of palm-wine drawers. Under these palms were little clearings where men of an age-set would set up their looms, keep their whetstone, and where they repaired to work, gossip and take their meals.

Women whose huts were on the same site of the village shared a mortar for pounding grain, and an oil-press. Paths wound between the palm trees through the grassland out to the forest in whose depths lay the stream whose accessibility had decided the precise site of the village.

The villages of the Western Lele, the subject of this study, were strung out along the watershed between the Loange and Lumbundji rivers. According to their tradition, they had entered the country from the south-east, having crossed the Lumbundji river at a spot somewhere near the site of Karanenge village. According to Vansina[17] their arrival would have been at some time in the 1730s or 40s. When each of the original settlements divided to form new villages, the people associated with founding the parent village stayed near its original site, and the dissident group generally moved north to found a new village, no doubt pursuing the better forest and soil in the north. As a result of this process the pattern of settlement in the whole area is one of groups of villages united to one another and distinguished from other such groups by a tradition of common origin. The member villages of these groups are often widely dispersed; some have stayed within a few miles of one another,

[17] *Zaïre*, 1959.

and others lie separated by the whole distance from Karanenge to the northern boundary and by many villages of different origin.

Lele insisted that all those which had split off from a single parent village were as one village. They had a common name, such as Mbombe, or Homba, which would be qualified for each village with a distinguishing nickname or epithet. When a man in a northern village said that he had been born in the 'down-stream village' or the 'middle village' it was perfectly clear to which member village of their group he was referring. They phrased the relationship between villages of a common origin in terms of descent, saying, 'We are all one village, we are children of one mother, we came from the same womb.' I would like to adopt their usage and refer to such a group of related villages as a 'family of villages' but the word family has such a well-defined meaning already that I will merely write of a group of brother villages, sometimes distinguishing the original village as the parent village.

The sense of relationship between members of a group of villages was maintained not only by the common name and inter-marriage with all the coming and going the latter entailed, but also by alliance in war and some collaboration in ritual. Ritual experts would be lent by one to another brother village on easier terms than the normal charges made to unrelated villages. Initiations to cults would be held jointly if the distance between them were not too great. Brother villages would combine to provide a wrestling team to oppose the team of a rival group of villages. Since the member villages of a group were spread out in a haphazard way their nearest neighbours would as often as not be unrelated villages to whom they would show strong rivalry, even hostility.

Table 3. Grouping of villages in the Western Chiefdom or Secteur du Loange

Name common to group of related villages	Individual village names
Mbombe group	Mbombe buho bola
	Mbombe Kumaket
	Bwene
	Ngoie
	Imbondo
	Yamba

Name common to group of related villages	Individual village names
Ibombo group	Iboanjali
	Iboa
	Ibombo
	Ibombo west of Loange
	North Ibombo
Malonga group	Lupekula
	South Malonga
	Ibanga
	Malonga Kanjoko
	Malonga Mituli
	Malonga Bwanga
Mwabe group	Mwabe
	Mwabe across the Lumbundji
Malembi group	Great Malembi
	Little Malembi
	Malembi across the Kasai
Mikope group	Bushongo Bwankapa
	Mikope Miakol
	Mikope Miamwab
	Mikope Mianjali (1950 the village had merged with the Admin. H.Q. called Basongo)
Njembe group	Mobendi
	Mapangu

The map showing the positions of the main groups of related village families suggests many lines of inquiry which I could not follow. From a thorough historical survey of the relations between the villages it would have been possible to estimate the rate of fission. To get an objective measure of past time would have been difficult, for the Lele tended to use their village sites as points of reference. My limited inquiries showed a tendency to collapse down the list of past sites to only a few significant names. For example, South Homba, from which North and

Middle Homba had broken off, recalled only thirteen names of village sites in all, seven of which were within the range of living memory. Of the rest, one was the original site after the crossing of the Lumbundji river, only about five miles away near the present village of Bushongo, the next was the birthplace of the first village head, the third was where North Homba had hived off. Numbers four and five were named, though not distinguished for anything, but number six was the site at which Middle Homba split off in its turn. North Homba was now a good twenty miles to the north, but there only the names of three early sites were known, followed by a detailed list of six sites occupied since 1920. Either they made big treks in the first three moves, or (more likely) many intervening sites in a more gradual shift northwards were forgotten. The odds were against the sites being remembered more accurately, since men did not normally grow old in villages in which they had spent their youth.

Shifting from one site to another took place at irregular intervals. An average of eight to ten moves would include sites at which a village stayed for fifteen years on end, and others where it stayed for only two years. Whether they moved far or near, shifting was a major undertaking. Old decaying huts would have to be completely rebuilt; huts in new condition would be lifted, wall by wall, and set up on the new site, if it were not too far away. Usually they tried to keep near enough to their old palms to be able to draw wine and raffia from them. South Homba had never moved more than six miles in its whole existence, and the four previous sites of Ngoie were well within two or three miles of the current site. Indeed Ngoie moved in 1950, after thirteen years on one spot, to a place only a few hundred yards away. Moves were not always dictated by the need to reach new forest for clearing. As often as not they were inspired by the wish to escape from sorcery.

There is evidence that the northernmost villages have been in position for at least fifty years. The early years of their expansion through this area were probably the time of maximum prolifera-tion of new villages, and of movement. Once they reached the north, where the bend of the Kasai makes a barrier not easily crossed, and where they had to fight the hostile Nkutu tribes, if they wished to establish themselves on the other side, the process of fission slowed down. A drift northwards then seems to have taken place. Individuals left the southern villages to join northern ones where there was more palm wine and meat to be shared, consequently villages in the north tend to be larger.

At the time of fieldwork I heard more of villages having been merged together than of villages splitting. In fact only one was planning to split, Yunda, which consisted of two villages which had been merged by order of the administration, and which was seeking a chance to divide again. The villages which had merged were Bushongo Bwabwani with its brother village, Bushongo Bwankapa, Makuba with Makuba across the river, and Middle Homba, which, after its first separation from the parent village, failed to establish itself and rejoined it, until it separated again in about 1880.

It is disappointing not to be able to say anything more precise to support my belief that the rate of fission had been very slow for a long time.[18] Village gossip harped continually on the prospects of changing to a new site, only in the solitary case of Yunda did I ever hear talk of a division. Within a village no one behaved as if they expected a division to take place, threatened to provoke one, or suggested that it would be a good or bad thing.

We can compare this general impression with reports on the age and stability of villages in other Central African tribes in the Congo and Northern Rhodesia which practise slash and burn cultivation in forest parkland. We should, of course, distinguish ordinary villages from those which have a special position in the wider political framework. Among the Bemba of the Great Plateau of Northern Rhodesia the politically significant villages, those of the hereditary councillors or Bakabilo, retain their identity and remain near the same site for very long periods, but commoner villages are very impermanent.[19] The same applies to Chokwe villages in the Congo[20] and Ndembu[21] in Northern Rhodesia. The evidence for the Luvale is not quite clear, but C. M. White[22] says that their very small villages tend to split on lines of descent. Where there are political forces raising a village

[18] Professor Vansina has made a detailed study of village histories which shows that for the Bushong it is true that the rate of fission has been very slow over a long period (private communication).

[19] Richards, 1937, p. 109.

[20] Struyf, 1948.

[21] Turner, 1957.

[22] White, 1955, p. 88; 1961, pp. 10–11.

above its fellows, and giving it a position which its members have an interest in preserving, and, alternatively, where there is fixed property obliging succeeding generations to remain in place if they are to lay claim to its use, villages endure. Otherwise nothing stops them from dividing or dying out when quarrels split them or deplete their numbers. As the Lele villages I am writing about are of the latter kind, ordinary villages, not the traditional headquarters of the aristocratic clan, their relative permanence and greater size are at first sight surprising.

Among the Western Lele the average size of villages to the nearest round number is 171. There is a tendency for villages to be bigger in the north and for a few northern villages to be very big indeed. Their populations according to the 1953 Census are given on Map No. VI. The differences between north and south can best be summarized thus:

Table 4. Size of villages

	South of Gt. Bamba	North of Gt. Bamba
Range in size of villages*	24–244	29–482
one quarter of the villages are less than	85	87
one half of the villages are more than	144	159
one quarter of the villages are bigger than	183	335

* The figures exclude the populations centred on European bases at Brabanta, Lumbundji and Basongo.

It is not easy to compare the size of these villages with other Central African figures because these are based variously on the number of huts, taxpayers, adults or total population. A Lele village with a total population of 160 will have about 45 huts, and 35 adult men. Take six tribes in Northern Rhodesia and Nyasaland: in Ndembu villages the mean number of huts per village is 13,[23] in Bemba villages it is 30,[24] and in Plateau Tonga villages, the average number of taxpayers is 20 and total population of adults and children 100,[25] in Yao villages the optimum size has long tended to be 10–15 huts (unless the village is politically important),[26] Chewa villages average a population of just over 100,[27] in Luvale villages the range is from 5–20 huts per village.[28] Lele villages tend to be distinctly larger than these.

[23] Turner, 1958. [24] Richards, 1937.
[25] Colson, 1958. [26] Mitchell, 1956.
[27] Marwick, 1952. [28] White, 1961.

II

THE PRODUCTIVE SIDE OF THE ECONOMY

Fixed Resources

LIVING so sparsely scattered, Lele were not conscious of any land shortage, and nothing in the way of fixed equipment acted as a magnet to attract groups of people. Disputes about land did not occur. Rights in cleared forest land, in fish ponds and in palm trees were heritable but not sufficiently valuable to have much effect on the pattern of settlement.

Their staple foods were maize and manioc, garnished with vegetable, meat or fish relish, and washed down with palm wine. The basic team for cultivating maize and manioc were man and wife. He cleared the forest patch, and burnt it. She planted, hoed and harvested, with occasional help from him. She also cleared a smaller plot in the grassland, near the village, which was entirely her own concern, in which she grew the hard ground-nut, *voandzeia*.[1]

All land rights were vested in the village, rights to forest for hunting, or for clearing, for gathering firewood and wild relish, and rights to streams for water and fishing. Each year new forest was cleared. It was not so much allocated, as chosen in a very informal way by individuals. A man might sometimes favour a plot near his brother, or equally one where his wife would be able to work near her sister or mother. Once the branches were lopped and the smaller trees felled, they were fired as they lay, without being piled into heaps. Nothing more was done to prepare the ground for cultivation. The half-burnt branches strewed the field. Eventually when they had rotted to a condition soft enough to be chopped by women, they would be carried away for firewood. In the meanwhile you had to pick your way over them as best you could. After the first rains had made the ground soft, maize was dibbled in with a long stick. Later manioc shoots

[1] When ground-nuts were introduced by the Belgians, they quickly displaced *voandzeia* from normal cultivation.

were stuck in between the growing maize plants. Round the clearing the man would plant seedlings of raffia palms, and banana shoots, and the woman would interplant peppers, and occasionally pineapples and sugar-cane with the maize.

The maize ripened first. After it had been gathered, the remaining crops had to be kept clear of weeds, though the rest of the field would be allowed to return to forest. Manioc was not dug until the second year. Raffia palms took about five years to mature. Each man would have a number of plots in the forest around the village to which he returned, and in which his rights were alive. After he had drawn wine from the last palm, having no further interest in his old plot, he allowed it to revert to forest. A site was judged good for a new clearing by the size of the tree trunks, and an active man would not want to re-cultivate land which was still in the process of regeneration. However, rights in cleared land, *mayungu*, were valued by anyone who was not strong enough to clear fully regenerated forest, a widow, or a woman whose husband was sick could claim the *mayungu* once cleared by her brother or mother's brother.

Fish ponds were another form of fixed property, also passed down between females. Women of a village would combine to bank up a little stream, so as to turn part of a valley into a marsh, in which they individually built a series of little ponds, one leading into the next. Here they could grow salt plants for making salt; open little dams and set fish traps in the channel; or dig deep holes filled with branches, where fish could breed. As every woman was expected to provide fish for the household economy, to be without a pond was a serious disadvantage. Ponds (*madiba*) were passed down from mother to daughter, and a woman who did not like her daughter-in-law or co-wife could not be induced to give her a corner of her pond. Transmission in the female line had a small side-effect in supporting the preferred marriage.[2] A woman whose daughter had been married to a man in another village would use her influence to get her daughter's daughter married in her own village, mentioning rights in her fish ponds as an inducement to persuade the girl.

Where men were concerned, rights in land were never an influence in decisions to move from one place to another.

[2] Expressed as marriage with the mother's father's clan, see Chapter VII, p. 117, and also p. 127.

Although the wine, wood and fibres of the raffia palm were essential in their economy, rights in palm trees only had a mild delaying effect. A man would try to plant twenty or so shoots roughly every two years of which, say, half would grow. He normally had about thirty growing palms scattered over his previous farming sites. Raffia palms do not grow in large groves, and they do not mature at the same time.[3] Those planted in the moist soil of the forest often yield better than those planted for convenience near the village, but the latter mature sooner. The technique of drawing wine was to make an incision in the crown of the palm, just at the time that it was ready for its first flowering. If this moment was missed, the palm was left to run to seed. A man had to be alert, watching his palms to see when they were about to flower. If two or three matured at the same place at the same time, he was lucky. If they matured in far separated spots, he had to ask for help in drawing the wine. When first cut a palm should be tended three times a day, later twice a day. Morning and evening a few new chips should be made in the stem, and the calabash re-attached, new leaves placed over the runnel so that rain and dirt did not get in. When the sap had all been drawn, the palm was dead. They stripped its ribs and fibres for house-building, and left the trunk to rot. Wine was not normally brought back to the village until the evening, unless there was a special call for wine to offer to a visitor, or to feed a newly delivered mother.

Everything to do with growing and processing the products of the raffia palm was the exclusive concern of men. The labour involved offset the attractions of ownership since yielding palms had to be tended in all weathers, at least twice a day. Often they were at some distance from the village and far apart so the owner of several yielding palms would need help, which he rewarded with a share in the wine. Although it was a skilled task, and some men were reputed to have a better 'arm' for it than others, no team collaboration was involved, and help could be asked of any thirsty man, on the most casual basis. Ownership of palms about to mature only entered marginally into a man's calculations about whether to move to another village. Wherever he went, he need not go short of wine if he was willing to help draw it. When he

[3] Pieraerts, 'Contribution à l'étude de deux espèces de raphia du Congo Belge', *La Revue Congolaise*, 1912, pp. 264–439.

died, a man's palm trees belonged to his local clan section, who should arrange for them to be tapped and the wine distributed according to the late owner's obligations of kinship. If quarrels arose about rights to palm wine, they were not about ownership of palms, but about the distribution of drinks.

The general effect of palm-tree ownership on the economy was less in influencing individuals to live with this or that group, than on the changes from one village site to the next. Raffia palms acted as a brake. Other crops capable of being stored and transported were not an important consideration affecting the choice of a new site. But men would be loth to move their whole village to a spot from which all their standing palms were inaccessible.

In short, neither land rights, nor raffia, nor oil-palm rights,[4] nor fishing rights made a marked difference to the pattern of settlement. The most significant characteristic of the Lele economy was the relative value of materials and labour. There were no possessions, land, equipment or trees so valuable as a man's work. A strong man felt free to go where he liked and be welcome anywhere, because he added to the manpower, in the hunt, in clearing and in palm-tree cultivation. The Lele were conscious of a shortage of labour. We shall see that this was not entirely due to underpopulation. In one direction there was a failure of authority and of incentives to undertake productive work, and in another manpower used to be diverted to raiding and defence.

In their lack of valuable fixed resource the Lele contrast with the tribes of the Lower Congo. The Yombe and Kongo live on more fertile land, at a greater density of population, have a more diversified economy, and principally, they exploit the *elaeis* palm for oil.[5] In consequence, their economy is based on two kinds of fixed capital assets, land, and palm groves. For them cultivable land is scarce, which makes it important for a man to make good his rights in his matrilineal lineage. The oil palm is cultivated quite differently from the Lele treatment of raffia palms, which were fully exploited and finished in five or six years. The short life of the raffia palm meant that no one left a heritage of raffia palms

---

[4] Oil palms were not cultivated crops. The fruit was cut from natural palm groves in the forests belonging to each village. The palms themselves were not owned privately.

[5] Gourou, P., *Atlas Général du Congo Belge.*

that would endure more than a few years after his own death. On the other hand oil palms[6] are a much more permanent and valuable form of fixed property. This may well account for the more rigid rules of residence and succession in the lower Congo tribes, where well-defined local, corporate matrilineages provide the framework of the society.

Division of Labour

The different work allotted to women and to men made each sex dependent upon the other. A man's work was arduous, physically exacting, and took its toll of his powers, but he was not fully engaged in it until after marriage. A small boy of 6 or 7 was given a little bow by his father, and played at shooting butterflies or small birds, in and around the village. He would soon begin to set snares and to go with older boys to help them set larger snares and traps. At 9 or 10 he began to learn the various processes of weaving raffia cloth. His father would have planted some palms for him, to teach him about the growth of the tree, and to learn when it was ready for tapping. At about 14 he would be expected to draw palm wine, and to follow the hunt. His first kill was a matter of great pride and congratulation. He did no agricultural work, and spent much time in the company of his age-mates. As a young man he cleared no fields of his own, but was expected to help his mother, his father, mother's brothers, or his elder brother if they asked him. Of course, he could not help them all simultaneously and equally, and if he helped one, he could not be expected to do as much for the others. He should help his father or mother's brother with house-repair, building, fencing, making sleeping mats and benches. When he was betrothed, his father-in-law could send for him when he needed work of this kind done. The age of betrothal for men varied very much. A man of 20 might be betrothed to a girl of 3 or 4. A fortunate minority might be betrothed while they were still boys of 10 or 12, but more usually they did not know who their future fathers-in-law would be until they were in their twenties. The demands a father-in-law could make on a boy's time were not continual, but sporadic. There was nothing like

[6] Unwin, *West African Forests and Forestry*, p. 241, says that they may live for up to 100 years.

the regular bride-service performed by young men in other parts
of Central Africa. After marriage, regular cultivation was added
to his programme.

Some men took up blacksmith's work in their spare time, others
carved bowls and beakers, bellows, drums or door-posts. When
the infirmities of age made it impossible for a man to follow a
hunt, shoot straight, or climb palm trees, there were some odd
jobs he could do if his eyes were good. He would be able to make
raffia cloth, and sew. He could twist cord, mend cracked gourds,
whittle a wooden stopper, or arrow, make a comb, and such small
inconsequential tasks. But for the normal male contribution to
the domestic economy, providing meat and wine, he was largely
dependent on the punctilious generosity of junior men, or on his
privileges as a cult member.

In their old age women were not at the same disadvantage.
A girl of 5 started to accompany her mother to the stream to
fetch water, and at home she would learn to watch the fire, hold
a baby, strip a maize cob. Soon she would be in demand as a
responsible baby-minder for any kinswoman in the village who
needed help. At 9 or 10 she would be helping in all the tasks of
a woman, pounding grain, cooking, gathering vegetable relish,
caterpillars, firewood, fishing, salt-making. At this age she might
well be planting, hoeing and harvesting with her mother or
mother-in-law, as girls were married before the onset of puberty.
From this time onwards, she would be set on a long career of
work, broken only by the holidays of rest which followed her
pregnancies.

Pollution fears[7] made every grown woman dependent on
others in her menstrual periods, for she was not allowed to cook
food for a man at this time. A child or old woman was called in
to stir the pot or tend the fire. Nor could she enter the forest,
and so had to beg for water or fuel if she had not forestalled her
need.

When she was past child-bearing, but strong enough to fetch
wood and water, to weed, harvest and cook, she would never be
without a husband if she wanted one. As an old woman her share
in the domestic economy was more valuable than that of a man
of her age. Two old women living together, with occasional help
for house-repair or clearing, could be much more comfortable

[7] See Chapter VI, p. 123.

than two old men. Even a very old woman, confined to the village, could still perform useful services in her daughter's home, such as tending the fire and the pot, amusing the baby. Old women were not such a burden on the village economy as old men. Further, because of the long association of mother and daughter, after a lifetime of helping in sickness and child care, an old woman had a secure niche in her daughter's home.

In sum, the division of labour was unfavourable to old men.[8] Without help from younger men for clearing forest, drawing wine and bringing home meat, they could not make the male contribution to the domestic economy. This disadvantage exaggerated the effect of the lack of fixed assets from which disobliging young men could otherwise be disinherited. If young and old quarrelled, there was little material reason to stop the young from taking their manpower elsewhere. These disadvantages of the older generation of men give the background for the social institutions in which they strove to lay young sons-in-law under heavy obligation, and stressed their solidarity against the young.

Slavery

In pre-colonial days, the Lele had a system of domestic slavery. Slaves were captured men or women from neighbouring tribes, especially Dinga, and Luba, and also Lele from distant parts of the country. Belgian rule allowed slaves to become free, but if the system had ever been at all extensive, one would have found many former slaves in 1950. In practice, I met very few— one deaf-mute, one woman who was not supposed to know about her own slave origins, one young man who remembered all the circumstances of his capture as a child and the efforts his captors had made to hide him from his relatives.

As slaves were mainly kept to be killed at important funerals,[9] there were naturally few alive to be emancipated. The males were killed, the females married, and their children might be counted as free, since free adherents were as precious to a man as anything else. A Lele who travelled far from his home might be

---

[8] From another hemisphere the signal importance of such a bias in the division of labour, with remarkably comparable consequences in social organization, is analysed by Hart and Pilling, *The Tiwi of North Australia*, 1960.

[9] Compare 'The Nkumu of the Tumba' by Brown, *Africa*, 1944.

4

suspected of slave origins, unless any of his own kinsmen was well known. Since anyone who travelled unprotected risked being killed, the chance of a slave surviving his escape was small. Slaves were bought and sold, for 100 raffia cloths or their equivalent. A slave was a kinless person, with no one to demand blood-compensation if his life was taken. Consequently his owner could kill him at will. This gave the latter an authority which he could not exert over a free man—with one exception, a future son-in-law could be sanctioned by withholding his wife. Wife and life were equated in Lele calculations of indebtedness, and so it is no coincidence that the future son-in-law formed with the slave the only class which could be compelled to work in all weathers.

A slave is a man who will do as he is told. If you send him to draw palm wine in the rain, he goes. You call him brother, age-mate, put your arm round his neck, give him palm wine and meat, so that he is happy. He thinks you love him. Then, when your mother's brother dies, you kill him to bury with your mother's brother. A slave knows that you can kill him. He has no clan to ask compensation. When you tell him to clear the forest or work in the rain he has to do it.

This text confirms the impression of a general inability to command labour in less unequal circumstances.

Scale of collaboration

Hunting was the only occasion when the Lele combined regularly, and in numbers. Most of their other work was individually performed, except for the occasional help of an age-mate or brother. Their rare occasions of collaboration are worth examining, since they show how little their social grouping was based on co-operation for work.

Table 5. Range of collaboration

Productive work Women	Range of collaboration
Agriculture: sowing, hoeing, harvesting	Wife alone, with occasional help from mother or sister
Cooking	,, ,,
Fishing: a) dry season: with poison, expeditions	All women of the village

Productive work	Range of collaboration
Women	
b) regular local fishing	Individual woman with mother or sister
Fetching wood and water	„ „
Salt-making	„ „
Gathering relish, vegetable or insects	„ „ or parties of children
Basketry	Individual leisure-time specialists
Pottery	„ „
Oil-processing	Women living on one side of village combined to use oil-press and pit installed there
Men	
Hunting:	
a) communal forest hunt	All men of the village
b) annual grassland hunt	Men of several villages
c) bow, snare or pit-trap	Individual man
Agriculture: clearing land for cultivation, burning	Individual man, or two age-mates or brothers
Occasional hoeing	Individual alone or with wife
Raffia-palm cultivation	Palms individually owned and worked except for sending a junior for wine
Weaving	Individual work
Oil-palm cultivation	Individual cuts fruit from palm for wife to process
House-building	Sons, brothers, age-mates, son-in-law give help
Blacksmithing	Individual leisure-time specialists, collaborating with charcoal burner and bellows boy
Wood-carving	Individual leisure-time specialists with occasional junior help

Women nearly always worked alone, or with help from a female relative, though they often gave one another companionship in going for water, firewood, fishing, pounding, etc. The only time they co-operated to use a piece of equipment was when the women whose huts were on one side of the village used the oil-press there. They dug a pit in which to leave the nuts to soften, built a fire on which to warm them, set up a press, in twisting which they took turns. Each carried home her own

gourdful of oil at the end of the day. This took place every two
months or so, or more frequently in the north where oil palms
were more abundant. The smell of the heated oil was regarded as
obnoxious, so the press was placed at a little distance from the
village, and the women who used it were simply those who lived
nearest to it. As residence in the village was according to the age
of the men, this meant that the presses were used by the wives of
men of the age-sets on that side of the village. They were also
liable to be called out to do a communal chore together as the
wives of such-and-such age-sets—occasional chores such as
clearing the site of a new village, bringing water or firewood to a
visitor. Apart from this, they did not have other occasions for
co-operation as a group of wives of men of an age-set.

In the dry season, when the rivers ran low, all the women of a
village went together on a two-day fishing expedition, to take (if
possible) large stocks of fish for storage.

Men, too, worked alone, or in twos, except for hunting and
house-building. The latter was a task in which a man would
expect his fellow-clansmen, his sons and sons-in-law, and his
age-mates to help him. The only help he could absolutely count
on was from the son-in-law of the wife for whom the hut was
being built. Otherwise, he would prepare the materials for the
hut alone, or with an occasional afternoon's stitching of thatch
from an age-mate or brother. When it came to assembling and
erecting the hut, he called for volunteers, and anyone who was
free at the time might lend a hand. There was no special in-
centive or reward, such as a beer party, and the claims of reciprocity were difficult to enforce for an occasion which came up
so irregularly, at intervals of five years or so.

Hunting was the most important sphere of collaboration in
their whole economy. It was important at all seasons: in the dry
season the animals were thirsty and withdrew to the heart of the
forest, hunting was difficult because dry twigs cracked and gave
warning of the hunters' approach; in the wet season a shower
would spoil the scent and hide the tracks. But hunting still took
place at all times. When they had nothing better to do, the men
of a junior age-set would band together and try to round up
some game. But the really important hunt was the communal
village hunt in the forest, in which all the men of the village
took part. It might be arranged at two or three days' interval or

every ten days according to the success or failure of previous hunts. Fifteen to twenty men, with ten dogs, were reckoned enough for a good hunt. They met beforehand to plan which coverts they should draw, then set off to surround a chosen piece of forest. Some of the hunters stood, with their arrows on the string, at regular intervals round it, waiting for the game to be put up by the dogs. The latter had wooden clappers tied to their bellies to frighten the animals, and green leaves tied to their backs so that they would not be shot in mistake for antelope or pig. The dog owners ran through the undergrowth with them, coaxing them on with calls and whistles. The game was expected to rush out towards the waiting marksmen, who liked to be able to shoot at very close range. If the game escaped through their ranks because they were too widely spaced, any men in the village who had deliberately stayed away were gravely reproached. Even old men and boys whose shooting was not sure were needed to help stop the gaps through which game might slip away.

This communal village hunt held a central place in Lele culture. It was not merely a matter of hunting being valued for its own sake, as it is among some peoples. Since they believed that spiritual beings punished their offences by inflicting hunting failure on them individually and collectively, and also that sorcerers could spoil the hunt out of spite, it was valued as much as a test of goodwill and harmony as for its yield in animal protein. Therefore, when we note that the hunt was the only occasion of regular collaboration between a large number of men, it was not an insignificant matter. In one sense we can even say that the village was a hunting unit.

Once a year, when the grassland was burnt, several villages combined to ring the area around, and kill the escaping game. This was the largest scale of collaboration the Lele ever achieved, but it was temporary, not very well co-ordinated, and rarely passed off without a row. In the old days they used to fire the grass after the first August rains, with the serious work of the year behind them. Each named stretch of grassland was apportioned between the villages around it, whether they were enemies or friends. The oldest village in the area had the right to name the day of firing, and sent a man round to discuss and settle the matter. They agreed on what positions they would take, and on the signals to co-ordinate their advance.

It was an occasion for great rivalry and display. Whereas in forest hunting men wore their oldest rags, for the grassland hunts they came out in all their finery, with new skirts and monkey and civet hats. A village lost prestige if another killed more game. After the fire had burnt out, the hunters moving forwards, bow-strings taut, following the contracting circle of flames, finally met in the middle of the burnt grass. Women and children followed them, with long palm-rib swats, swooping down on singed birds and grasshoppers or cane-rats caught by the fire. When they came to a standstill, panting and hilarious, they would find their men arguing fiercely over the kill. Finally the different villages would re-form their ranks, and set off for an agreed spot, in which the unsuccessful hunters hoped to take their revenge in a wrestling match.

It was difficult to co-ordinate hunting on this scale. One side might light the grass before the others were in place, so the game escaped unhurt. Or someone would forget to give the signal to fire, or to advance. One hunter might shoot the first arrow that checked an animal's flight but a hunter from a rival village might finish it off and not admit the other's claim. These hunts were more likely to end in quarrels and frustration than in increased respect. They were not an exception to the rule that relations between rival villages were competitive and bordering on violence.

Apart from house-building and hunting, men performed their other tasks alone. Many could be divided up so that one process could be entrusted to an assistant, also working on his own. For example, a length of woven raffia cloth might represent the work of three or four men, but each would have contributed his share alone. One might gather the yellow fronds, separate the soft inner cuticle, dry it in skeins on his roof. Then he might store it to use himself, or give it to a friend short of strands for his loom. Combing the strands into fine threads, and preparing the heddle were long and tedious tasks, suitable for an old man. Once the loom was spanned the actual weaving was very heavy work again, and an old man might pass it to a younger one. Weaving a few lengths prepared in this way by his father-in-law was one of the regular tasks of a young bridegroom.

In cultivation and in drawing palm wine a man might similarly be helped by a junior without necessarily having to accompany him. Hunting was the only aspect of their economy which imposed a minimum size on the local group. A village of less than twenty men found it very hard to muster a hunting team; one of more than fifty men had to be in an area specially well supplied with game to be able to reward its hunters. Between the family, consisting of husband and wife, which was the unit for cultivation of maize, and the village, the unit for the communal hunt, there were no social units which emerged as a result of collaboration in productive work.

Their techniques of production, involving so little regular co-operation, had one effect which aggravated the relative disadvantage of old men in the economy. In large-scale enterprises an old man's experience and skill in handling personnel might be an advantage for the community at large, and consequently valued. But by definition in a primitive economy, there are few such roles, and for the Lele they scarcely existed, even at the political level.

Calendar of work and comparison with the Bushong

To get an idea of the efficiency of Lele techniques and of the amount of effort they put into exploiting their environment, we need a basis of comparison. We have compared the density of their population and fertility of their soil with tribes to the west of them, the Suku, Chokwe and Pende, and to the east, with the Bushong. Although the western tribes lie in roughly the same geological formation and poor environment as the Lele, they belong to a different culture, and base their economies on different staple crops. The Pende eat millet, the Suku and Chokwe manioc. The Bushong,[10] on the other hand, live, like the Lele, on maize mixed with a little manioc flour. They are historically related, and share many values. On the surface, Lele material culture looks so like a counterpart of Bushong that it is worth comparing the two tribes. Both cultivate maize in the ash of burnt forest clearings, both build their homes from palm-tree fronds, both drink palm wine, weave raffia and hunt. The one tribe is poor compared with the other, not only in our terms, but in their own.

---

[10] The comparison is only possible because Professor Vansina has been generous with information about the Bushong drawn from his own research among them.

Whereas Lele produce for subsistence only, sharing their goods, or distributing them among themselves as gifts and fees, the Bushong have long been used to producing for exchange, and their economy was noted early for its use of money, and its specialists and markets. Everything that the Lele have or do, the Bushong have more and can do better. They produce more, live better, as well as populating their region more densely than the Lele.[11] From the comparison we should be able to draw some general conclusions about conditions predisposing to economic backwardness.

Briefly, the Lele are poorer than the Bushong because in hunting, fishing and house-building the Bushong use more specialized equipment, in cultivation they spend more energy and time over a greater part of the year, and in craftsmanship they have more skilled specialists.

Take hunting first, since Lele are passionately interested in it, and pride themselves on their skill. Among neighbouring tribes it seems that they are notoriously inefficient, as they never use nets, and only rarely make pit traps. Using nets, the Bushong need a team of only ten men, and can hope to do well with as few as five.

Why should the Lele not use nets, and rarely make pit traps? Lest it be thought that they neglected capital-intensive aids because hunting was a sport, a pleasure, and even a religious activity, let me deny any parallel with English fox-hunting. They eagerly bought firearms whenever they could get the money and the licence, and would have applauded Conan Doyle's French Brigadier who slew the fox with his sabre. Making a net is a long task, allocated to women among the Bushong. Lele women do a larger share of the total of agricultural work than Bushong women, so that some of the answer may lie in the division of labour between the sexes. Both pit traps and nets represent a long investment of time and work. Making a pit trap requires a stay in the forest of several days and nights, or regular dawn journeys and late returns. The pits are hard to dig, with only a blunt matchet for spade; once set, the traps need to be watched.

[11] Europeans who know the Bushong but not the Lele will be surprised to find them used here as a model of a go-ahead economy, productive and efficient, since they are normally compared unfavourably with people who have made a better adaptation to European conditions (see Nicolai, 1954), but this recent adaptation is not strictly relevent here.

Since there is less forest, and so less game, on the Lele bank of the Kasai, the amount of game caught is often less worth the labour of making traps than it would be on the Bushong side.

Another possible reason for their neglect of nets and pit traps is that their constant search for spiritual causes for their hunting failures may have blinded them to technical deficiencies. Whatever the reason, their inefficiency in hunting is consistent with a general tendency in their economy not to invest time and labour in long-term productive equipment.

In fishing the Lele were also inferior. Their country was well watered with rivers and streams, and bounded on two sides by the great Kasai, and on the west by the swift-flowing Loange.

Along the banks of the Kasai the men of fishing villages have dotted the river with elaborate traps and platforms. The villages are Dinga or Bushong, not often Lele. Compared with the Bushong the Lele in general are not good at fishing, or at canoe-making. This is not the place to describe in detail the diversity and elaborate character of Bushong fishing equipment, but in some types of fishing, using several canoes trailing nets, a team may consist of twenty men or more. Lele mostly left fishing to their women, whose techniques were crude by comparison. A morning's work draining their little marsh ponds and catching the floundering fish would yield a bare pint or so. In the dry season they made expeditions to the Lumbundji river, where they spread a saponaceous poison over the low waters, and pulled out the suffocating fish by hand.

In housing and in furniture, the Lele do not compare well with Bushong. Their huts looked much alike. They were low, rectangular structures, roofed with palm thatch, the walls covered with rows of split bamboo or palm rib, lashed on to layers of palm-leaf, on a frame of strong saplings. Deceptively, Lele huts when new looked much sturdier than those of the Bushong, but in practice they lasted less well. The Lele hut was more roughly and quickly made. A well-built one lasted at most about six years without repair, and as they were capable of being renewed piecemeal, by replacing a wall or roof, they lasted about twelve years before they disintegrated. A hut in good condition would be transported to a new village site, with from six to eight men carrying the roof, and four at a time carrying the walls.

Bushong huts were also transportable. For the roof thatch

they used leaves of the raffia palm, like the Lele; for the walls they used the reputedly more waterproof leaves of a dwarf palm growing in the marshes. Over this, instead of palm ribs split in half, they sewed narrow strips of bamboo, where available—Lele held bamboo to be tougher than palm, but it was rare in their region. The narrow strips were held in place by stitching in pleasing geometric patterns.[12] A rich Bushong man, who could command labour, could build a solid hut that would last up to fifteen years without major repairs. The palace of the Nyimi at Mushenge, still in good condition in 1956, had been built in 1920.

The Bushong used an ingenious technique of ventilation, a movable flap between the roof and walls, to let out smoke. Either their building was too solid to let the smoke filter through the walls, or they were more fastidious about ventilation than the Lele, or they minded mosquitoes less. Lele expected their huts to retain smoke to keep off insects.

Within the hut, the furnishings show forth the difference in wealth. The Bushong met their needs with greater ingenuity and refinement. They sat on stools, laid their heads on carved neck rests (often necessary to accommodate elaborate hair styles). They ate from fine basketry plates, with spoons. They had a bigger range of specialized basketry and wooden containers for food, clothing and cosmetics. A man who has more than one hat naturally needs a hat box, and something to keep his hat pins in. Lele did not make fibre hats, and only a few men in a small village would possess a skin hat. The beautiful Bushong caskets for cosmetics are prized in many European museums. To have enough cosmetic to need a box for storing it says something about the standard of living. When a Lele woman prepared some cosmetic from camwood, she used it at once, and there was rarely enough left over to store. Only a newly delivered mother, cared for by her own mother, had time to grind camwood for herself and the baby, and stored enough for a few days in a little hanging basket, hooked into the wall.

Professor Vansina was impressed with the high protein content of the Bushong diet, with the large quantities of fish and meat they ate, and the variety of their food. The Lele gave an impression of being always hungry, always dreaming of meat, often

---

[12] See Nicolai and Jacques, *La Transformation du Paysage Congolais par le Chemin de Fer, l'Exemple du B.C.K.*, 1954, pp. 272 seq.

going to bed fasting because their stomach revolted at the idea of a vegetable supper. They talked a lot about hunger, and *ihiobe*, a word for meatlessness and fishlessness.

As to village-crafts, such as carving and smithing, the best of the Lele products compete in quality with Bushong manufacture, but they were much scarcer. The Lele were more used to eating and drinking out of folded green leaves than from the basket plates and carved beakers common among the Bushong. Their medical instruments, too, were simpler. If instead of simply cutting down a gourd top, they carved a wooden enema funnel for a baby, they made it as fine and thin as they could, but did not adorn it with the elaborate relief pattern found on some Bushong examples.

The method of storing grain is a rough index of output. Both Lele and Bushong houses were built with an internal grain store, suspended from the roof, or supported on posts, over the hearth. Here grain, and even fish and meat, could be preserved from the ravages of damp and of insects, by the smoke of the fire. Most Lele women have no other grain store. Bushong women found this too small, and used external granaries, built like little huts, raised a few feet above ground. These granaries, of which there might be one or two in a Lele village, were particularly characteristic of the southern Bushong villages, while in the north huts built in the fields, for a man to sleep in during the period of heaviest agricultural work, were used as temporary granaries. The Lele were not in the habit of sleeping in their fields, except to shoot wild pig while the grain was ripening. This may be another indication that they did less agricultural work than the Bushong.

The techniques of cultivation reveal many contrasts. The Bushong planted five crops in succession, in a system of rotation that covered two years. They grew yams, sweet potatoes, manioc, beans, and gathered two and sometimes three maize harvests a year. Their cultivated tree crops included citrus fruits, pineapples, pawpaws, mangoes, sugar-cane and bananas, which were rare or absent in the Lele economy. The Lele practised no rotation, and reaped only one annual maize harvest. The two agricultural cycles show that the Bushong worked continuously all the year, while the Lele had one burst of activity, lasting about six weeks, in the height of the dry season. Hence their dread of that season. The Bushong, working all the year round, like the European, welcomed the period from mid-May to mid-August as the 'cold season'. But the Lele, enduring the sun beating on them from a cloudless sky, while they were trying to cram in all their agricultural work for the year, suffered relatively more from the dust and impurities in the atmosphere and from the greatly increased insolation, and so dreaded it as a dangerously hot season.

Table 6. Annual cycle of work

	Bushong	Lele
Dry Season		
Mid-May	Harvest beans, maize II, yams. Clear forest. Burn grassland for hunt.	Hunt, weave, draw wine.
June	Hunt, fish, weave, repair huts	,, ,,
Mid-July to Mid-Aug.	Burn forest clearings, gather bananas and pineapple. Plant hemp. Hunt, fish, plant sugar-cane and bananas. Send tribute to capital— period of plenty.	,, ,, Clear forest for maize. Women fish in low waters. Burn forest clearings. Sow maize.
Wet Season		
Mid-Aug.	Lift ground-nuts.	,, ,, Fire grassland for hunting.
Sept.	Sow ground-nuts and maize I. Collect termites.	,, ,, Sow *voandzeia*, collect caterpillars, plant manioc,[13]
Oct.		,, ,, bananas, peppers;
Nov.		,, ,, sugar-cane, pineapples (occasional) and raffia palms in
Mid-Dec.		,, ,, forest clearings, with maize.
Little Dry Season		
Mid-Dec. Jan.	Sow maize II, sow *voandzeia*.	,, ,, Green maize can be plucked.
	Sow tobacco, sow maize II.	,, ,, Maize harvest.
Wet Season		
Feb.	Lift ground-nuts, sow beans, collect termites and grubs. Reap maize I (main crop).	,, ,, Lift *voandzeia*.
March	Reap maize I. Sow tobacco, beans, yams, manioc.	,, ,, Collect caterpillars.
April to Mid-May	Gather beans, sow *voandzeia* and tobacco.	,, ,,

[13] Manioc can be dug up for use at any season.

Apart from the difference in crops cultivated, there are differences in emphasis and timing. Lele gave ·hunting and weaving a high priority throughout the year, while the Bushong thought of them as primarily dry-season activities. Bushong burnt their forest clearings in the middle of the dry season, Lele burnt theirs when it was practically over. According to Lele belief, the rain clouds are attracted by heavy columns of smoke going into the sky from the burnt clearings. The smoke brings the rain. Laggards who had not finished their clearings begged their neighbours not to fire theirs until everyone was ready, lest the ensuing deluge ruin later attempts at firing. Should heavy rains set in before the clearings were fired, the disgusted farmers blamed the downstream people for bringing rain with their smoke. Since the downstream Lele got their rain some days in advance of the others, and had to adjust their calendar of work accordingly, the belief in the connexion between smoke and rain clouds was annually upheld.

Traditionally, the Lele used to burn the grassland for the big hunts in which five or six villages combined at the end of the dry season, when the bulk of their agricultural work was done. If the first rains had already broken, so much the better for the prospects of the hunt, they said, as the animals would leave their forest watering-places to eat the new shoots. As the end of the dry season is the time in which the firing could do the maximum damage to the vegetation, it was forbidden by the Colonial Administration, and if permission was given at all, the firing must be over by the beginning of July. The Bushong used to burn the grassland in mid-May or early June, at the beginning of the dry season, when the sap had not altogether died down in the grass.

The cycle of work described for the Lele is largely what the old men describe as their traditional practice. It was modified by the Belgian agricultural officers. Lele were encouraged by them to sow maize twice, for harvesting in November, and in April. Manioc was then mainly grown in the grassland, instead of in the forest clearings as formerly. There were also some changes in the plants cultivated: *voandzeia* was replaced by ground-nuts, some hill rice was sown, and beans in some parts. These were largely treated as cash crops by the Lele, who sold them to the Europeans. One other new occupation competed for their time, cutting oil-palm fruits for sale to the *Huileries du*

Congo Belge.[14] The fruits tended to ripen in larger quantities in the dry season, and so this work coincided with the time of maximum effort for clearing forest on the Lele traditional programme.

In one field at least, the weaving of raffia, the Lele were considered to be better craftsmen. Their cloth was of closer texture, because they used finer strands, produced by combing three times, whereas the Bushong combed only once. As Lele cloth was too fine to be suitable for the velours embroidery of the Bushong, the comparison of their textiles shows that they had specialized in different directions. Plain woven cloth held a special place in the Lele economy. One length was their standard value for counting debts and dues of all kinds in internal transactions, and it was their principal export. This accounts for their pride in making cloth of a fine, regular weave. The economy of the Bushong was far more diversified, and they made use of various currencies as media of exchange in internal trade. No one commodity held such a central place for them.

After this survey of techniques, if we ask why one tribe was richer than the other, the difference in environment still explains something, though not enough. The Lele worked less at producing the things which made their wealth. They did not build up producer's equipment, such as nets, canoes, traps and granaries; nor did they work so long at cultivating food crops, and their houses wore out quicker. Their economy was geared to a shorter cycle. To some extent their poorer environment would account for this. It is arguable that on their soil much more intensive cultivation would start a degenerative cycle, and that hunting nets and pit traps are less worth while in an area poor in forest and game. But there are other differences in the two economies which call for a different kind of explanation.

On Lele time-tables there are no heavy schedules of work which might suggest full employment. Yet an apparent shortage of hands confronted anyone who sought collaborators. When a sick man wanted to send a message, or needed help to clear his fields, or to repair his hut, or to draw palm wine for him, he would often be hard put to find anyone whose services he could command. His fields might well lie uncleared, or his palm trees run to seed, for lack of incentives and authority, not because

[14] See Chapter XIV, p. 263.

every able-bodied man was working from dawn to dusk. The Lele were less fully engaged than the Bushong on productive work. They gave more time to raiding, ambushing, abductions, negotiations for loans and compensations. To push the comparison any further we have to try to assess their different attitudes to the rewards and inconveniences of productive work.

For the Bushong work was the means to wealth, and wealth the means to higher status, so that they valued individual effort and achievement. Nothing in Lele culture corresponded to the Bushong striving for riches. Bushong talked constantly and dreamed about wealth, while proverbs about its being the stepping-stone to high status were often on their lips. Riches, prestige, and influence at court were explicitly associated together.[15] By the combined mechanisms of market, money and elective political office, oiled by generosity, production was geared to the attainment of prestige. But the Lele for their part talked as if the most satisfying roles fell into an individual's lap in the ripeness of time, provided that he was normally virile. Their society held out its best rewards for middle life and after, and these were attained through marriage and parenthood. In spite of their disadvantages in the productive side of the economy, older men made for themselves a comfortable position, to be defended against the encroachments of the young. Since prestige and production were divorced, the spirit of competition did not prevail. The one economy had a restrictive bias which the other had not.

Summary of causes of Lele economic backwardness

Apart from the attitude to work, the main differences between the two economies are as follows. First, the Lele lived in a less favourable environment. Second, though in both economies the division of labour between the sexes was unfavourable to old men, Bushong society had more prestige-carrying administrative and political roles, in which age and experience were not a loss. The small scale of their society and their more rudimentary technology put Lele old men at a relative disadvantage. Partly in consequence, their authority over their young men was weak. Boys would be boys, until their middle thirties, leading a

[15] Vansina, 'Les Valeurs Culturelles des Bushong', *Zaïre*, Nov. 1954, p.9.

good life, of weaving, drinking, and following the manly sports
of hunting and warfare, without continuous agricultural responsibilities.[16] Third, marriage among the Bushong was monogamous,
among the Lele polygynous. The Lele system of prolonged
bachelorhood, with polygyny in middle life, was central to the
tribal economy. It provided social security for the old men,
otherwise at a serious disadvantage. We can compare it super-
ficially with an ambitious old-age pensions scheme costing more
than the society reckoned. Through polygyny tradition, seniority
and male dominance were maintained to the end. But among the
costs were delayed marriage for young men, and inter-village
raiding. By meeting the problems of polygyny the way they did,
Lele were committed to small-scale political life. The diversion
of young men's energies to raiding girls from rival villages was
one cause of the low level of production. Raiding gave rise to
such insecurity that at some times half the able-bodied males
were giving armed escort to the others. In the old days, a man
did not go to the forest to draw palm wine alone, but his age-mate
escorted him, and stood with his back to the tree, arrow on the
string, watching for ambush. Travelling between villages, men
as well as women were escorted. Such insecurity is obviously
inimical to trade.

Small-scale political life has other repercussions on an
economy. The Bushong managed to develop a well-organized
political system[17] embracing 70,000 people. Authority was
decentralized from the *Nyimi*, or paramount chief, to minor
chiefs, and from these to canton heads, and from these to village
heads. Judicial, legislative and administrative powers were
delegated down these channels, with decisions concerning war
and peace held at the centre by the *Nyimi*. Political office was
elective, or by appointment. To be chosen, a man had to be rich
and generous as well as capable. Appropriate policing powers
were attached to leaders at each point in the hierarchy. The
Nyimi maintained his own army to quell rebellion. Leaders
themselves were checked by variously constituted councils.
Tribute of grain, salt, dried foods and money was brought into
the capitals, and redistributed to loyal subjects and officials. The
chiefs' courts provided good markets for craftsmen's wares, so
that regional specialities were saleable far from their source.

[16] See p. 103.   [17] Vansina, 1957.

I a.
Boy drawing palm wine

I b.
Bringing in raffia and palm wine

II a.
Diviner with rubbing oracle

II b.
Feeding hunting dogs

Even before the advent of Europeans, there was a food market at Mushenge, the *Nyimi*'s capital.

By contrast, the largest political unit of the Lele, the village, was smaller than the smallest political unit in the Bushong system.[18] Beyond the village, there was no ladder of status on which a man could honourably climb, to satisfy his competitive ambitions. There was no series of offices for which age and experience qualified him, so that in his physical decline he could enjoy respect and material rewards. Lele damped down individual achievement, and shunned overt leadership. Their truncated status system turned the village on itself, to brood on quarrels and sorcery accusations, or turned it against other villages. The final paradox is that the general insecurity, making markets impossible, and production above home needs pointless, aggravated the precarious position of the old.

From another angle we can summarize the differences between the two economies by comparing their use of manpower. At one end of the life-cycle, young men joined the productive effort later among the Lele, and at the other end, old men retired from it earlier. The Bushong could use their older men in various administrative roles which maintained the security and order necessary for prosperity. Their young men were married and fully engaged in agriculture at twenty, compared with thirty-five or forty among the Lele. Add to their more continuous time-table of production the fact that a larger proportion of the male population was involved in it, and we have a simple statement of how one economy was richer than the other. The environment laid down the initial disadvantage for the Lele, but the social organization intensified it.

[18] Lele villages averaged 170 compared with 210, the average population of a Bushong village.

III

DISTRIBUTION OF WEALTH

BY FAR the larger part of their daily work went to produce perishable things, drink that had to be consumed the same day, grain that barely lasted to the next harvest, clothing that wore out in a few months. Even their houses and beds only lasted about ten years with much repairing. Durable goods were rare and valued accordingly. They were distributed on quite a different basis from the things in what we can call (not very accurately) the subsistence sphere of the economy.

Distribution of subsistence goods

All perishable goods were used within the village in which they were produced, except for transfers between close kinsmen of different villages.

Each married woman controlled her own stores of grain, roots and ground-nuts. She could give them away as she liked. Her daughters or sisters or other close relatives in another village would count on her help in time of need. Every day when she had cooked food, she divided it up. Her menfolk received baskets to share with their age-mates, one basket for her husband, one for her unmarried sons, possibly another to her brother if his wife was away. Before she sat down to eat with her children she might call one of her clanswomen to join her. Cooked food was distributed right through the village. Husband and wife, although they produced it together, rarely ate together.

Uncooked meat and wine also circulated through the village, on different sets of rules. A hunter was not free to dispose of game caught by himself unless it was too small to be worth sharing. The back and haunch of a large animal he owed to his mother's brother, the other haunch to his father, who shared it among his clan resident in the village. The chest was the prerogative of initiates of the Begetters' Cult.[1] The diviners took the head of a bush pig to share among themelves. The hunter

[1] Chapter XI gives an account of the cult groups.

might sell some of the carcase, if he could persuade his father and mother's brother to give up their share to help him to meet an urgent expense. To sell meat he had to go to a village where the claims of kinship were not importunate. His wife always expected to get a good cut for drying. Sometimes the whole of the animal might be claimed for cult purposes, and the hunter would get no more of it than his cult standing warranted.

Game killed in the communal hunt was divided between all the hunters, with special shares earmarked for rewarding particular efforts. The man who had shot it took one haunch and one foreleg; the dog owners took the place where the dogs seized it, the neck; the men who carried it home on their shoulders took the shoulder. The smiths who forged the arrows sometimes took the stomach. The village head was entitled to one haunch, and the official diviner of the village[2] to the intestines, and a little sinew in each limb. Chest, foetus and young were the sole prerogative of the Begetters' Cult members. The rest was divided equally between all who had taken part in the hunt. Each man who received a portion, however small, divided it again among his womenfolk and old men. After such a general share-out, men would carry home bits of meat the size of a little finger.

Since there was virtually no one in the village who could not trump up some claim or other, a single hunter in luck had to expect to give something to everyone to avoid ill-feeling. If he felt he could not face the begging and recriminations which followed any distribution, a man was tempted to carry his kill home after dark to eat secretly with his wife and children.

Every evening the men who had yielding palms went or sent someone to draw wine. Before they brought their calabashes back to the village they met on one of the paths to the forest. Friends or relatives without palms, invited to what Torday aptly called the men's drinking club, would saunter along at dusk with beaker or folded leaf in their hand. It was rude to drink palm wine standing up, or armed. Each man laid his matchet on the ground and sat on it. For an hour or so they discussed the quality of the wine, the prospects of the hunt, and any matters of general concern. The wine that was carried back to the village later was mainly for women.

[2] Chapter XII describes his role.

Apart from food and drink, some other goods not strictly perishable circulated mainly in the village. Containers, whether baskets or calabashes, and native salt were for the producer's own use or for kinsmen, who might not always be in the village. By and large each village was self-sufficient for these things. It was impossible for anyone to predict or budget for their future needs because they never knew who might come to the village with claims to food. If there was a death the chief mourners would stop all forest and domestic work for at least six months. If their mourning started during the dry season, their fields were simply left uncultivated until the following year. They would have to be fed by their close kinsfolk. No one could say in advance how many they might suddenly be called upon to support. The wife would take on whatever catering duties fell on her, spreading her resources as best she could, and reckoning that she could go to a sister or daughter in another village if her supplies ran out. Before the harvest there used to be much purposeful visiting of women from different villages.

Poultry and dogs were not normally sold, but transferred between friends and kinsmen on a deliberate parallel to the transfer of women in marriage. The recipient of a hen or bitch had to make a return in kind from his first brood or litter, just as a man had to give his daughter to his wife's father.

Bartered durable goods

Certain durable goods were imported into Lele country. Iron bars, tools and weapons came from the Njembe and the Pende. Bars of red camwood which was ground down into a paste for anointing the body, came from north of the Kasai, from the Nkutu. Copper wire which was used to be bent into anklets and bracelets came from the Kuba and Luba, but was rarely seen in 1950.

Others were of Lele manufacture. Any man or boy could weave raffia cloth. Old men kept the secret of making coloured borders for the most admired dance skirts. Specialist craftsmen worked in iron or wood to make arrow heads, gouges for drawing palm wine, razors, needles and knives, wooden bellows, beakers, plates, beds, chairs, pestles, drums, shuttles and bows.

The imported goods were bartered for plain raffia cloth. A man and a boy would go on a bartering expedition to one of the neighbouring tribes carrying commissions to sell raffia cloths for their friends. The man would have been before as a boy, and have a trading partner[3] who guaranteed their security, and gave them hospitality, which they would return when he visited them in their village.

Raffia was also given in barter for the products of Lele craftsmanship if the ties of kinship were not strong enough for the thing to be transferred gratuitously. If the village, or a cult group or age-set in it, wanted a new drum they would commission their own craftsman if he was good enough, and reckon to pay him in raffia cloth half what they would have to pay to a crafts-man of another village. But since the remuneration was small, he would take his time over the job, and they might well decide to pay more and order the drum for 100 raffia cloths from a stranger with a good reputation. Good craftsmen were not to be found in every village, so people were often obliged to pay raffia cloth if they wanted wood or iron things finely wrought, but for ordinary things, like plates, arrow heads, needles, bows and shuttles, there was generally a local craftsman who would do the job in recognition of his kinship obligations. From bartering between men of different villages or tribes there arose a raffia price for the valuables which were obtained in this way.

Formal prestations

So far we have distinguished two kinds of distribution. First, there was a subsistence sphere, in which food and drink and containers and other small items were given to kinsmen and neighbours who made return, not directly, but by innumerable services and gifts which were required of them also on the basis of kinship and neighbourhood. This took place mainly within the village. Second, there was barter of durable goods for raffia cloth between strangers or trading partners, which was therefore mainly external to the village.

There was also a third sphere of exchanges, that of formal prestations.[4] For entrance fees, fines and compensations, mar-riage dues and fees for ritual services, only certain standard goods were accepted in payment. These were raffia cloths,

---

[3] Called *mbai*, age-mate, see Chapter IV, p. 73.

[4] A term which I retain because of its association with Mauss's study of *The Gift*.

camwood, axes, in the old days copper wire or slaves, and in
1950 goats or Belgian Congo francs. All the dues were fixed in
quantity in terms of raffia cloth, but could be paid in any of the
standard forms, 100 raffia cloths being equivalent to three large
bars of camwood or five small, one full-size copper bar or a slave.
The normal unit of raffia cloth was *iboka*, a bundle, which
consisted of either nine or ten cloths. A debt of 100 cloths could
be settled by paying 90 raffia cloths, though the same 10 per
cent. latitude was not allowed for the equivalents of raffia.

It is not quite true that these objects circulated in an entirely
separate sphere of exchanges. Individuals who were well-placed
for direct barter with foreigners could obtain any of them for
raffia cloth, and any Lele man could weave the latter. Craftsmen,
drummers and dancers were paid in raffia cloth. People also
obtained raffia cloth through spontaneous gifts. But there was a
strong tendency for this class of things to circulate from hand to
hand in settlement of the various dues and debts which collectively can be called prestations.

Uses of raffia cloth

The value of raffia cloth was greatly enhanced by its use in
barter and in settling debts. Its intrinsic value was, of course,
as a textile. Two lengths sewn together, plain hemmed, made a
man's normal loin cloth. Two lengths, with a strip cut off to
make them shorter, made a woman's skirt, hemmed or fringed.
Five lengths, sewn together and hemmed, made a semi-formal
skirt, *lupungu*, for men. Ten, sewn together, and with a coloured
appliqué border at each edge, made a dance skirt, *mapel mahangi*
(glad clothes), or *mapel milunj* (clan clothes). The latter was one
of the valuables counted as an heirloom of a local clan section.
Ordinary skirts would be worn out in use in three or four
months. The others did not get regular use, being only worn for
special occasions. Any member of a local clan section could
borrow one for a dance, but could not dispose of it. Its ultimate
fate was to be used as a burial gift, since they honoured the dead
by burying them dressed in all available finery, and stuffing the
coffin until it could hold no more.

All social relations, even the closest, were smoothed by informal gifts of raffia cloth.

A husband should frequently surprise his wife with a gift of two cloths, neatly folded and tied together, which she would store in her basket, for him to make a skirt for her later, or for herself to give away when occasion demanded. Her sons, and her sons-in-law should also make occasional informal gifts of raffia to her. If her son was to be congratulated for a kill, or for drumming or dancing well, or if a kinsman visited her, or recovered from illness, she could give a raffia cloth from her store. Raffia was the great sweetener of relations between men and women. If a man insulted one of his wives, by committing adultery or by unduly favouring her co-wife, or if an apology was ever called for between any two persons, a peace-offering of raffia was the proper way to end the quarrel.

Some standard gifts of raffia could only be neglected at risk of rupturing specific social ties. On reaching adulthood a man should give twenty raffia cloths to his father. Until he had done so, he would be ashamed to ask his father's help for raising his marriage dues, forty raffia cloths for the mother and fifty for the father of the girl. A man had to give twenty raffia cloths to his wife on each delivery of a child which qualified him for entry to a cult group,[5] or she might repudiate the marriage, saying that he had cast her off. He should come to her parents' burial with a mortuary gift of at least twenty cloths. If she reported to him a would-be seducer he should reward her fidelity with twenty cloths, or she would not be virtuous a second time.

These semi-formal gifts were never forgotten, and were totted up whenever a new outlay or the end of the relationship was being discussed.

Apart from these gifts required from a man by his father, and his wife and her parents, there were heavy dues for entering a cult or age-set. Entrance to an age-set varied from six to ten cloths, entry to the Begetters' Cult group, 100, to the Diviners, 100, to the Twin Diviners, 40, and 20 for the Pangolin Cult. Ritual services were also paid in raffia: minor oracular consultations might cost one or two cloths, major ones forty, fifty or a hundred for a cure. If a man wanted to buy the right and the power to perform a ritual, whether for divination, or for hunting success or fertility or healing, he had to pay from forty to a hundred cloths again.

Raffia was also paid to restore good relations after an offence

[5] See Chapter XI.

had been committed. Adultery damages were a hundred cloths,
fines for fighting in the village, from two cloths upwards according to the amount of violence or bloodshed. A form of tribute
was also paid to aristocrats[6] in raffia cloths.

Raffia distribution restored advantage to older men

Since so many aspects of social life were regulated by payment
of raffia, it is natural that raffia should have acquired value over
and above its simple value as clothing. Most young men were
urgently needing large quantities of raffia, for paying entrance
fees, marriage dues and fines. The heaviest charges fell on a
man in the early years of his life. By the time he had entered an
age-set, married, entered the Begetters' Cult and become a
diviner, he would have disbursed a minimum of 300 cloths, and
certainly have spent as much again in maintaining good relations
with his wife, his in-laws, his own father and mother and settling
adultery damages, to say nothing of medical fees for his wife's
confinements. Once these payments were behind him, his
position improved. He himself received payments from other
young men, entering the cults he had joined or marrying his
daughters. If his wife committed adultery he would be paid
damages in raffia. Fatherhood, cult membership and the practice
of a specialist craft or ritual gave an older man sources of raffia,
while the younger men were working to produce raffia to achieve
these positions. Young men were constantly in need of large
quantities of raffia cloth, while older men were constantly
receiving it. The latter thus had funds of raffia from which they
could reward their juniors, bolster up their own prestige and so
compensate for their declining effectiveness in the system of
production. Young men did not expect to weave enough raffia
for their own needs, so they went to some of the older men to
ask for help in raising raffia to pay other older men. Thus an
asymmetry in raffia indebtedness went some way to redress the
disadvantages to which older men were put by the productive
side of the economy.

Raffia, being divisible and portable, is suited to a kinship
system which emphasizes both sides of the family. Men trying
to raise large sums of raffia would draw on any ties of kinship or
affinity which they felt would bear it. Unlike a heritage in land,

[6] See Chapter X.

wealth in the form of raffia cloth does not incline the society towards unilineal descent, but is compatible with mobility of residence, and with bilateral recognition of kinship.

If all the materials were prepared and his loom spanned ready, a strong young man could weave five cloths in a day, or two in an afternoon. This meant hard, concentrated work. It does not follow that he could make fifty in ten days, since he would never have so much dried raffia, combed and ready for weaving to be able to work uninterruptedly so long at his loom. So when a man was faced with a demand for 100 cloths, he never thought of weaving it all himself. He would weave some, say ten, and try to collect the rest.

In the 1950s there was an acute shortage of raffia for paying fees and fines. Lele attributed it to the new demands on their time. Before the Belgian occupation there may have been more woven raffia in circulation, as young men were not expected to cultivate fields, and did not earn wages. But I believe that the modern shortage of woven raffia was due to a more complex relation between prestations and rights over women in the blood-debts system.[7]

Raffia was not a medium of exchange. It did not help to pump the circulation of goods through the economy. Its transfer was only used to express status, and to pay for services which were not productive of material wealth. Although the occasions for paying raffia were standardized, they were not limited. Services to be paid for and offences to be fined could be multiplied, and rates for fines raised indefinitely, without regard to the supply of raffia or of its equivalents.

There was nothing to stop the demand for raffia from soaring away as new demands and new credit expanded. If it had had a real monetary role and the demand for it had been in fact a demand for purchasing power, then either prices would have gone up or the demand would have been satisfied by an increase in supply of the things raffia bought. But there were no prices to bring supply and demand into equilibrium. Except in the narrow field of barter the equivalent values expressed in raffia referred to substitution not to exchange and they were more or less fixed. The demand for a means of expressing status may never be satisfied. Furthermore, Lele expected to meet demands for raffia

[7] See Chapter VIII.

by expanding credit further and further into the future, not by starting a commerce in it. Kin ties inhibited the outright sale of raffia to the needy; indeed, for a man to be driven to buy raffia would be felt as a failure of all the social bonds which were expressed in gifts of raffia. It would be almost as distressing as the imaginary case of an Englishman reduced to buying Christmas cards to adorn his shelf. A Lele man would feel a complete failure if he had to admit that there were no sources he could hope to tap for raffia. So far from admitting that the costliness of fees deterred them from applying for cult initiation, men generally boasted of devoted kinsfolk lined up ready to help. For the same reasons, no one would expect to have to find all his raffia needs by sitting down and weaving cloth for himself. The normal response to demands for raffia was to call in outstanding debts or to create new ones.

Lele were constantly turning over in their minds ways of meeting their financial commitments, counting their assets, and possible future expectations. Among the young especially there was a feeling like financial pressure. A man would make promises on the strength of his unborn daughter's future bridewealth; any insult or injury would be almost welcomed as possible subject for a claim. They hoped to meet their demand for raffia by increasing the velocity of circulation rather than by increasing supplies. No one was expected to be anything but quick in making claims, or ruthless in pursuing debtors. The result was an inflationary pressure on the available supplies of raffia: too few raffia cloths circulating after too many debts and promises. Raffia was no sooner paid over than it was transferred again to liquidate debts of ten or twenty years' standing.

Divination was one field in which new debts could easily be created. A diviner was paid when he achieved a cure. Certain beliefs secured both that the cure would be admitted and the payment made. A patient under treatment was made to accept a number of irksome restrictions on his food, sexual relations, clothing and travel, which could only be lifted by the practitioner who had laid them on him, at risk of new complications in his disease. Therefore, at the first abatement he was usually ready to concede that he had been cured. Once the final ritual had been performed, unless he paid the diviner's fee for a cure, he risked a relapse. One diviner was temporarily cured of the symptoms of leprosy by another, who charged him 100 raffia cloths. The patient raised an instalment of thirty cloths, by borrowing from a colleague, and was casting about for more credit, when he heard that his healer had fallen ill with intestinal trouble. Quickly dispatching to him a remedy, with full instructions, he gleefully reckoned that he would charge seventy cloths for a cure.

Raffia in the transition to a market economy

After the Belgian occupation, the Lele started to extend their commercial experience from barter to the use of money. Europeans found that they could enter the barter system if they had supplies of the always acceptable raffia cloth. They allowed taxes to be paid in raffia. In 1924 the official rate was two cloths for one Congo franc. The district tribunal allowed fines to be paid in raffia in lieu of francs. In 1950 the rate was up to five francs to one cloth and in 1953, to ten francs. Its value had gone up because francs gradually became less scarce in the economy, while the demand for raffia never relaxed. The retail shops also occasionally accepted raffia cloth as payment. Raffia paid as fines at the tribunal was taken by court clerks and police, who liked the chance to change their wages into raffia cloth at the official rate for the sake of their marriage payments. Since this was the only point in the economy in which raffia could be bought for money, there was hardly a free market. In 1949 raffia cloth, as the most widely acceptable barter commodity, seemed ripe for developing into a supplementary currency. But this did not happen.

Lele society at that time was only on the brink of entering a market economy. European enterprises started at the mission and at the oil-palm concession at Brabanta, and at the administrative headquarters at Basongo, brought more strangers into contact than ever before. The workers who left their villages temporarily became dependent on one another for food and lodging. Either they forged links of friendship on the model of brothers or age-mates, or they entered market relations, buying food and clothing at the stores. Their pressing need for Congo francs for the necessities of life turned many of them to trade in their own villages on their holidays, when they hawked small quantities of anything they could acquire. The coming and going of so many strangers, with money but no kinship ties, broke down the old rules of hospitality. In villages near the work centres it became the custom to sell palm wine by the beakerful, or meat, or even, more rarely, flour. Things in the subsistence sphere, which had never had any price before, began, albeit only occasionally, to acquire a price in francs.

In the sphere of prestations, one valuable only could be bought with francs . . . camwood, which was stocked in the retail shops. Lele generally preferred to buy camwood through their traditional channels of barter, since they did not trust European traders' judgement of quality. Indeed, they sometimes travelled with their money forty miles to the shop, inspected the stock, and returned without buying any of it. But if they liked the quality, they used Congo francs to buy camwood, which would be accepted by the old men for marriage fees or cult dues. Apart from this, francs were only seeping into the economy around the centres of wage-earning where Lele were displaced from their villages. Away from these centres, in 1949 at least, francs had little purchasing power in the native economy. People said that they only earned money in order to pay their taxes and fines at the tribunal.

By 1953 a big change had taken place. Congo francs were desired for the sake of the trade goods in the shops. Guns had always been much sought after, but their acquisition was limited by licence. Now bicycles, sewing machines, clothing, paraffin lamps were seen everywhere and men who did not have the use of such things might well be found to be laboriously saving up for one. Old men helped and encouraged their nephews to buy guns because they hoped to use them in the hunt themselves, and bicycles because they could send the owner on messages, or be taken for long rides to visit distant kinsfolk on the handlebars.

However, raffia cloth, which had seemed well placed for acquiring a real monetary role, since it was highly acceptable, and was already a standard of value, had not become a supplementary currency.[8] It was still much desired, but there was simply no market in it at the official rate of ten francs, and no black market at any higher rate. As soon as I acquired a store of raffia cloth, through the Tribunal, I was offered baskets and carvings which nobody would part with for the equivalent sum

---

[8] Thus Lele raffia cloth constituted an exception to Karl Menger's expectation that the most highly saleable barter commodity tends to become an acceptable medium of exchange. (Menger, 1892.)

in francs, which showed that the official rate of exchange under-
valued raffia. In truth, Lele who were at the receiving end of the
traditional prestations did not want a more realistic rate of
conversion, since they had good grounds for resisting the flow
of francs into their economy.

Only in special circumstances could francs be substituted for
raffia cloth in prestations. A rate of substitution is not the same
as a price, and raffia in fact could not be bought. If a payment
was made in raffia cloths, the number could be 10 per cent.
below the nominal amount due, but in any other of the acceptable
goods, it usually had to be the full amount. Young men would
accept francs, and older men if goodwill prevailed, but any
angry husband asking adultery damages would try to insist on
raffia or camwood.

In their old society, raffia transactions marked out all the
statuses and relations between men. A free market in raffia would
have disrupted these established patterns. Raffia had been a
valuable which young men had to pay to older men, and which
they begged from their senior kinsmen. If it could be acquired
simply by buying it with earned francs, raffia would soon be
accumulating in the hands of the young, since they were the
wage-earners, and many old obligations would be dissolved.

There was another reason why money could not perform the
same role as raffia cloth. Just because it was a medium of
exchange which bought bicycles, guns and sewing machines,
once it was acquired it tended to be taken out of the cycle of
prestations. With a thousand francs a man could buy the cheapest
kind of muzzle-loader, whereas the obvious way to use 100 raffia
cloths was to pay an outstanding cult due of that amount. If
muzzle-loaders or bicycles had been accepted in lieu of raffia for
prestations they would have had the same effect as money in
tilting the distributive side of the economy in favour of young
men, and they would have blocked the circulation of prestations
by being taken straight into use. Another kind of society would
have been shaped.[9]

Although they tried to stop the tendency of young men to
offer francs in lieu of raffia for prestations, Lele allowed a

[9] Compare Oliver's study of the economy of a Solomon Island in which the
pattern of distribution is not tied to a rigid status pattern but used to reward
enterprise. The position of older men is correspondingly without honour.

completely new form of wealth to be freely substituted for raffia, that is goats. Previously they never kept goats, and even in the 1950s they had no use for them. In their hunting culture the idea of eating domestic animals or drinking milk was utterly repugnant. They kept goats because Luba, employed in thousands in Brabanta, ate the meat and paid readily for it in Congo francs. In 1950 Lele bred goats not for slaughter but for use in their prestations. A man did not expect to sell his goats for cash but passed them on in settlement of marriage fees and cult dues, and the recipients likewise. At any time they could be converted into Congo francs, so they were a store of value, and, like raffia, a standard of value, but not a medium of exchange. If a man needed francs suddenly, he could sell a goat, but usually there was no need to sell it for francs, since any Lele creditor would accept it in lieu of raffia or francs.

The rate of equivalences for raffia in 1953 was as follows:

Table 7. Raffia values

Accounting units of raffia	Equivalents in things	Congo francs 1953
1 *iboka* (plur: *maboka*) 1 bundle (9 or 10 cloths)	= 1 axe	100
2 *maboka*	= 1 bar of salt (obsolete) *nghei* (plur: *mihei*)	200
	= 1 three-foot bar of camwood	
	= 1 he-goat	
4 *maboka*	= 2 bars of trade salt	400
	= 1 large bar of camwood (five feet long)	
	= 1 she-goat	
3 *mihei* (60 raffia cloths)	= 1 she-goat gravid	600
1 *lutuku* (body) (90 or 100 cloths)	= 1 slave	1,000
	= 1 copper bar (obsolete)	
	= 5 bars of camwood	

Rights over persons

One hundred raffia cloths used to be equal to one slave in outright purchase, also to compensation for one blood debt, and also to a full marriage payment. Thus the sum of 100 raffia cloths, *lutuku*, a body, entered into another sphere of exchanges, of rights over persons. Except over slaves, these rights were not strictly buyable.[10] Blood debts[11] and marriage dues could not be paid or claimed at will. No one who had a claim, either to demand a girl in payment of a blood debt or in simple marriage, would give it up for the sake of valuables, unless he saw no other way of realizing the claim. Just as no one possessing prestation valuables would dream of exchanging them for anything in the subsistence sphere, so in the prestation sphere everyone wanted to convert camwood and raffia into rights over women. But possessors of these rights disposed of them only according to elaborate rules and not to the highest bidder.

Although they were not completely watertight and separate, there were four distinct spheres[12] of exchange, ranked in prestige, so that no one would voluntarily 'convert down'[13] from a higher to a lower one, though severe straits might force him to do so.

It was not an arbitrary matter of the prestige of the things themselves which stopped a man from converting down his wealth from a higher to a lower sphere, but a sensible recognition of the way their distribution was arranged in the economy as a whole. All their institutions were so biased that no one could rise far in status without marrying wives and having daughters and granddaughters. Marriage fees were not prices. However well endowed with material wealth a man might be, to be accepted as a suitor he needed a supplementary title distinguishing him from other competitors, and ratified by the current generation of fathers and gradfathers of girls. The blood-debt system and preferred marriages were like rationing coupons— in reverse. A real rationing system aims at giving equal access to scarce commodities, allowing no one special privileges over his fellows. The Lele system restricted access, so as to underpin their status pattern.

If either natural selection or market principles had had free

---

[10] Unenforceable blood-debt claims could be sold, see Chapter VIII.
[11] A blood debt was equivalent to a claim over a marriageable girl, see p. 143.
[12] Subsistence exchange, barter, prestations, and rights over persons.
[13] The existence of distinct spheres of exchange in primitive economies has often been indicated (E. Hoyt, F. Steiner, C. Dubois, P. J. Bohannan). The latter uses the term 'conveyancing' for transactions within such a sphere, and 'conversion' up or down for transactions between two of them. I am much indebted to him for suggesting this approach to the analysis of distribution.

play, the strong, handsome young men would have carried off the girls. There would have been an end to polygyny of older men with all it meant to the Lele for seniority, tradition and the rest. Nothing the Lele could do would change the supply of marriageable girls. The pressure of demand merely forced their age of marriage down, so that girls were pledged in infancy, even before birth. Their great value and relative scarcity were axioms from which the rest of Lele culture flowed. In truth, the rationing system is a bad analogy, since the allocation of several girls to older men in fact created the scarcity which it also regulated.

The distinct spheres of exchange emerged because men were naturally reluctant to give up rights to what was most scarce and valued for the sake of anything more easily acquired. Further, to give up a claim over a woman for the sake of nominally equivalent material wealth was to give up a position of social advantage in which indefinite quantities of material wealth would automatically accrue. More wives meant more daughters, more raffia from sons-in-law, more daughters' daughters to marry off, more blood debts to pursue, and so on.

There is nothing mysterious about the existence of distinct economic spheres whose mutual penetrability is deliberately limited. Restrictions on the saleability of social status are found in even the most commercialized of modern economies. There are always some official posts, titles, honours, and marriages which cannot be had for money, and yet which once acquired bring in an indirect revenue. The Lele refusal to do commerce in raffia cloth in the 1950s was like a rear-guard action to delay the revision of their social system on market standards.

The high value of raffia and its equivalents was largely because 100 raffia cloths counted traditionally as equal to a transfer of rights over women. A man oppressed by debts in raffia might be forced to convert some of his rights over women into raffia cloth. He could always liquidate an excessive pile of raffia debts by giving a girl pawn[14] or daughter's daughter to a friend who would pay his raffia debts. This meant that the tendency for credits in raffia cloth to expand indefinitely used not to be limited merely by the extent of the lender's gullibility. Under the old system an advance of 100 raffia cloths was covered by the security of womenfolk over whom the borrower had rights. If repayment

[14] Chapter VIII describes the system of pawnship for settling debts.

III a. *Woman baling out fish pond*

III b. *Women pressing oil*

IV a. *Arranging folds of dance skirt*

IV b. *Men eating together*

were to be refused indefinitely after a quarrel, public opinion would applaud the creditor for taking a woman by force. Thus the inflationary trend was transferred from raffia to rights over women, with obvious effects on their age of marriage, and other aspects of Lele society.[15]

In colonial conditions this control on lending had gone. Not only did the administration try to liquidate the system of blood debts, by forcing claimants to accept Congo francs in settlement, but it restrained them from capturing women. This explains the continual shortage of raffia under the colonial régime. The behaviour of raffia in the 1950s, its scarcity, high value and unsaleability, only makes sense in the full context of changes in marriage and blood compensation, to which the whole distributive system used to be tied.

---

[15] See Chapters VII and VIII for the account of the communal village-wives and of pawnship.

6

IV

THE VILLAGE: OFFICES AND AGE-SETS

THE VILLAGE was the social unit which the Lele valued most. Its members strove consciously to maintain its membership, canvassing young men from all quarters with a zeal which later set problems of authority and co-ordination. New members from other villages had to be welded into a corporate group, so tendencies to split the village on lines of descent were checked. Other principles of organization dominated, less liable to provoke rifts than kinship.

Village head

Every village had its chief, *kum a bola*, a semi-hereditary post, in so far as one (or sometimes two) of the original clans which founded the village had the right to put its senior member into the office.

The principle of seniority by age was strictly followed; the oldest old man of the privileged clan was automatically indicated and there was no question of election from several candidates. No special investiture was performed. When one headman died, his successor was known and referred to at once as the new village head.

No other qualification than seniority in years was needed. He did not have to belong to a particular cult group, or to have achieved any particular success, or to have attracted a personal following. He only needed to have outlived his fellows. He was not the focus of village unity. People did not join the village on his account, or leave it if he became old and weak. Indeed the titular village head was often a tired old grey-head, who spent most of his day resting in the shade. Since his role demanded no special qualities of leadership or judgement, it did not matter if he was not a vigorous personality. He did not govern, allocate resources, adjudicate disputes.

The method of his selection and his unprominent role made it certain that the office stood outside any field of competition.

Men did not cherish dreams of headmanship or resent the incumbent of the day. A possible source of antagonism and of fission of the village, if we judge by the experience of some other Central African tribes,[1] was altogether eliminated.

The office of head was the apex of village society since it fulfilled the two principles of precedence in the village: precedence of a particular clan in that particular village and precedence of sheer age. The Lele thus saved a cherished ideal which hard economic and political facts put in jeopardy. Other old men might, for individual reasons, fail to deserve the respect due to seniority, but the precedence of the old *kum a bola* demonstrated that age in itself gave a claim to prestige.

His duties were to represent the village. Decisions which he voiced were not his, but arrived at in a meeting of all the men of the village. His prerogatives were portions of meat and wine. From the communal hunt he should receive one haunch of antelope, and from wine tappers one calabash of palm wine, but when meat and wine were short, he did not complain if he received less, or none, so long as he was supplied on the occasions when he had to receive guests on behalf of the village.

His one sanction against disrespect was his curse, a penalty he wielded together with a number of other people in the village. A man feared to be cursed by his own father, father's sister, or mother. The curse, *mihangi*, was in effect an appeal to God to witness and punish a slight to a person entitled to respect. A diviner could curse his patient. Anyone calling himself a *munabola*, owner of the village, could similarly curse the whole village. Members of founding clans, twins, and members of certain cult groups were owners of the village in this sense, and able to call on God to uphold their rights.

If the village head spoke in anger or even felt silent anger against the people of his village, nothing they did would prosper. They had to apologize, and ask him to remove his saliva (*cwei mahoynyi*). This action was the normal form of blessing. A diviner transferring one of his powers to another or treating a patient while uttering his blessing gave a very delicate and

---

[1] I refer to the analyses of Mitchell (1956) and of Turner (1957) for the Yao and Ndembu and to White (1955) for Luvale. In these societies competition for the office of village head was liable to split the villages along lines of descent.

conventional appearance of spitting on his outstretched hand. It was more an articulated word, 'Cha!' than expectoration.

As a sanction it should not be underestimated. It was a considerable satisfaction to the old village head to know that if anyone were to insult him sooner or later they would be heard confessing their fault in public. If the offender did not himself raise the matter, anyone who knew about it would feel bound to do so. If the hunt went off in ignorance, the offender would not be surprised if he repeatedly missed his mark. If the whole hunt were a failure, the hidden matter would come out afterwards and the offender be reproached for wasting everybody's day by keeping it secret. Called upon to give his blessing, the village head would know how best to exploit the situation launching into a long, complaining speech, insisting that he felt no rancour, but listing all the occasions when he had not received his due.

Some of our examples of actual quarrels and insults may suggest that Lele life was characterized by much spontaneous violence. Nothing could be further from the truth as far as village life was concerned. Lele were constantly preoccupied with keeping the peace. Not merely the officials in a village, but every man and boy was ready to step between combatants, to scold both parties to a quarrel, and to hold before them the accepted ideals of conduct.

Men prided themselves on their eloquence (*lutot*), on being able to cool one another's passions and bring out the true, best nature of their neighbours. They were all keen judges of oratorical style. Young men, whom respect forbade to speak in the presence of their seniors, would develop their talent in their age-set quarters. They knew how to begin speaking in a very low voice, compelling attention by their very quietness. A good speech, witty and packed with proverbial allusions, would be delivered with elegant gestures of the hand. Rhetorical questions punctuated it, so phrased that the audience was impelled to break in with the proper elicited response.[2] Often the speaker would round his peroration with the verse of a song in which others would join the chorus.

If Lele cherished the skills of rhetoric, it was because they valued full communication. They wanted to reach each other's hearts and to coax out of them any lurking grudge or spite that

[2] Tew, 1950.

might be there. Peaceful living together was a constant pre-occupation. Believing jealousy to be its main enemy, they tried to avoid conspicuous leadership. They eschewed direct authority, and resorted to numerous, overlapping, indirect means of control. Of these, the most important was the automatic religious sanction of failure in the hunt. This imposed on every man the obligation to declare his animosity and to promise to let it rankle no more, on pain of rendering the hunt fruitless. When people quarrelled, they said, the forest went hard, no game came to the hunters' arrows or traps, the people suffered. Diviners could put it right with ritual, but not before the disputants had paid a fine. At the time of my visit it had become the custom to perform a rite, *ndengu*, after every quarrel. But I heard this was an innovation, and that within living memory it had been considered enough to collect a fine for minor quarrels.

The hunt is obviously well adapted to uphold these beliefs. Any man may misfire, trip and fall, or lose his arrow, and the more he is worried and nervous the more likely his misfortune. Men liked to go to the hunt confident of their standing with one another, all grievances aired and settled. Their regular pre-hunting surveys of faults and omissions built up the sense of community. What is striking about the Lele is not how often they quarrelled, but how much it worried them when they did.

If in the course of the hunt the first two or three draws produced no game, they might hold another meeting and go through a ritual of appeasement. Two men would exchange weapons in the name of disputants, known or unknown, so that the hunt could proceed in good heart to the next draw.

If we needed other evidence for their concern for peace, their nightly exhortations, plaints and appeals provide it. If anyone had a grievance against his fellow, he would raise it, in a loud ringing voice, in the late evening or just before dawn. Anyone could speak thus, member of the village or not. But if he wished to delegate his matter, he could trust it to the *Itembangu* or village spokesman.

Spokesman

The spokesman was informally elected, or chosen by his pre-decessor, for outstanding personal qualities. He should be eloquent, judicious and gentle. He was a young man, blessed with a clear, carrying voice and skilled in the rhetorical arts. He spoke for anyone in the village, delivering messages and warnings, making announcements for the next day's hunt or work. If someone had broken a calabash, or an unknown borrower not returned a woman's axe, he would exhort them to make themselves known, lest people quarrelled for such little things or he might warn that the owner was going to consult an oracle if it was not replaced in the morning. He put into his speech anything that struck him as worth mentioning. If someone's carelessness had nearly set the village on fire, he recalled a previous disaster, and begged people to be careful. Or, if he had had a bad dream, he might mention it. If someone was sick, he certainly would ask people not to make a noise with drumming until the danger was past. He usually got up to speak when people were finishing their evening meal. They stopped their quiet gossip to listen. When he ended, he would say, 'Now I have spoken! Go into your houses, and sleep well. *Polo!*' In some large villages he spoke twice, at both ends of the village, in others there was a raised platform for him, but usually the villages were so compactly built that he could be heard from all corners.

Besides speaking, his duties included keeping the treasures of the village. He would collect fines when they were to be paid. He accepted all goods paid into the village treasury, and brought them out of his hut to transfer to creditors as occasion demanded. He also had to carve up the game from the village hunt, allocating to each his due amount.

These tasks demanded a conscientious, good-tempered performer, but not any exercise of authority. The conventions of the post indicated a young man (young by Lele standards, 40–45), courteous and correct. There was no need for him to make enemies in the exercise of his duties. He was a servant of the village, in no wise its master. Therefore he was jocularly called wife of the village, because he kept their possessions in his hut, and had to be discreet and impartial. If anyone struck or wounded him, they owed full blood compensation to the village, whereas for wounding a private person the compensation could be paid in raffia cloths.

The ritual of the hunt and its chancy outcome fastened attention on breaches of harmony. The village head and village spokesman gave expression to the desire for unity. But they were expected to do little to impose it. Order in the village was expected to arise from the principle of seniority. Between any two men, the senior always had precedence, and the junior showed respect by avoiding him. Precedence settled rival claims in favour of the elder, avoidance eliminated friction. Logically, therefore, between co-evals there could only be ease and good-will. On this basis, men of all clans were banded into age-sets, to share a common life, and even a common wife.

Age-mates

The word for age-mate was *mbai*. It carried strong emotional overtones. Boys who had been born at the same time, within a few weeks or a month, would have been taught from infancy to love and be loyal to one another. By reason of the very formality which separated a boy from his own brother because of the several years between their births, so his relation with his true age-mate was close and intimate. The bond between age-mates was contrasted with that between brothers, in a way that sharpened and emphasized each. If two brothers were born at the same time, then they were anomalous in several senses,[3] but socially because they combined the characteristic of age-mates with the opposite characteristics of brothers.

That the Lele were aware of these contrasts and likenesses was evident from the play they made of the relation between twins. To have been born from the same womb at the same time was such a striking anomaly that it overrode the distinctions of sex. Lele normally distinguished very carefully girls' names from boys' names and there would be no possibility of confusion between them. But in the case of twins, regardless of sex, only two names were permitted, Ihaku for the twin that was delivered first, and Mboyu for the second. Thus, by the distinctive naming, seniority was introduced into their relations and the social anomaly in their situation reduced.

Lele idealized many of the relations between men. They rhapsodized about what a man should do for his father, what a father should do for his son, the devotion of brothers. The love of true age-mates for one another was even more a favourite theme. Age-mates should have no secrets or reserves. They should share their goods and bear one another's hardships. No

[3] Douglas, 1957.

sacrifice was too great for an age-mate. In a fable, the eagle and the tortoise made a pact of friendship (*ku wat bumbai:* to tie the bond of age-mates). Each promised to the other the most precious thing he possessed. The tortoise asked the eagle for his feathers, which the eagle forthwith plucked out for him. Then the eagle asked the tortoise for his shell, and the tortoise gave it to him. The eagle's feathers eventually grew again, but the tortoise had not hesitated to sacrifice his life. My cook, who had previously never worn anything but raffia cloth, to illustrate the completeness of the sacrifice entailed in such friendship, declared: 'If my age-mate wanted the very trousers I stand up in, yes! the ones given me by Madam for my work, I should take them off at once, and hand them to him!'

Age-mates spent most of their day in one another's company. When they were nine or ten years old, they would be turned out of their mother's hut at night, and thenceforth they slept together in a boys' dormitory hut. As they grew older, they fed together, their mothers sending them baskets of food to share. They hunted, set snares, drank wine together, worked at weaving in the same shelter. If one was sent to do marriage service for his father-in-law, the other would go too, to help him. If one got into trouble, the other would plead for him.

For example, a boy, Polidor,[4] committed adultery with the wives of two older men who were age-mates. One of them had accepted the usual fine in his own case, but when his age-mate's wife was also seduced, he was so outraged at the double affront that he tried to use his influence with Polidor's future father-in-law to get his betrothal cancelled. However, Polidor's own close age-mate, who was of the father-in-law's clan, pleaded successfully for his age-mate to be forgiven.

An age-mate extended classificatory kinship terms to his age-mate's family, avoiding his mother-in-law, calling his wife 'my wife', and his children 'my children', and coming to his home to ask for food, as of right. But he should never make any sexual approaches to his age-mate's private wife.[5]

Although the relationship was supposed to be based on the co-incidence in time of two men's birth, *bumbai* age-friendship

[4] Bwenga, 13—see Fig. 13, Appendix A, p. 277.
[5] As distinct from a communal village-wife, see Chapter VII.

could be 'tied' between any two men with some of the emotional associations of a shared childhood carried over into a straight-forward contractual relation. A man could make a bond of age-friendship with one of another tribe, thus assuring to each safety, gifts and hospitality, and the basis for a profitable trading partnership. *Bumbai* in this, and in its other sense of a volun-tarily assumed relationship, is comparable to blood-brotherhood in other parts of Africa.

On this basis of perfect friendship the Lele system of wife-sharing was established. When boys reached the age of eighteen or so the hardship of their bachelorhood began to press on them. Yet it was quite likely to last another twenty years. Lele said that the whole object of their age-set organization was to alleviate the trials of bachelorhood. An unmarried man in their society was an object of pity. He was compared to an orphan, always hungry and neglected. Only a married man was certain of two square meals a day, because he could beat his wife if she failed to cook to his satisfaction. But bachelors had to wait on their mothers' inclination. When the food-baskets were sent to them, they sat around hungrily, until four or five baskets had been sent, then twenty young men would share them out, taking small handfuls in turns, until the food was gone. They protested that they were never satisfied, and would go round to their kinswomen, scrounging more. In the evenings, when married men had long since retired to sleep with their wives, the bachelors whiled away the night, dancing to the drum, singing songs by the fire, asking riddles or playing games. The hunger, homelessness and wifelessness of *baput*, bachelors, gave intensity to their shared life.

In a sense they seemed to have formed a little society within the larger society of the village, with their own criteria of prestige which might well run counter to the codes of village life. One would celebrate an act of daring by planting a banana or palm tree; when it fruited or yielded wine he would share it with any others of his age-set who had equalled his exploit, whether it be killing a leopard, an eagle, or a man. Such a tree was always planted by members of a newly formed age-set, its fruit to be shared by those who had committed adultery. Boys excluded from the feast would be mercilessly ridiculed.

It is not surprising that the bachelors in their age-set quarters were treated as if they were not full members of society. Ribald and violent as they were proud to be, women and older men were half-afraid of them. The respect which was a father's due was ensured by the father not approaching his son when he sat in the company of his age-mates. Mothers and sisters never approached their quarter, but sent food by the hands of a child. At one point their code was consistent with that honoured in the village, that is, the rule of seniority. Therefore they were sometimes asked to form a court to judge one of their members for a failing in this respect. That he might deceive or insult his kinsmen in general was not a matter which concerned his age-mates, but that he should respect the rights of a senior brother was consistent with the rule on which their whole association was based. So a man could complain of disrespect to the age-set of his younger brother, and they would settle the case with a singing contest: they accusing him with well-known tags of verse, and he rejoining as best he could with others. The outcome was certain if the facts were agreed. If he had failed in respect towards an older brother, he had to pay a fine, usually two calabashes of wine, one to the brother and one to his age-set.

Everyone recognized that the young unmarried men coveted the wives of their seniors. Indeed, one of their pastimes was to plan seductions and the man who boasted of none was derided. Since the old men wished to remain polygynists, with two or three wives, and since adulteries were thought to disrupt the peace of the village, Lele had to make some arrangement to appease their unmarried men.

Therefore, when a sufficient number of them reached the age of eighteen or so, they were allowed to buy the right to a common wife. Four or five of them would pay ten raffia cloths apiece, and in return be given a name, in recognition that they had formed an age-set and been given the right to build a hut for their wife in their quarter of the village. Whether the girl was allotted to them or abducted by them from a rival village, it made no difference to her standing in the village, which was very honourable. The rules regulating sexual intercourse with her, protecting her from dangers in childbirth and establishing her family as children of the village will be discussed later.[6]

In a Lele village at any one time there would be about six age-

[6] Chapter VII.

sets currently established. The establishment of a new set was entirely a matter for the individual village. It would be aware of what other neighbouring villages were doing, but did not attempt to co-ordinate closely its age-sets with theirs. The main factors which they took into consideration when deciding to open a new set were the number of young men in the last-formed set, and the span of years they bridged, the numbers of boys claiming the right to form a new set, and the effect of a new set on the balance of sets in the village. When they formed a new set, roughly every fifteen years, the oldest would be dying out, only three or four old men belonging to it still left alive in the village. Age-sets in a small village would number fewer men, and there would be fewer of them. For instance, in South Homba, the oldest set, Manyamangele, with only four or five old men had, to all practical purposes, merged with the Yulu, also a very small set. If the last set had been formed there would have been exactly four sets. By contrast, in Ngoie, a much bigger village, if the last set had been formed, a very numerous one, even though the two oldest sets were merged together, there would have been five full sets in being. In other words, new sets were opened more frequently in the big villages.

Only a rough co-ordination of age-sets from village to village appeared. It was not one of the aims of the age-set system, and discrepancies between villages did not worry anyone. When a man changed his residence from one village, where he had been formally admitted to age-set D, say, he could expect to be allocated either to D in the new village, or to C, or even E, according to the numbers in the sets, and according to a comparison of his age with that of the members of the sets. The name of the set to which he had belonged in his village of origin was not necessarily found in the system of sets in his new village. The only thing that mattered was that he should be accepted in a set of his contemporaries, and allowed to pay a fee giving him right of access to the village-wives.

The names of the age-sets did not follow a strict recurring cycle, although I was told that they did not ever wish to let the names of former sets be lost and intended to revive them one day. In practice the wish to repeat the names of previous age-sets was hampered by the fact that in any village the older men, natural repositories of tradition, would not have been born or brought up there, but would have come in from a number of other villages, each with its own tradition of age-set names.[7]

Table 8. *Age-set names*

Yunda	Ngoie	S. Homba
	*Tamananji	*Itaka La Yang
*Tamananji	*Njobamwai	*Koku Mangamba
*Ngwangele	*Njumbangele	*Ngamba
Ilebo (2 alive)	Ilebo (1 alive)	*Luang
Luong	Luong (4 alive)	Manyamangele
		(4 still alive)
Yuli	Taka	Yulu
Tamananji	Tamananji	Tamananji
Ngwangele	Luang	Luang
Young Christians	Njumba	Young Christians
	Young Christians	

* Members all dead.

In each of the three villages the age-sets were terminated by a band of young Christians who dissociated themselves from village polyandry. Some of the old names crop up again, but not regularly. A small village, S. Homba, has fewer sets to embrace its living men than a big village, Ngoie.

The age-sets were the basis of residence in the village. A man built near his age-mates, and away from his parents. Beyond the huts of an age-set were their groves of palms, and their weaving shelters. Here they would rest between work, wait for food or wine and do occasional sedentary jobs, repairing weapons, etc., if they could not find a place to set up a loom. One of the paths to the forest went past their shelter, leading first to a clearing where their wives pounded grain together, and then farther on, to another clearing where the wives pressed oil, and then down to the water and the cultivated clearings.

Each age-set had its treasurer-spokesman, and *itembangu*, who carved the meat when occasion demanded, stored the valuables or divided them amongst the set. In the north each set received the entrance fee of new sets on its own side of the village and they either applied the wealth to some common purpose, such as the marriage fees of a new wife, or shared it out. In the south the fees were generally paid into the village treasury.

Each age-set was separated from those immediately preceding and following it, by alternation. Sets one and three would be ranged together opposite sets two and four (see Table 9). The

[7] I had difficulty gathering the names of previous age-sets, but the lists for Ngoie, Yunda and S. Homba will illustrate the small degree of co-ordination.

Table 9. Arrangement of residence according to age-sets

On the most usual pattern the square of the village was split in half by an imaginary diagonal, on one side of which were ranged the huts of the men of the most senior set, 1, together with those of the second youngest set, 3, while on the other side were the huts of the men of the second oldest set, 2, with those of the youngest, 4. This pattern held for Yunda, North Homba, Ibombe and Ngoie. The two sides or halves of the village were not named.

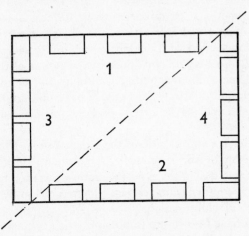

In Malembi the village was divided into three, so that age-sets 1, 2 and 5 formed a unit separating set 3 from set 4.

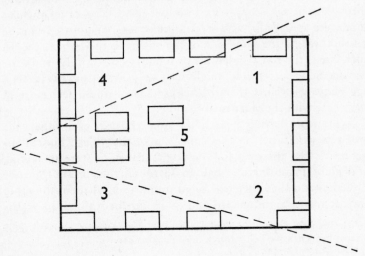

oldest set, dying out, would be tacked on to number one, and the youngest, awaiting admission, or newly admitted, would either be treated as an appendage to the next youngest, until it was formally opened, or it could anticipate its association with number three.[8] The alternation of sets divided the village into two halves, or hands (*iac*). The reasons given for the avoidance between successive sets was that they were natural rivals, and so likely to fight one another. In practice alternation achieved a neat balancing of opposed interests in the village. Each of the two senior sets was allied with one of the two junior sets. One of the two bachelor sets would thus be attached to one of the two sets of married men. They acquired common interests which their competitive interests might otherwise have obscured. In South Homba residential age-quarters were not so clear as in other villages.

The junior set on one side of the village referred to its senior set as its elder brothers, or their grandfathers. In other words, they were treated as of the same generation, not therefore obliged to avoid one another from respect.[9] These kinship terms had no reference to kinship relations.

It would have been quite impossible to co-ordinate biological relationships with the age-set system. Lele were used to living with glaring discrepancies in their kinship relations, and it was certainly not their idea to tidy up loose strands of kin behaviour through their age-set system. I noticed many cases of men whose sons were spread through several junior sets, one of them in the set that was on the same side of the village as the father's set. In such cases, the son avoided his own father respectfully, and if he was specially susceptible, might also keep away from his father's age-mates as well. Others of his age-mates would feel more at their ease with the older men than he.

Apart from having their living quarters near each other, the two sets associated on the same half of the village hunted together. When the men for the communal hunt were mustered, and plans made for one half to surround the forest from one direction and the other half to go round to meet them the other way, it was straightforward and quick for them to fall in on the

---

[8] G. Brausch, one-time administrator of Basongo District, reported other arrangements in some Lele villages. See Brausch, 1951.

[9] See Chapter V, pp. 104-5.

basis of the age-halves of the village. Thus the juniors had the benefit of the experience of the seniors of their own half, while giving the latter the advantage of their strength, speed and accuracy.

After a hunt, when the game was divided up, certain parts would be reserved for the members of the hunt who had not a claim to a specific part as reward either for shooting or for carrying home the animal. For instance, two forelegs, and one hindleg of a pig were given to the two halves of the village, to be divided by the spokesmen of the sets. In a large village, where there would be several evening drinking clubs, these would be formed on the same basis, so that the young man without palms and the old man without strength to draw wine would still get their share.

As far as meat and wine were concerned, the young men more than contributed their share to the senior set. But it was the turn of the latter to help the younger men when they got into trouble. If they committed adulteries, or if they were restless because they were not being given enough wives, the senior set on their side of the village would speak up for them, ask them to be forgiven, try to allocate them a wife. The senior set was supposed to allocate to them their own daughters' daughters. This was following the regular pattern of Lele preferred marriages, by which a girl should be given to her mother's father to dispose of in marriage. Thus the daughter's daughter of a village-wife was destined from birth to be the wife of a new age-set, the younger brother set of those who begot her mother. Since brothers were supposed to help one another to get wives, and older brothers supposed to allocate to their classificatory younger brothers their daughters' daughters, the analogy with clan brotherhood was well developed. I found many cases of wife-giving between age-sets on this basis.

Villages north of Yunda and including it, had elaborations of the age-set system which the southerners declared were innovations contrary to the old easy-going system which they still practised. In the south if a woman was set up as wife of an age-set, she was the village-wife in the sense that any man of the village could have sexual intercourse with her in the forest, and moreover, this grace was extended to all men of all the brother villages. 'Are we not all one village?' they would ask. The same hospitality was extended to visitors from friendly neighbouring villages, which did not claim a common origin.

In the north, however, a much more jealously possessive code was practised. If a man moved from one village to another, the fee he had paid in the first place did not entitle him to access to the village-wives. He had to pay again, in some villages it was ten cloths, in others only three, according to their attitude to recruits. If a man tried to make the village-wife his own, to keep other men away from her, as they put it: 'tried to beget her children all by himself', he would be heavily fined or beaten up, and the same if a man from another village had sexual intercourse with her without having paid the fee.

In the north the age-set itself would be divided into several sections, *njong*. The men of the front section, who opened the age-set by paying their fee to the senior men on their side of the village, ten or twenty cloths according to local custom, kept their first village-wife to themselves. They did not allow the younger men of the next section to enter her hut until they had paid their fees, not to the senior set this time, but to them as the front section of their own set. The senior set on one side of a village could have free access to the wives of juniors, but the latter should not approach theirs. Nor should the village-wives on one side of the village cross over to have sexual relations with men of age-sets on the other side of the village. The greater precision and narrowness in the formulation of age-set rights in the north obviously is a response to the larger scale of northern villages. All the men of the three Homba villages combined were not more numerous than those of Ngoie alone. The larger villages had correspondingly greater problems of organization.

The age-set system performed several functions in Lele village life. It provided a universally applicable scale of priority between men, regardless of their other affiliations—thus it promoted order. It built up the sense of community between men of different clans, and men coming from different villages—in this way it aided the assimilation of new arrivals, vital for the survival of the village, as well as binding together existing members. It prevented the male population from splitting on the line of their opposed interests in the competition for wives: youths against elders, or rather, bachelors against married men. It stopped the young men from disrupting the village by seducing the wives of their seniors because it went some way to meet their claims to women, and this in a fashion which turned their attention away from their own village, to the girls of other villages. This meant that peace within the village was saved and its political rivalry with other villages promoted. When the young men succeeded in abducting a girl from another village all the existing tensions and hostilities would be forgotten in a general flush of pride in their deed. In the south at least, the age-set system promoted harmony in the village by turning the young men's attention away from the restrictions and temptations that beset them there, and faced them outwards, towards the glory to be had by raiding and capturing girls from other villages. In the north more complex functions for the internal relations in the village followed from the greater elaboration of the system.

Probably the most important contribution that the age-sets made to the Lele way of life was to enable the young men's social maturity to be delayed well after they had passed their physical prime. In his study of age-organization[10] Eisenstadt has made a distinction between age-sets organized on a tribal basis, whose initiation ceremonies are co-ordinated from district to district, and age-sets organized on a narrow, local basis. The first kind provide a criterion of status extending as far as the tribe itself and transmit in ceremonial common values throughout the whole area it occupies, from generation to generation. By contrast, the other kind of age-sets are not co-ordinated from one locality to the next, not charged with ceremonial or direct teaching of the youth, in short with no large-scale integrative role. According to Eisenstadt these latter, small, localized age-groupings arise when the social maturity of youths is deliberately delayed by older men who control wealth, wives or office. Consequently behaviour of these age-sets is characterized by hostility between the generations. So far from seeking to integrate the different elements in the whole society, they express the resentment of the young against their immediate seniors in their own locality. How far this correlation holds good is doubtful, since even in the tribal-wide age-organizations of East Africa there are signs of hostility between the generations and of delayed social maturity. But certainly the Lele fit the second type. Their age-sets offered their young men prizes which consoled them for their long

[10] Eisenstadt, 1959.

7

bachelorhood. Therefore the system propped up the polygyny of the old men, not without generating hostility.

We have now given the formal framework of village organization: the old village-head at the apex of the age-set system; the spokesman, a civil servant not a political leader; the age-sets themselves banding together the men of different clans into a single polity. It is still impossible to say where authority resided. The age-set system achieved balance, rather than hierarchy, for the two oldest sets opposed each other, on two sides of the village, each ranged with its associated junior set. In spite of their regard for seniority, their political inclinations tended always towards balance, rather than to authority delegated from any peak to subordinate points in the system. Indeed, anyone who has lived with the Lele will agree at once that there was no authority. There was no person or body in a village who could give orders, and expect to be obeyed by anyone else. Lack of direct authority in the strict sense of legitimate power went right through their culture.

Lele themselves explained this in terms of basic personality structure. They said that they were inherently envious by nature and could not abide a friend's success. If any man became a conspicuous leader, he would be dragged down and killed by jealous sorcerers. It was just not safe to excel. We can go a stage further. A lion-tamer without a whip can only wheedle and bribe his lions to perform. So long as they wanted a distribution of status and authority at variance with the real distribution of power in hard economic terms, Lele were bound to use indirect techniques of control. We have seen that the productive side of the economy put the old men at a disadvantage and that the distribution of raffia cloth somewhat strengthened their position. Their lack of authority in village and clan organization shows that their privileges were none the less precariously held.

V

CLANS

THE LELE seem to have entered their present territory in small bands composed of men of several different matrilineal clans with their wives and children. In each band one of these clans was the acknowledged leader and the members of the others their followers. The clan structure of present-day villages has kept a similar form. In a group of related villages the descendants of the clan which led the migrating party remains dominant in the parent village, and descendants of its original followers remain also represented there. Subsequent fission makes no difference to this pattern of clans in the parent village. In the new village which has broken away the same pattern is repeated with different emphasis. The clan whose members led the break-away becomes its dominant founding clan while descendants of their companions or wives count thereafter as founding clans of that village. Since a system of preferred marriages continued to link the members of the separated villages in ensuing generations, the pattern of founding clans tended to be unchanged, so that they continued to form the permanent core of a village, while members of other clans also tacked themselves on at different times.

The clan had no corporate character whatsoever. It was an amorphous collection of individuals who never assembled or took common action of any kind. Its members did not know each other. Responsible men tended to know from fifty to sixty fellow-clansmen living in about fifteen villages, but they also recognized the existence of many more they could not name. All that clansmen had in common was the name of the clan, a number of songs and proverbs associated with it, and personal names handed down to members and their children and children's children.

Members of a clan were not evenly dispersed. Isolated members might be found anywhere and everywhere, but there would always be a few local concentrations, which we call local clan sections. They tended to dominate, numerically and socially, in a

85

village which their ancestors had helped to found.[1] The village might be called after the foremost of its founding clans. The men of that clan would occupy the four corner houses. The village

Table 10. *Founding clans*

Number of founding clans represented by adult males in a village and proportion of founding clans to total male population, 1950

Village	Total males	No. founding clans	No. other clans represented by adult males	Men of each founding clan	% of total males
Ngoie	77	2	10	36, 9	59
Little Bamba	25	3	2	6, 5, 9	80
Great Bamba	30	3	6	4, 5, 13	73
North Homba	43	3	8	9, 16, 4	67
Middle Homba	29	3	3	9, 6, 8	79
South Homba	35	3	4	11, 9, 4	66
Hanga Yulu	35	2	3	8, 16,	68

head was always its oldest male. One way or another through its long association with the village, it was able to attract young men to marry a good proportion of its womenfolk locally, and so build up a large section, holding many cult positions in the village.

The members of a founding clan, *malunji mahin* or *bina mbanj*, had a certain superiority over stranger clans of later arrival in the village. The distinction between original clans and strangers is more highly developed among the Bushong and other Congolese tribes. Among the Kele, on the right bank of the Kasai, the descendants of the original clans of a village, *mimbangata*, had clear-cut privileges and political duties assigned to them; the election of the village head from among their number, rights to parts of game killed, and so on. Among the Lele the pattern was there, but different, since clanship itself was not the main principle of association in the village. True, the office of head of a village was hereditary in one of the founding clans, but it was not elective. Food privileges were certainly not allocated on this basis, with one exception, the right to partake of pangolin meat, in the cult of the pangolin.[2] Candidates for this cult had

[1] It was rare for one of the founding clans to constitute a majority of the village population, but the sum of all the founding clans usually outnumbered the members of other clans living there.

[2] See Chapter XI. The pangolin is a scaly ant-eater.

to be members of founding clans of the village, who had each married a woman of another founding clan and begotten two children, one of each sex by that wife. Thus the cult did much to honour the founding clans.

A young man was not likely to join a particular village with the hope of one day becoming its head. Nor was the prospect of occupying a corner hut an inducement, since it was thought to be an exposed position, vulnerable to outside sorcery. The knowledge that his senior clansmen would be members of the Pangolin Cult was double-edged, since it implied that they were capable of sorcery, to protect or to kill him.

The prestige of living in such a village was intangible. It meant the difference between being at home, a member by full right of birth, or being an outsider. Certain people in a village were called *muna bola*, owner: the village head, the senior cult officials and any members, male or female, of the founding clans. Anger on the part of any of these was thought more potent to spoil the hunting than anger of any other ordinary members. Founding clansmen enjoyed being asked to give a public blessing as sign of their goodwill. I heard a sick woman, whose sister in the next village was inviting her to live there, emphatically declare that, if it cost her her life, she would never leave the village where she was *mwana mbanj*, child of the foundation.

Although people felt the original clans ought to be permanently represented in the village which they had founded, sometimes one would die out, or the last member move away. Then the connexion tended to be forgotten, so there was no lasting affront to their sense of continuity. More usually the other clans tried to plan intermarriages so that the dwindling clan would remain represented in the village it had helped to found.

Founding clan sections were distributed in a quite haphazard way through the different groups of villages. One section of a clan might have founded a village in one group of brother villages, which might be traditionally at enmity with a village founded by another section of that same clan. The related clan sections would not be able to stop the two villages from fighting, and their members could take opposite sides in the fight so long as they took care not to kill one another. If by mischance they should recognize a fellow-clansman in a fallen enemy, convention required them merely to refrain from mutilating his body.

Although the clan as such had no corporate unity, yet membership of a clan was important for every Lele. It gave them each a claim they could make on any fellow-clansmen they chose to join. It was like a blank ticket or coupon which might take one anywhere or entitle one to anything, according to the circumstances. The man who travelled could use it to claim hospitality. If he made friends with his hosts, he could use it to beg a wife, and the right to settle down with them. They might adopt him as fully as if he were a son of their own mother, or they might only accept him after a trial period, or they might pay lip-service to the claims of common clanship but never really accept him as one of themselves. When he realized this, he would get up and try somewhere else. Two things only were necessary for a man to become a full member of a local section of his clan, with every expectation of being allocated wealth when he needed it and a wife. One, of course, was clanship. It did not matter how he was related, near or distantly or by no known links, so long as he was a fellow-clansman. The other was friendship, readiness to behave to one another as brothers should. Some men were born in their local clan section, and stayed in it. Others chose it in adolescence, and settled down for life, while others experimented here and there, before finally settling down in one village. When Lele said that a clan consisted of brothers, children of one mother, they were accurate to the extent that belonging to a clan was like holding an option which could be taken out with any local group of clansmen. If a man chose to fill the role, he could indeed become one of a band of brothers.

Choice of residence with local clan sections

Lele valued their freedom to live where they liked. They denied any necessity to join any one section of one's clan or any particular group of mother's brothers. If there was a general rule of residence, it would be that a man had a duty to live near his father as long as the latter needed him. When his father died, he could stay on or move, as he liked. Often he would feel unwanted by his father's clansmen when his father was dead. So far from feeling a pull towards a large local clan section, many said they would naturally prefer to join just one or two fellow-clansmen, there being less quarrels in a small than in a large clan section.

Since women went at marriage to live with their husbands, and since villages were not endogamous, the concentration of adult clansmen in a village resulted from a complex set of movements. If they were born where their own clan was not dominant, men left their village of birth to join some group of their own clansmen. Roughly two-thirds to three-quarters of the young men used to leave the village of their birth.[3] In Ngoie, for example, out of twenty-five men over fifty, only four had been born in the village. The same general trend emerged from a survey of the clan composition of men's age groups in seven villages. The two senior age groups generally represented only three or four clans, the middle and junior sets spread through a much wider range of clans; these juniors, born in the village, could be expected at some stage to go away if they did not happen to belong to one of the founding clans. In Ngoie, twenty-four of the twenty-eight oldest men belonged to only two clans, and the thirteen men of the middle age-sets included nine from these two clans. The junior sets were heterogeneous from the point of view of clan composition. (See Table 11.)

When he moved a married man liked to take his wife with him. But women did not like to leave their homes, and often successfully resisted plans to make them do so. A girl's first choice would be the village of her own birth; her second choice the village of her mother's birth, where her grandmother might still be living. If neither of these could be conceded by the men arranging her marriage her last preference would be to live at least within easy visiting distance of her mother and sisters.

[3] Percentage of male residents over 50 born away from their village: Ngoie, 80%; North Homba 64%; Middle Homba, 78%; South Homba, 75%; Hanga Yulu, 90%; Little Bamba, 38%; Great Bamba, 72%.

Table 11. *Clan and age-set composition of seven villages*
Only a few clans represented in the older generations.

Village	Clans	2 Senior age-sets	Middle set	Junior set	Summary
Ngoie	Not known	3	–	–	Membership of
	*Bulumbu				2 senior age-sets concentra-
	Bwambala Njok	19	8	3	ted in 3 clans
	*Bulumbu Bwa				
	Yengo	5	1	1	
	Bwene	1	–	3	
	Kombe	–	1	1	
	Holo	–	1	–	Membership of
	Nghang	–	1	3	junior sets
	Ngwapanji	–	1	–	spread over 8
	Imonu	–	–	1	clans
	Kamba	–	–	1	
	Bwaya	–	–	1	
	Ket	–	–	–	
	Ngondu	–	–	–	
N. Homba	*Bulong	3	5	1	Membership of 2 senior sets concentrated in 7 clans
	*Bwekamba	1	–	–	Membership of
	*Bulomani	1	–	–	junior sets
	Bieng	2	1	2	spread over 6 clans
	Ndong	1	–	–	
	Kamba	3	7	6	
	Ket	1	1	1	
	Yongo	–	1	2	
	Luta	–	2	–	
	Lubelo	–	–	1	
	Mabenge	–	–	1	
	Ngwapanji	–	–	1	
M. Homba	*Lumbunji	4	3	2	Membership of 2 senior sets concentrated in 3 clans
	*Hanja	3	2	1	
	*Bucwa	2	3	3	Membership of junior sets spread over 6 clans
	Njembe	–	2	2	
	Ndaba	–	–	1	
	Bwenga	–	–	1	
S. Homba	*Lubelo	6	–	5	Membership of 2 senior sets concentrated in 4 clans

Table 11 (continued)

Village	Clans	2 Senior age-sets	Middle set	Junior set	Summary
S. Homba (cont.)	Ndong	1	1	2	Membership of junior set spread over 6 clans
	*Bwenga	1	5	2	
	*Bulomani	–	–	2	
	Ngondu	1	1	1	
	Ket	–	1	2	
	Mbwe Kamba	1	–	–	
Hanga Yulu	*Ndaba	8	2	6	Membership of 2 senior sets concentrated in 3 clans
	*Pata	2	5	1	Membership of junior set spread over 5 clans
	Bulong	–	1	2	
	Lung	–	1	2	
	Lumbunji	–	–	1	
Little Bamba	*Ngondu	2	2	2	Membership of 2 senior sets cover 4 clans
	*Bwaya	2	2	–	
	*Luta	1	4	–	Membership of junior set covers 3 clans
	Ket	3	5	1	
	Lemba	–	–	1	
Great Bamba	*Lubelo	2	1	2	Membership of 2 senior sets concentrated in 4 clans
	*Lembe	3	1	9	
	*Luta	1	1	2	Membership of 2 junior sets spread over 8 clans
	Pata	1	–	2	
	Ngondu	–	1	2	
	Ngwapanji	–	–	1	
	Monu	–	–	1	
	Bwene	–	–	1	
	Ket	–	–	1	

* Founding clans.

The tendency for junior men to come from a wide variety of clans would be even more marked if Christians had been included in this count. In Ngoie twenty-two Christians in their twenties came from ten clans.

VILLAGE A   VILLAGE B   VILLAGE C

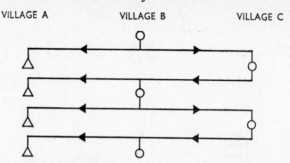

Fig. 1. Relation between residence pattern and preferred marriage

In village 'A' are men of a local section of a clan ('a') who have been born in villages 'B' or 'C'. In villages 'B' and 'C' are men of local sections of clans 'b' and 'c' respectively, who by the rule of preferred marriage have rights over their own granddaughters of clan 'a'. The diagram shows four generations of men and women of 'a' clan, descended from a woman married in village 'B'. Her daughter is married in village 'C', her granddaughter in 'B'; her great granddaughter in 'C' again, and her great-great-granddaughter in 'B'. None of these women ever goes to live in village 'A', the village which their own clan founded, and where their menfolk have been at home for generations past.

If a woman talked sentimentally about her birthplace as her home she might be derided by a man, saying: 'A woman has no home.' In a sense this was true, since a woman was never a member of a village in the same way as a man could be; and in another sense this was how men wanted things for they liked women to have no local attachments, so as to be freely disposable throughout any part of the country. Nevertheless, women had a strong sense of home, and succeeded in restricting the range of intermarriage. It follows that men did not either have to go far afield when they changed their father's for their clansmen's village. Each village lay in a field of intermarriage whose area covered the range of movement normally open to individuals changing their residence for whatever reasons.

Distance far or near was never a simple matter of geography. The field of intermarriage included villages of the same family, and also one or two other villages in close proximity, with whom alliances had been established, so that it was different for each brother village in a given family. South Homba, for example, as

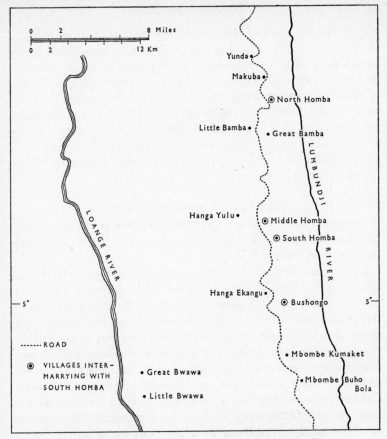

Map VII. Field of intermarriage of South Homba

well as intermarrying with the two other Homba villages, intermarried with its old ally Bushongo and with Mbombe. Only
seven of its thirty-seven adult men and twelve of its forty-seven
women were not born in one of the three Homba villages or in
Bushongo. But Bushongo did not intermarry with Mbombe, or
with other members of the Homba family, though it did so
regularly with Hanga and Bwawa villages. For its part Mbombe
had an old series of marriage exchanges with other Mbombe
villages to the far north. In the days when these patterns of intermarriage were formed all the villages were nearer to the river
valleys, and the highland between them a barrier rather than a
route. North Homba was close to the Loange river and South
Homba close to the Lumbundji river, yet they intermarried.

Nearly twenty years of close proximity since they were brought
close to the road in 1935 had not changed the habit which made
the Homba villages strangers to the Hanga and Bamba villages.
The main movements of population took place within the limits
of alliances between brother villages, and between others brought
near by the hazards of shifting. When Torday and Simpson
recorded that the Lele seemed not to know the path to the
nearest village to their own, and armed for war when obliged to
carry loads thither, they showed that even then the nearest were
not the friendliest villages.

Recruitment to village through local clan sections

Every village wished to expand its membership. They would
have liked to have kept their own sons, at the same time attracting
boys from elsewhere.[4]

In the competition to recruit new members, there was always
the possibility that a village might lose on both trends. In such a
case the balance of the generations would be lost. Lele openly
recognized that a village of old people was not viable, and
referred to this danger when urging old men not to press their
claims too severely against the young. Bystanders used to beg
disputants to compose their differences, lest quarrelsomeness
gave their village a bad name, and kept off possible new-comers.
Canvassing new members of local clan sections went on all the
time. Sorcery fears were played on and illness made the occasion
of a special drive to bring in a potential member. The conventional way of cheering a sick man was to assure him that his
neighbours were poisoning him, and that if he would come to
live with his other kinsmen he would recover at once. Long
journeys would be made to visit sick clansmen to persuade them
to come away, and even their transport by litter or bicycle
assured. It was offensive to refer to the reduced size of a village,
since this implied that the sorcery of the senior members had
driven the youth away.

Although they said that villages had divided in the distant past
because they grew too big for the game to be shared among so
many men, in practice they recognized no limit to the desirable
size of a village. The communal hunt needed a team of twenty

---

[4] The familiar dilemma of matrilineal descent systems in which marriage is
virilocal. Turner's study of Ndembu (1957) develops the theme very fully.

men, but the average male membership of villages was much higher than this; forty in the southern half of the country and nearly seventy in the northern villages. The local clan sections, likewise, saw no practical reason for setting an upper limit to their expansion. As recruitment to the village was done through clan sections, it was to the general interest that they should not discriminate, but should welcome new-comers from all quarters. It was an offence against clan solidarity to make distinctions between clan members on any basis other than age, and sex of course. All senior men were supposed to have an equal and like authority over all junior clansmen, and all juniors had the same right to share in any distribution that was being made. In the name of clan unity, the local clan sections competed to gain membership at one another's expense.

It follows logically that the very arrangements which made it easy for young men to change their residence made it difficult for old men. A young man came in at the bottom of the status ladder in a local clan section, and he brought his strength to the hunting, forest-clearing, wine-drawing and house-building. But the same principle of seniority meant that an old man would expect a niche at the top without adding to the manpower. This made for a practical age-limit for easy transfer from one village to another and the time came for each man when he had to decide to settle down permanently. It is very important to realize that every village was composed of a younger generation which was expected to go away, and an older generation which was in permanent residence. Conflicts between old and young men, normal in Lele society, were coloured by the fact that the young men were able to move, though everyone wanted them to stay, and the old were not able to move away and could only be attacked through sorcery accusations.[5]

The distinction between a long visit and a permanent change of residence was not always clear. In every village, around the settled core of each large local clan section there would be a fringe of new-comers working to make good their membership or trying to decide whether they liked it enough to stay on. At the same time there were the young men, born in the village and regarding it as their home, and yet who were preparing to leave unless a very tempting proposition was made.

[5] These residence factors are relevant to Chapters XII and XIII.

In some situations an ambiguous status is better than a well-defined one, since definition means separation and a cutting-off of claims. Membership of a local clan section was such a case. A man knew that if he did not reside and co-operate with one group of his fellow-clansmen he could not make claims on them for wives or help. But he foresaw a time when he might quarrel or be driven out, and he would like to keep similar claims warm in another village. *Mwana mala mapende kung wak yungu bo*: 'The child of two villages won't die.' Consequently men kept up close, friendly contacts with other local sections of their clans and when they were ill might shunt back and forth between them. All this adds to the difficulty of saying precisely who composed the local clan sections.

Composition of local clan sections

The method of recruiting men to the local clan section gives the lie to the notion that they consisted of close matrilineal relatives. In South Homba only one clan section was composed of descendants of a common grandmother (Ndong, see Appendix A, Figure 14) and indeed only a fraction of her living descendants were there. Yet Lele liked to talk about the local clan section as a devoted band of brothers.[6] It was living together and sharing resources which made this kind of brotherhood, not descent from one mother. The members would have mostly come together because they liked one another, and would be ready to put much effort into creating a close relationship.

In the small clan sections with only three or four men the ideal was realized impressively. In the larger clan sections brotherly goodwill fell short. By comparison with other parts of Africa a group of ten men and their wives and children would never be called large, still less too large for harmony. But for men trying to live together, expecting so much devotion and self-control while doing so little to define their relations, it is a large group —too large for a spontaneous, domestic style of solidarity. The several old men would find themselves heading factions; there would be a fringe of men with a chip on the shoulder who had found assimilation difficult in small sections of their clan in other villages, whose very presence undermined solidarity. The harmony in the small sections showed up the wrangling in the

[6] In what follows it is rarely necessary to distinguish full brothers from clansmen.

larger ones, and made the latter's members feel cheated of the peace to which Lele culture seemed to entitle them.

The local clan section was not strictly a working unit, nor a residential unit within the village, nor the group which took food together. It was rather the group which shared rights to wives and to wealth. A new arrival could work, eat, hunt, sleep in the village for a long time without knowing for sure whether he was accepted in the local section of his clan. The test would be inheritance.

Inheritance

When a man died the Lele did not select a general heir to take over his offices and possessions. Hereditary offices went to the senior resident of the appropriate clan. Seniority meant everything, closeness of relationship within the clan nothing, so there was no need to call in an outsider more closely related to fill the post. The possessions, debts and claims, and the widows of the dead man reverted to his local clan section. This sounds simple enough until we remember that membership of that group was vaguely defined. In practice the right to share in inheritance was based on a combination of matrilineal relationship and co-residence. For very close relatives matrilineal succession gave them a claim, whether they were living with the dead man's clan section, or not. Locally resident members of the clan section also had an automatic claim, whether they were close relatives or not. Thus a man discovered whether he had become a member of the local clan section on the death of one of the other members.

Bundles of raffia and bars of camwood were the most prized material parts of an inheritance. If more than one local clan section claimed the dead man as member, the wealth might be divided between the heads of each, after suitable provision had been made for his children. In any case the elder of the local clan section took over control of the things, and was expected to use them to help his juniors.

Far more important than the material wealth were the widows of the deceased. A widow would not be allocated until a year of mourning had elapsed, in which time various suitors would try to woo her, since her preference would be respected by the heirs. A man's claims to allocate young girls in marriage were just as important a legacy as his own widow. If he had not arranged

the marriages of his daughters' daughters, this right would fall
to the inheritors, adding to the stock of marriageable women
which the clan section claimed to dispose of. Apart from good
fellowship and security, the object of joining a group of fellow-
clansmen was to stake a claim in their pool of rights over women.
A new-comer who was allocated a woman by the local clan section he was hoping to live with had no further doubts about
whether he was a full member or not. One who was passed over
more than once might have to think about packing up to go.

Transfer of wives within a local clan section

Giving a wife to a new-comer was the accepted way of making
him welcome. If there was no widow or unmarried girl to give,
the host might well part with one of his own wives. This was the
ideal of the generous brother. He parted with the most precious
rights the Lele knew, for the sake of brotherhood. Although they
held certain women in a village in common,[7] a man's rights over
his own wife were clearly demarcated. Any infringement was a
grave insult. Although brothers addressed the wife of one of
them as 'my wife', it was known she was only their 'wife for
food' not for sleeping. When a wife was transferred from one
brother to another, sexual rights over her were given completely
and exclusively. Yet the fact that she might be transferred was
an important expression of the solidarity of clansmen. They were
able to function literally as equivalents in the one situation which
defined the status of a man, marriage. Whether an old man
betrothed a child in his own name, or in the name of a junior
clansman, a new-comer or a full sister's son, the relevant point
was that she was betrothed to the men of such and such a clan
—any one of them might be selected to put her in his house (as
they said), any other one might take her over later if the marriage
did not work out well, or subsequently inherit her. She was
married to the men of a dispersed clan, not even to the men of a
local clan section, since it was never certain which men of a
dispersed clan might end by joining a particular section in a
village. The system was flexible. It enabled adjustments in the
choice of partners. A man whose wife grew up into a scold was
able to make a gesture in giving her to a needy brother. But it
also invited conflict. A bachelor who noticed a fellow-clansman

[7] See Chapter VIII.

having domestic strife might suggest that the girl would settle down better with himself, or he might be tempted to sound her out on the subject first, or the initiative for a change might come from the woman. But the actual husband might take the suggestion so badly that the village became too small for both men. Both cases, of brothers quarrelling or being united over the transfer of a wife, crop up frequently in case histories. In a small clan section men were on the whole more conscious of the obligation to respect one another's wives than in large clan sections. In these small sections the interest in recruitment was also greater, and the stock of rights over unmarried girls smaller. The transfer of a wife was often the only way of consolidating the clan section.

Seniority

Seniority in years was the main principle which regulated the men of a local clan section. Of any two full brothers, unless they were twins, one was senior to the other by at least three years; thus inequality was part of the nature of brotherhood. The elder should protect his younger brother who should show him respect, and bring him the product of his labours. For example, if the younger were given two chickens or raffia cloths by his future father-in-law he should forthwith show them to his elder brother who would decide with him where they should be kept. If the younger brother brought palm wine or game the elder brother decided the distribution. A little boy was expected to be like a devoted servant, rewarded with promises of help with his marriage and cult dues.

The principle worked well enough when the boys were young, and if there were not too many of them in a family or local clan section. It was supposed to govern their relations all their lives. At any crisis, the elder full brother was responsible for helping the other. If the younger lost his wife, and if the elder brother had two, he should take one and give her to the bereaved brother. Lele spoke movingly about the relation between full brothers. In practice it was true that if one man went to prison, his brother sent him food or raised money to pay his fine; or if one went to hospital, his brother would carry him there, and feed him; if a clerk or shopkeeper was caught embezzling, the brother was expected to repay the amount for him. If a man was charged with sorcery, his brother defended his innocence.

8

Such devotion did not always hold between all the brothers of a big family. Boys would start by trying to 'build up brotherhood' with all their brothers, but their obligations were so unspecific and so all-embracing that they would end by counting their own contributions and measuring the size of their rewards. A promise broken, or counter-gift refused, and the relationship soon became prickly with disappointment. Having calls on his help at all times, from all directions, a man might easily be reduced to measuring their urgency and calculating his best outlay, a calculus quite contrary to the spontaneous generosity he was supposed to show his brothers and fellow-clansmen.

Avoidance of competition between brothers

Competition between brothers and fellow-clansmen, which might spoil their affection, was to some extent ruled out.[8] There could be no competition for leadership of the local clan section. The elder was unambiguously selected as the oldest male resident. The position of elder of the local clan section was not very important, in spite of his apparent control of all resources. In a small clan section he was controlled as much by the men he represented, as they by him. In a large one, there would be several factions, each with a *de facto* elder at its head, who held a nominal position as spokesman. As we have said, the clans were not the main units in village organization. The clan-section elders would be rivalled in influence by cult officials. Since the position of elder of clan section was a relatively inconspicuous one, offering no scope for rivalry, a common cause of village fission was eliminated.

They also tried to eliminate competition on the part of younger members. That brothers might feel jealous, even hate one another, was admitted. The two words for jealousy distinguished *tainy*, sexual jealousy, a trivial emotion, from *bupih*, envy or malice, which a man feels when he is surpassed by others in any sphere, and which tempts him to kill them by sorcery. Women were said to be less likely to feel *bupih*, probably

---

[8] Yet the field of greatest tension, competition for wives, was not regulated —compare the Plateau Tonga who held jealousy between full brothers to a minimum by the rule that they could not inherit one another's wives (Colson, 1958).

because their world was not governed by ranking. But it was always likely to colour the relations of men of the same clan, if one were eclipsed by a junior's achievements. Since prestige was ideally supposed to be distributed according to seniority, and since seniority was no guarantee of outstanding performance, little boys had to be taught not to rouse the jealousy of older brothers.

If one brother practised a special skill or craft, and his junior started to show an aptitude for it, the latter was warned off by his mother or friends, and advised to try his hand at something else. 'Why compete with your elder brother, if you don't want to die young?' they would say. Often when I asked a man whether he had tried drumming or carving, he would answer shortly, 'No, my brother does.' If the younger persisted in developing his talent in a direction in which his brother already excelled, it would have to be with the consent of the latter, and with the clear understanding that when the junior had become proficient, the elder would retire in his favour. The convention was well established, not only for full brothers but for any two kinsmen who practised the same trade. Whether they were father and son or uncle and nephew, the younger would for a time act as apprentice to the senior, but when the latter saw himself being outstripped in skill, he was expected formally to resign. Then no one would reproach him, if the younger were to fall ill, of having jealously practised sorcery against him. Restriction of entry into skilled professions was one reason why the Lele had fewer specialists than their neighbours, the Bushong.

These practices were not so much signs of incipient hostility as realistic recognition that it was necessary to avoid competition in order to realize the ideal. Seniority in years is a crude and inadequate principle for allocating roles. Lele did not refine it with the secondary principle of distinction between descent lines. Their rule worked excellently in the small domestic unit, but as soon as there were two or three men of the senior generation, it broke down. To any young man all the clansmen of his mother's generation had a theoretically equal claim on his services, her full brothers and classificatory brothers alike, except that the elder took precedence over younger men more closely related to him. Exact genealogical links were often hard to unravel and were treated as irrelevant.

Genealogical distinctions disapproved

If the Lele clan elders had wished to set up a fagging system like that run by the Kongo elders[9] they would presumably have had to distinguish the children of own sisters, from those of mother's sisters daughters, and allotted them each to the eldest full brother of the mother. Thus well-defined matrilineages would have emerged, within the local clan section. The pattern of residence accordingly would have had to be more clearly defined. Among the Kongo little boys of ten years old were invariably sent to their own mother's brothers, a contrast with the uncertainty of recruitment to the Lele clan sections. As the Lele did none of these things they did not succeed in creating a strong chain of command, and their boys had an easier time.

The rule of seniority by age and by generation is clear enough in a small group, and in a big one if it is only a question of requiring formal deference. When it is a matter of allocating conflicting claims to services among several senior men, something more precise is needed. The fact that a young man was not attached to the service of one mother's brother more than to another, but should help them all, meant in effect that in a big clan section he owed full-time service to none. The various senior clansmen found themselves fishing together in the same undifferentiated labour pool. The nominal claim of one was only as good as, not better than the others of his generation. A sister's son helping one man with a few days of clearing could not simultaneously be expected to draw palm wine for another or build a fence for a third. There was scope for playing one elder off against another. A boy's obligations were so general that he could skip out of them if he wished. For all their formal subservience, the youth held the whip hand, at least in saying how much they could contribute to the productive side of the economy.

The weakness of defined authority favoured factions in the larger clan sections. We have seen that even between full brothers, a man had, by gift and service, to build up brotherhood into a strong relation. Even more, the relation between mother's brother and sister's son had to be made good by personal effort.

[9] Van Wing (1959, p. 229) compares the life of a Kongo boy living at his mother's brother's beck and call with that of a slave.

Men had their favourite nephews and uncles, who helped them, the junior with services and the senior with contributions to the fees and fines the latter had to raise.

Even the fact that the junior came cap in hand, as it were, to ask for material help did not give the senior an effective sanction for his authority. Men trying to raise 100 cloths would collect ten here, five or two there, from clansmen, father's clan, mother's father's clan, and father's mother's clan, throwing the net as wide as they could. Refusing to contribute to a young man's raffia needs was not an effective way of bringing him to heel as he could usually collect from other quarters. Though the older men as a group had a collective advantage over the younger men, in their control over wealth and wives, it was not a direct source of power for the individual old man. If he was generous he would have young friends; they would bring him palm wine and a share of meat; he would not be accused of plotting sorcery. If he was mean and disagreeable, he risked isolation. Since the system did not allow them individual authority the older men relied on their collective authority. Thus the tendency to think in terms of an opposition between *baotale*, the elders, and *babilenge*, the youths, was enhanced. Old men were not afraid to make a collective threat of sorcery to defend their privileges though they would hesitate to do so to defend their private interests.

Avoidance

Smooth organization requires more precise indications than the Lele social system provided. Conflicts constantly threatened. The characteristic response to a risk of conflict was avoidance. *Cin*, to avoid, was the way to show respect. A man had to avoid his elder brothers and, by implication, his younger brothers too, his mother's brother, his father, and his wife's father, mother and mother's brother. It was a serious injunction. A man could not be at ease or speak freely or intimately with any of his own clansmen as they were all older or younger than he.

Age-set behaviour was the other side of the medal. Age-mates were by definition a group of equals, intimate and free. Their ease underlined the distance between clansmen. Men of an age-set divided their world into two, those immediately above and below themselves, and all the rest. Generations within a clan section were similarly divided into relations of ease and respect.

Men received and owed respect to the generations only immediately above and below them. Stringent rules of avoidance acted like air-cushions separating men whose interests might bring them into conflict. For other relatives with whom intimacy was allowed the obvious model of behaviour was that of coevals. So the relation of a man to his old mother's mother's brother was treated in kinship terminology as if they were in one sense brothers, in another sense age-mates. The child calling his mother's mother's brother 'my big brother' did not have to avoid him as he would have avoided an elder brother, and could equally call him *mbai*, age-mate.

The association together of alternate generations never means quite the same in different societies.[10] Among the Lele its role is negative. To treat certain kinsmen as if they were coevals throws into relief the distance which should separate others whose relationship is more constrained. But when it comes to the preferred marriage the same theme is used to a different end. Here it corresponds to the scarcity of marriageable girls. By giving a man rights over his daughter's daughters, and putting those female descendants into his own generation, control of women is secured for the most senior men.

Examples from South Homba

Here there were four small clan sections and two large, each true to type. The genealogies as best I could discover them are given in Appendix A. The numbers refer to position on genealogical charts. Since genealogical prying was not rewarded in their culture, memory for genealogical facts was accordingly very weak. I choose the Ngondu clan, but any of the other small sections of the village would furnish as good an illustration of the points I have made.

[10] Among the Plateau Tonga (Colson, 1958, p. 48) it is applied within the matrilineal group to enhance solidarity. A man has authority over his sister's children, but her children's children are classed with his own generation as siblings over whom control is left to his sister's sons. Thus the equation of alternate generations within the matrilineal group eliminates conflict between men of proximate generations. Among the Ndembu (Turner, 1957) it applies within the village, giving a man a prescriptive right to marry girls of his children's children's generation, thus checking the tendency to village fission. In the first case it has a regulative function, by separating potentially conflicting roles, in the second it has a consolidating function, by justifying intermarriage. Lele equate alternate generations in both these ways and yet make a somewhat different pattern.

Small clan section

Ngondu (see Figure 17 in Appendix A)

Five or six years before fieldwork there had only been two males, old Njoku (1 in Figure 17) half blind and senile, and Jerome (7) a young leper; three females, the old mother (2) of Jerome, and two married sisters, Niabwani and Pahimba (4 and 5). Then they were joined by their brother, Ngwe (3), strong and active, who left Bushongo in anger because his first wife had been taken over by his clan brother. With his full brother, Oscar (8), he came to South Homba to live near his sisters, and to let his second wife be near her brother. Ngwe was at once given another wife, from the Lubelo clan which had begotten his own mother, and Oscar was given a young Christian girl,[11] whom he later took back to live in Bushongo. Ngwe was made junior official diviner. Next he was joined by Makum (6), from Mobendi in the north, who left home because he attributed a festering sore to sorcery there. He was wifeless, but at that time a girl, Biong (Bwenga, B15) who had been originally betrothed to Ngwe, but whom he had earlier transferred to a wifeless brother, came home to her mother in S. Homba saying that her husband neglected her and that Ngwe was her true husband. He, with two wives already, gave the girl to Makum. Later another woman of the Lubelo clan, Mihondo (Lubelo, A8), accusing her husband of the deaths of her children, came to her clansmen in South Homba and was willing to be offered to Makum, who then had every reason to feel securely established in the village. He and Ngwe cleared their fields together, shoulder to shoulder; when Ngwe's wife was sick, he called each day and collected herbal remedies. At first neither had palm trees, but later, when Ngwe's palms matured, they took turns with the chore of drawing wine, old Njoko getting his due share as mother's brother. When Makum was fined at the tribunal, Ngwe helped him to pay, after first asking to see Makum's reserves of cash and raffia, as an elder brother was entitled to do. Thereafter they pooled their resources. When Makum killed game, Niabwani and Pahimba claimed the share of the hunter's sisters. When Jerome went to Brabanta as an out-patient to the clinic. Makum and Ngwe sent him cash and food. Makum and Ngwe were in a few years more aware of brotherhood than was Ngwe with his full brother Oscar in Bushongo. The following summary of the way in which they raised their most important fees shows that the new-comer, Makum, gained more than he gave to Ngwe, and Oscar, Ngwe's full brother, is not in the picture at all.

---

[11] See Ket, Chapter VIII, pp. 149-50.

Table 12. *Raising of fees in Ngondu clan*

		Wealth		Provided by
Ngwe		for his two marriages		
		5 camwood bars		His fathers, from Bushongo village treasury
		1 " "		His mother
		10 raffiia cloths		
		10 " "		His father (house-)
		1 axe		" "
		200 raffia cloths and one axe.		
	Diviners' cult	50 raffia cloths		His lords, S. Homba section of Lubelo clan. (See Ch. VIII on blood debts)
		10 " "		Father's sisters
		40 " "		Mother's mother's brother and Father's father
		100		
	Twin cult	40 " "		Ngwe himself, helped by his sisters in S. Homba
Makum	Diviners' fees	50 " "		His father, in Njembe village
		50 " "		His mother's brother in Njembe village
		100		(Not sure of details)
	Begetters' cult	10 " "		Njoku
		20 " "		Ngwe
		30 " "		Makum himself
		20 outstanding		
		80		
	Twin cult	20		Niabwani and Pahimba (classif. sisters)
		40 (one goat)		Ngwe
		30 (camwood)		Makum himself
		90		

Nestor (Ngwe's sister's son)
    for first part of
    his marriage dues

20 (camwood)		His father			
30 (paid in					
— francs)		Ngwe		100 francs	
50 cloths,		Makum		100 "	
completed payment to bride's		Mother		50 "	
father; when child ready to		M. Sister		50 "	
come to his house, he would					
have to raise another 40 for her				300 "	
mother					

The effective head of this clan section was the new-comer Ngwe, a vigorous man in his forties. The true elder, Njoku, had lost his memory and could not function even as nominal head, except on rare occasions. If Ngwe died, his full brother, Oscar, in Bushongo, and his clansmen in that village would have as good a claim on his widows as Makum, since Ngwe kept in close touch with them. If Makum died, his close clansmen in Mobendi would have little claim on his widows, as he had lost touch with them, and they never helped him after he left. The same tale of generous solidarity goes for the Ket and Ndongu clans and also for the Bulomani where there were only two men. For the Lubelo and Bwenga it was a different story.

Large clan sections

(a) *Lubelo* (see Figure 12 in Appendix A)

The members of the local clan section derived from five descent groups (A, B, C, D and E) which could not trace any connexion whatsoever. In 1949 Ngapici (C1) was village head, and when he died he was succeeded by Kombe (D3), while the administration named as *Capita* Makaka (E6). The latter was highly intelligent, nervous and strong-willed. He made enemies easily, outwitted them and tenaciously got his own way. By 1950 he was middle-aged; his three wives were not on good terms with one another; he had quarrelled with both his adult sons, who had left the village. He was senior official diviner of the village, and skilled in ritual knowledge. He had quarrelled with his own clansmen and was not even on speaking terms with Pung and Kombe (D3 and 2); young Clement (C12) left the village on account of disputes with him. Outside his own clan he had other quarrels, concerning women. As official diviner he was supposed never to have sexual intercourse with any of the communal wives of the village, but he had pursued one so jealously that she had finally been relinquished to him as his private wife, and another had published his advances to her. On both scores the village and his own wives were very angry with him. The village was so conscious of his resentment and of fear of his ill-will that every illness raised the same tacit query: if it was illness in his own clan, Makaka was thought to be attacking his own sisters' sons again; if it was illness in any other clan, he was suspected of using sorcery to promote Lubelo interests. In 1953 his reputation as a sorcerer was putting him into a dangerous position.

The only other older man in the clan section who had any following was Ngomabulu (B5), a slow gentle character, who had no pretensions to leadership.

(b) *Bwenga*

This clan section consisted of four descent groups (A, B, C and D in Figure 13, Appendix A) which collaborated little with one another. Of ten men seven were established members, if we include two boys at the mission, and three peripheral members, either not fully accepted or not fully decided to stay. The elder, Bwato (D1), was one of these latter, who had been forced to leave two other villages on charges of sorcery. Once he had been a respected member of the clan, speaking with authority in clan disputes. Now he was wifeless, he had a mild form of leprosy. He was embroiled in quarrels with his own clansmen. He had twice tried to take Pero's wife (A5, Figure 13) and Manda (A14) believed him to have killed her daughter by sorcery. One of the village-wives accepted him in her hut, but he had little hope of being given a wife of his own. With him had come his sister's son, Bikwak (D12), and Kabenda (C7), both rolling stones who had spent their childhood in the village and now hoped to make it their home.

Kabenda had been born in Tundu, the chief's village, but on his father's death, his mother brought him as a small child to S. Homba, where he attached himself to an older man, Mukwa, whom he regarded as a brother. When he was still young, Mukwa was given a wife, but she refused him, and was taken over by one of their mother's brothers. Offended, Mukwa left for M. Homba, with the young Kabenda, who learnt how to weave there. Later, they went to N. Homba, where Kabenda learnt to draw palm wine. At some stage too they went to Domaie, and invested in a he-goat, which they left among their clansmen there. They returned to S. Homba, and this time Mukwa was married, to Mandong of the Lubelo clan. After begetting a son and a daughter, he died, and Kabenda was allowed to inherit the widow. On his version of the story, he was a good husband, he reared her first two children and begot two more sons. Then she gratuitously got him into trouble with the village, and he was forced to leave. On her version, he neglected her disgracefully, and rejected her, which seems possible as she was older than he. Leaving S. Homba for N. Homba, he was given a village-wife to live with. Eventually another man became her favourite husband, and he was ousted from her hut.

At this stage Kabenda set out in earnest to acquire a new wife of his own. First he went to S. Mikope, because a senior clansman there vaguely promised him a daughter's daughter. While waiting for this girl, Kabenda noticed that one of his other clansmen was getting on badly with his wife, and proposed that she should be given to himself, Kabenda, but they tartly refused, and he left Mikope feeling very hurt, to spend two months in Domaie, where he saw that his goat had been mated. Although, as he claimed, the Bwenga of Domaie insisted most

hospitably that he stay and let them find him a wife, the men of North
and South Homba also called him back, and he was tempted by the
prospect of living near his sons.

Bikwak was also set wandering by the early death of his parents. His
mother was married in succession to three men of the Lubelo clan in
S. Homba. She died when Bikwak was a small child, and the Bwenga
women let him starve, so his sister in Mikope took him away. He never
forgave his classificatory mothers of the Bwenga clan in South Homba
for their neglect.[11] He took work with the Europeans, for three years at
the oil-palm plantations, for nearly four years as a soldier, and for five
years with the police, coming home at intervals to South and Middle
Homba. With the riches he amassed in the police he betrothed and
married two girls, one the daughter of a village-wife in Hanga, distributing great largesse to his in-laws. In 1953 he borrowed a house in
S. Homba with a view to settling there, among his clansmen and
fathers, but while he was deciding where to build, he began to doubt
the wisdom of his choice.

In the first place, hunting was bad. In the second, there was much
sickness, including his own small children. Both indicated sorcery.
Lastly there was quarelling, a bad thing in itself. Throughout July
evening harangues against sorcerers showed that the Bwenga attributed
their misfortunes to Lubelo sorcery. Then the Bwenga got into a series
of disputes.

Lukondo, of Bulomani clan, violently demanded fresh payment of
adultery damages from Polidor (Lukondo's cousin, Bwenga, A13). The
village rate of adultery damages had recently been put up to sixty cloths,
so Lukondo decided to reject the original payment of some years back
of ten badly woven cloths, and receive it again at the new rate. The hunt
planned for the next day was forthwith cancelled because of his anger.
Before this could be settled, fighting broke out; Pero (Bwenga, A5)
attacked old Bwato (Bwenga, D1) for addressing his wife. Eventually
his wife, failing to calm Pero, laid him out flat with a heavy palm rib.
Now they too would have to pay a fine for spoiling the village. In the
evening a spate of speeches were made to reconcile the contenders, and
reproach the trouble-makers, especially Bwato for not leaving his
brothers' wives alone.

A few days later, at a general meeting, Lukondo was formally given
400 francs (from Polidor's earnings) and ten raffia cloths from the
village treasury, [12] and Buhinda, the mother's brother of Polidor, produced 100 francs. A friend of Lukondo tried to reopen another charge of
adultery against Polidor, for which he too had been paid at the old rate,

---

[11] Especially Mikic whom he later accused of sorcery, see Chapter XII.
[12] Polidor was a son of the village, see Chapter VII.

but this was quashed. Then Pero and Bwato were asked to provide chickens as fines for their fighting, so that ritual could be done for the hunting next day.

A week later Kapala, a leading Bwenga man in Mikope, who had been a benefactor of many of them, died[13]. The Bwenga in S. Homba closed their ranks, collected raffia and went off in one body to mourn Kapala. Kabenda made far the biggest contribution to the mourning gifts (ten cloths instead of two or one) by way of staking a claim to one of Kapala's three widows—a vain hope, since the girl was known to be unwilling to leave her home.

Only two weeks later the village was agog with news of Kabenda's adultery with the wife of Ngomabulu, the senior Pangolin man.[14] The outraged husband asked for exemplary damages, 100 raffia clothes, as the woman was not only his wife but his pawn[15] and two more and an arrow head as she was the wife of a cult official. If a woman were now to come free in South Homba, Kabenda would not be allotted one if Ngomabulu had any say.

The Lubelo clan, brothers of Ngomabulu, magnified the scandal; they pointed out that, as Ngomabulu was a son of the Bwenga clan, Kabenda had committed adultery with his classificatory daughter-in-law. They mulled over the previous cases in which Bwenga had deceived them, and agreed that Kabenda should be made an example of, thrashed as well as made to pay full blood compensation. But Kabenda's eldest son, a Lubelo, pleaded with his uncles and elder brothers, so they gave up the idea of the thrashing.

Kabenda, a marginal member of the local clan section, was driven to various shifts to raise all the payments he was required to make. For the marriage of his younger son he had contributed four raffia cloths and 100 francs borrowed from a friend in Middle Homba. For the eldest son he had given a female goat, worth forty cloths. He obtained her from a mother's brother in Mbombe against a promise of two goats of his own from Domaie, when his sick son should be strong enough to go and fetch them. The ten raffia cloths he gave for Kapala's funeral were out of his store. Called on to pay adultery damages with no time or credit, he produced in two days two bars of camwood and 100 francs. The cash was a generous gift from Lukondo, in the role of classificatory son-in-law of Kabenda. The large bar of camwood was lent to him by Kumaking (Bwenga, D9), his fellow-clansman, and the other by François of the Ndong clan, who both asked to be repaid in raffia cloth. He had to draw largely on credit counted on a narrow basis of loan and direct return, whereas the Ngondu clan section raised its funds by gifts to be reciprocated some day by suitable return gifts—not by loans.

[13] See Chapter XIII, pp. 252–3. [14] See Chapter XI. [15] See Chapter VIII.

Conclusion

The outrages by Bwenga recounted above, public reproaches, adultery and assault, would have been nearly unthinkable in any of the small clan sections. Among the Lubelo too some of the old men were not on speaking terms with one another, and there had been a steady loss of confidence in Makaka. By contrast, in small sections passions had to be more controlled and individuals enjoyed more moral support. The large clan section was a less comfortable group to live in, yet it was inevitable and necessary that there should be large sections of founding clans represented in every village. The very looseness of their structure made it easier for clansmen who had not found a niche elsewhere to attach themselves, and so to fulfil some of the expectations which Lele society raised.

Because of the lack of moral intensity, small quarrels did not necessarily drive the men of a large clan section out of the village. They could always remove their hut to the other end of the square, and behave as if their rival did not exist. By intermarrying the founding clans formed the permanent core on which the village was built. Since the intermarriages were planned when the men were young, and not living in the village of their final choice, there was little knowing in advance what pattern of intermarriage would link the different generations of the founding clans. For example, when Ngomabulu's wife was seduced by a Bwenga man, various relationships had been flouted. Ngomabulu's father was of the Bwenga clan, one of his classificatory brothers, Makaka, had a Bwenga wife, and one of his 'sisters', Mandong, had a Bwenga husband while his sister's daughter's son, Modest, was married to a Bwenga girl. By their very confusion and unpredictability the lines of intermarriage gave the leading clans resilience in their relations with one another.

Marriage into the father's clan was prohibited nearly as strongly as marriage into one's own clan, but marriage with a girl by her mother's father's clan was a preferred form. If the local clan sections had been simply local segments of a lineage these regulations would have emphasized the distinction of generations within the clan. The repeated pattern of intermarriage between local clan sections in a village, while linking them together, would have had the effect of focusing on certain affines as points where tension and conciliation met, and we might have expected customary joking and privilege as for example between cross-cousins in Yao villages. But as we have seen, the composition of a local clan section was based on election rather than descent. Each local clan section composed in this ungenealogical way, had its traditional set of inter-marriages with other clans. When their members moved else-where, they went as husbands and sons of other clans, and when they finally settled down as members of a local corporate clan section they were content to sort out their relations with one another without reaching any high degree of consistency. For example, of two men calling each other 'brother' because they regarded their respective mothers as distant classificatory sisters, a third would call one of them mother's mother's brother and the other, mother's brother on different criteria. No one worried about being classed in different genealogical generations. And so it could be that a man's own father and his classificatory brothers and sister's sister's son might all be married into the same clan.

In one way the big local clan section made it possible for the small one to realize its highest ideals, by giving a home to unamenable members. But as the difference was only one of degree, the same set of ideals was applied to both kinds of local group within the village. The success of the one mirrored more the failure of the other. Consequently the men of the larger sections were doomed to disappointment, and some were likely to be squeezed out in ignominy in later life. Later chapters will describe the alternatives that awaited the two stormy petrels, Makaka of the Lubelo and Bwato of the Bwenga clan.

VI

MARRIAGE

I. THE PRIVATE WIFE AND PRIVATE FAMILY

Social system based on men's control of women

A MAN'S position depended on his control over women, but women were not so easy to coerce. Their action was much freer than Lele institutions, described from the male point of view, would imply. It was not impossible for a woman to end a marriage which did not please her. If she transferred her attentions to one of her husband's brothers, her preference would be hard to resist. If she favoured a man of another clan, fighting might ensue; men might be killed, but not she. If she ran away to another village, her husband would be prevented from reclaiming her by the armed force of the whole village which had given her refuge. The self-confidence of Lele women gave them much of their charm.

Men spoke of women in several distinct styles. When they discussed a woman's looks, they spoke lyrically about regular proportions, slinky leopard's movement, a face like the rising sun. When there was prospect of a sexual adventure they spoke in a cajoling, teasing voice, as if to a child. But compared with men women were beasts, ignorant, unmannerly, worse than dogs. Capricious, weak and lazy, they could not be trusted, they did not understand clan affairs, they behaved badly on formal occasions.

Again, when sick, pregnant, newly delivered or barren, they were fragile, delicate creatures, with only a slender hold on life. This corresponded correctly to the high rate of mortality in childbirth.

When they considered that all their complex status system was built on such an uncertain basis, men would make a wry expression, saying: 'Women! Women! What can we do about them?' It was an axiom of their culture that all fights and quarrels between men were disputes about women, which was true enough, as case histories show. The notion that a woman's role

was to be completely plastic in the hands of men suited the way
in which men defined their relationship with one another, but it
was difficult to make women accept that role. When the mission
fathers taught the story of the Garden of Eden, and of Eve's
responsibility for the introduction of sin, they assented, pagans
and Christians alike, with deep conviction. But in all, men behaved as if women, in spite of their shortcomings, were the most
precious, desirable objects in their lives.

A man could not achieve any status without a wife. He could
not beget, and therefore was excluded from the most important
cult groups. Without a wife he could have no daughters, and so
could never play the coveted roles of father-in-law or mother's
father. Lele honoured fatherhood. Boys were taught: 'Your
father is like God. But for his begetting, where would you be?
Therefore honour your father.' They were taught that the debt
which they owed him for his care of them in infancy was un-
repayable, immeasurable. It was very shameful for a man to show
disrespect to his father. Fathers were expected to avoid their
grown sons, so that the latter should not feel bowed down with
the burden of respect. If a daughter disobeyed her father's wishes
in respect of her marriage, he was supposed to be able to curse
her fertility. In all important crises the father as well as the clan
of the person involved had to be consulted. The father took the
larger share of a girl's marriage payments, fifty cloths and an
axe, against forty for her clan. When a man looked for help for
his marriage payments, or for any other big dues, he should be
helped equally by his father as by his clan. In these matters his
clan and the father's clan took a long view, and generally con-
trived to strike a bargain for sharing the responsibility. For
example, if two sons were being married simultaneously, the
father might take over the whole responsibility for one son, and
the clan for the other. Or if the father had paid the whole of his
son's marriage dues, then the clan would offer to shoulder the
whole of his entrance fees to the Begetters when his first child
was born, or the cost of an expensive oracle consultation, or
adultery damages, according to the particular case. The bilateral
emphasis in Lele kinship flowed from the importance of fatherhood, in its turn inevitable in a society of men competing for the
control of women.[1]

[1] Again the Tiwi of North Australia offer a close parallel.

Preferred marriage

The form of the preferred marriage extolled the father's importance. Whenever a man begot a child, and reared it, his wife's clan was thereby increased. If he begot a female child the debt was greater, since she would bear more clansmen. However much the clan honoured its fathers-in-law or sons-in-law it could never cancel a debt of such magnitude. Piety and gratitude required them to offer another girl in marriage. This was how Lele explained the rule that a man could claim as of right his daughter's daughter. He could marry her himself if he wished, as a comfort for his old age, or he could give her to his brother, who was a classificatory mother's father, or to his sister's daughter's son. He was not supposed to give her to his own sister's son, although the latter might occasionally be allowed to inherit her as a widow. In the old days before monogamous Christian marriage had restricted the range of possible partners, a man could hardly have hoped to marry a girl as close to his own age as his mother's brother's daughter (see Fig. 2 below).

He could not marry his own daughter, of course, nor could he marry his daughter to any member of his own clan. The rule prohibiting any marriage with the father's clan underlined further the importance of the father. But he had the final say in the marriage of his daughter, and the right to take her daughters in marriage. So when a man of one clan gave a female member to another in marriage, in a sense it was giving the husband's clan a permanent right to interfere in the marriages of women descended from himself. Since there was a tendency for the men of a clan to gather in certain villages, and a preference on the part of women to live with their mothers and sisters, or mother's mothers, the preferred marriage of a girl into her mother's father's clan accorded well with other tendencies, and made for some stability in the local relations of clans with one another.[2]

The preferred marriage gave the father of daughters enhanced prestige in his own clan. He had a say in the disposal of marriageable girls, he could offer his daughter's daughters to individual clansmen whom he favoured, and he would try to use them to attract young clansmen to his village. In practice his right, as girl's mother's father, was limited by the similar right of her own

[2] See Chapter V, p. 93.

9

father, who had the advantage of being on the spot. The final result of their separate interests would be a compromise, the girl's mother's father's clan taking one of her daughters, the father taking another for his own father's clan, and the others being allocated to settle blood debts, or to marry men in their natal village. With all these influences pulling in different directions, the mother's father would often have to be content if his right to one of his daughter's daughters for his own clansmen was honoured merely by her being given to a fellow-clansman who happened to be living near her birthplace, rather than one who had joined his, the mother's father's village.

One of the most important consequences of the preferred marriage of a girl into her mother's father's clan was to place control over marriages securely in the senior generation of men, the fathers and grandfathers.

The rules of preferred spouses make more sense in the context of the average age of marriage, than considered in the abstract. Girls used to be betrothed at birth, and married very young, even before puberty. If she conceived before her first menstruation a girl was congratulated on giving such early proof of her fertility.[3] Consequently the generations of women descended from women (on whom the membership of the matrilineal clan was naturally based) succeeded one another very quickly— much more quickly than the generations descended from men. Figure 2 illustrates the imaginary case of a man born when his mother was fifteen and his father thirty-five. This was the average age of marriage, though some men might be married later, or earlier. For the sake of simplicity we assume that all males marry and beget at thirty-five and all the females at fifteen. Then, before ego has married and begotten his first child, his twin sister could be a grandmother. By the time ego himself has reached the age of sixty, he could see his sister's daughter's daughter's daughter married, though he would not have seen even the marriage of his own son. At sixty he would have seen, if we include his mother, five generations of his clanswomen married, of whom three alternating generations could have been allotted to his father's clan. Imagine the sense of continuity this would give to interclan relations seen from the male perspective. In his

---

[3] The special term for the child conceived before the first menstruation of its mother was *mwan 'ihutu*.

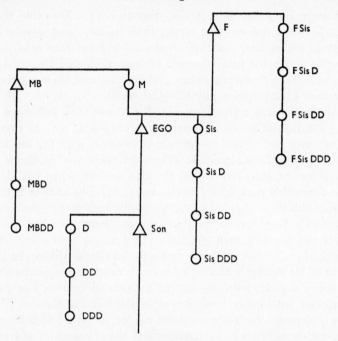

Fig. 2. Effects of discrepancy in age at marriage

lifetime ego would have twice seen his father's clan lay claim to girls descended from his mother, and he himself would have laid claim to girls similarly descended from one of his mother's brothers.

Lele were well aware of this discrepancy in the life-cycle of men and women. Boys of eighteen or twenty exclaimed humorously when their young sisters were married: 'Look! She is fully grown already, and here am I, still a child.' That boys grew up slowly, and girls quickly, they attributed to physiological differences, but there was an obviously large element of social maturity and immaturity which they discounted, based on the responsibility given to a girl from early years, and the easy life of youths. Take a brother and sister of nearly the same age, say in their early twenties. She would be broad-shouldered from pounding, with two or three children around her, in every sense a mature woman. He, light-hearted and dashing among his age-mates, slightly hangdog in the presence of seniors, would really

look more like a little boy. At the other end of the life-cycle, they
said that men did not live longer than women, and were even
likely to die earlier, but that on the other hand men remained
sexually active for much longer. Indeed, they said that with a
man sexual desire never finishes, and here, at least, their marriage
system catered for their physiological needs.

Why were senior clansmen not able to use their influence in
the allocation of wives in order to attach young men to themselves more firmly, and to provide themselves with the services
which they so much needed? Why were there any problems of
labour and of authority within the clan section, when the older
men controlled such an important sanction? The answer is that
in the old days they did not normally reckon to give their
daughter's daughters to their juniors, but kept them for themselves and for their own generation. A younger man's first wife
would often be his mother's mother's brother's widow. In the
event of his mother's mother's brother's death, he might be able
to marry a girl whom his mother's mother's brother had first
betrothed with every intention of taking her for himself. The
long-postponed marriage accounts too for the sense of competition and hostility which characterized the relations of old and
young men in the Lele village, for there was no surplus of females
allowing old men to be polygynists without delaying the marriages
of young men. They never went in for large-scale polygyny, but
an average of two or three wives per old man was quite enough
to dislocate completely the ratio of unmarried men and girls, to
give the young men a sense of grievance, and the old men
anxiety about preserving their privilege.

Role of the son-in-law

Although in principle both clans, husband's and wife's, were
on an equal footing, the one giving a wife, the other giving
children, there was no denying that the immediate beneficiary
was the husband, wives being precious and hard to come by.
Marriage payments from the bridegroom emphasized his debt: so
did his respectful avoidance of his mother-in-law, and his
obligation to work. Since the husband elect had a vital interest in
pleasing his in-laws, it was customary for the latter to rely more
heavily on him than on junior clansmen for services such as
clearing, or house-building. The service of a son-in-law was thus

a crucial element in the working of the Lele economy, since it made an older man less dependent on his clan fellows. It enabled him to sustain his role as polygynist, since whatever heavy task he had to do for his wife, he could transfer to the strong shoulders of her daughter's future husband. A man could not possibly refuse to come when his father-in-law sent for him to roof a hut, make a fence, do a stint of clearing land, or of weaving raffia. This does not imply that an ideal pattern of clan seniors directly controlling their clan juniors was replaced by an actual one of girl's fathers controlling their sons-in-law. The latter was the case in small Bemba villages; in Yao villages the senior clansman controlled men who married his female matrilineal relatives. If it also held good for the Lele that older men controlled their male affinal relatives it would contradict my general thesis that Lele old men had little control over young men of any description. But the Lele had nothing like groom service. A son-in-law did not change his residence to work for his wife's father or mother's brother. The services he gave were brief and irregular. A week's clearing in the dry season, some hut or fence repair every year, weaving five or ten raffia cloths when asked, this would be the sum of his obligation. He would work alone, never as part of a team. His contributions were very necessary to keep the old men's households afloat, but they still left the son-in-law very free.

A man's relation to his mother-in-law was unique. He and she represented each their own clan in the projected marriage, long before the bride was nubile. The man might easily be older than his mother-in-law. Their relation had to be one of collaboration and respect with no sexual overtones whatever.

Respect required a man to avoid his mother-in-law utterly. If he saw her advancing up a narrow path, he would hurl himself into the undergrowth, so as not to see her. If he found her in a hut he had carelessly entered, he jumped out backwards in dismay, squeaking apologies. Since there was never any direct contact between them, nothing that happened subsequently in the course of the marriage could affect their relation. 'In-lawship endures for ever.'

The relation between a woman and her daughter's husband would have been developed over the years, since her child's babyhood. A man who could say that he had reared his wife, by years of occasional working for her mother, earned his right to his marriage in a special way. It was as if he had been entrusted by his clansmen with the duty of keeping alive part of their common stock of rights to wives of other clans. The more conscientiously he performed it, the more he would resent encroachments from other men. His own clansmen would blame him if he were slack in his obligations. Until the girl was of marriageable age, he and his mother-in-law were the chief points of contact in this deal between their clans, and the chief beneficiary was she; once his wife had come to his house, it was he. His clan-brothers also had to show her formal respect, but he personally had to serve her. She was superior to him though merely a woman. Complete avoidance expressed the paradoxes of their relationship.

Yet it was capable of warmth. A woman whose mother was visiting her received a message from her husband asking his mother-in-law to delay her departure until he had found some raffia cloths to give her. She replied to the messenger that her son-in-law had given her two small grandchildren, which she could hug, one in each arm; that was all that she could possibly want, so why should she wait for raffia cloths?

Husband and wife

There was nothing uncertain or ambiguous about the relations of husband and wife. Lele recognized that their co-operation laid the basis for all social life. They would speak approvingly of a happy couple that 'they had made their marriage well'. Their religion inflicted penalties for breach of the rules which were supposed to govern conjugal relations. For example, it was the wife's primary duty to cook food for her husband, and if she refused to do so, without good reason, it was tantamount to repudiating the marriage; for the husband to refuse her cooked food was an equally grave insult; for him to strike her in anger, or for her to run away from him were serious offences against the village as a whole. It would be useless to go hunting until they had paid fines for their breach of the peace. The question of whether a particular woman had run away in anger, or whether she merely went on a normal visit to her mother used to be raised before hunting, and similarly whether a man had refused to eat his dinner in rancour against his wife, or whether simply because he was not well and without appetite. If there had been a quarrel they owed a fine to the village.

Husband and wife were bound to stay with one another in sickness as well as in health. To care for one another in illness was one of the major responsibilities of marriage. On the husband there lay the duty of finding a cure for his wife when she was ill or barren. He should travel far, if necessary, to find the best diviner, and be prepared to spend his substance on consultation and treatment for her. If he neglected her when she was sick, she would not be blamed for repudiating him and returning to her home. On her part if he was ill, she should not refuse him the shelter of her hut, she should feed him and wash him, and not shrink from the sight or smell of his sores. In effect, if a sick man were to be abandoned by his wives, he had little chance of recovering. A man who had two wives contracted leprosy. It was said that they refused to enter his hut to keep the fire going, put his food on a leaf, and walked backwards to put it on the ground sparing their eyes the sight of his mutilations. They were severely condemned for their neglect, even by their own clan, and blamed for his early death. Another man, not old, who had a wound in his side through which his innards bulged, was deserted by his wife. The whole village felt his plight on their conscience. They tried to remember to bring him water and food, and certain of his clansmen dropped in regularly with wine or meat. People who felt guilty about not helping him got into the habit of making a detour so as not to pass within earshot of his hut. When he was visited he always answered politely and bravely that he was feeling a little better right up to his death, and took care to utter no reproaches. No one called him a sorcerer. Everyone blamed his wife, whose failure to do her duty turned his pain and the disorder and dirt in his hut into a common reproach.

Most of the other obligations of marriage lay upon the husband as a polygamist. He had to treat his wife with scrupulous fairness, sleeping in her hut as often as he slept with her co-wives, providing her with the same goods and with the same help in her fields. If he kept a bow and arrows in one wife's hut, he had to put a duplicate set in the other's hut, and the same for calabashes and baskets. If he favoured one wife, he had to pay a propitiation fee to the other, or she might sulk and refuse to cook for him. If he committed adultery he would have to compensate all his wives.

The crops which she harvested, maize, ground-nuts, manioc, were under her control, and he could not dip into her store while she was away without express permission. The same for meat which he had given her and which she had decided to dry for storing, and the same of course for all her raffia cloths. Her store basket had to be inviolable, so that her brothers could store their surplus raffia cloths with her rather than with their own wives.

Each wife in a polygynous compound was entirely distinct and separate from her fellows. Ideally they were supposed to help one another in sickness, and feed one another's children, but in practice co-wives could rarely count on each other in a crisis. Each would put her own sisters and daughters first, and consequently each looked for help for herself outside her compound. There was too much strain and competition in their relationship for it to be otherwise. No ranking or priority of any kind regulated their relations to one another. Often after an ancient quarrel they would have lived for years in the confined space of the compound without addressing a word to one another. It was a curious experience to have a perfectly amicable conversation with two women, each of whom would address a third party, but not the other. A woman had little consolation of company in her co-wife, and one who was married in a village where she had no clanswomen tended to be very lonely. This aspect of polygyny partly contributed to the strong attachment between mothers, daughters and sisters.

Sex pollution

Lele ideas of sex pollution also contributed to the tension between co-wives, since deaths were frequently attributed to it, and figured in claims for blood compensation.

Any contact with a person who had recently had sexual intercourse was thought to endanger the sick or weak. If a person was ill, or if there was a newborn baby, yellow strands of raffia were strung across the entrance to the hut to warn sexually active persons not to approach. Illicit sexual intercourse was more dangerous. If a man was sick, and his wife committed adultery, he would get much worse. As soon as a woman conceived, her safe delivery was held to be imperilled if she or her

husband or any of her co-wives committed adultery, and
similarly the adultery of any of them would later endanger the
life of her newly born child. The conjugal group of husband and
co-wives was thus defined by its vulnerability to the adulteries
of its members. But the idea did not always operate for goodwill
and harmony. When one woman ascribed the death of her baby
to the promiscuity of her co-wife, relations between them became
understandably strained.

The fatal illness caused by sex pollution, *hanga*, as it was
called, also defined the privacy of a woman's hut. This time it
worked to distinguish each woman from her co-wives, sisters and
all other women. If she was pregnant or had a young baby, they
might both die of *hanga* if another woman had sexual intercourse
in her hut. A young Christian girl, Angélique, struck her mother
on the head with her hatchet when the latter, who had come to
help her, was found to be having sexual intercourse in Angélique's hut. The baby was very ill, and when it died it was
generally agreed that grave responsibility lay with its grandmother. The hut was like a sanctuary, private to a woman and
her husband and defiled by the sexual intercourse of others. The
final insult when two women quarrelled would be for one to
enter forcibly the hut of the other and sit down on her bed. No
one would blame the insulted woman for wounding the intruder
with an axe.

Excessive promiscuity in a woman was thought to cause
barrenness,[4] and in such a case the husband would blame his
wife severely. Furthermore, a husband's life was never safe if
his wife was promiscuous, for it was thought that a sorcerer,
by having sexual intercourse with her, could, by using charms,
strike the husband with sickness next time he touched the woman.

These anxieties about adultery correspond to the fact that
a man's status was severely attainted by infringement of his
sexual rights. His marriage was given to him, as it were, by his
clan, he held the wife on behalf of his clan, and when he died a
fellow-clansman would take her over. If he lost her in the meanwhile to another man, it was a general loss, in which all his clan
was concerned, but for which he was responsible. As we have
seen, when a man and wife were known not to be getting on well
together, his clansmen might suggest that she be transferred to

[4] See Chapter VII.

one more to her liking lest she be tempted to run off with
another man altogether and be lost to the clan. The usual
formula for seduction was to whisper to the woman that her
husband was not virile, to offer her palm wine, and suggest that
she try sleeping with a real man. It made a man very angry to
hear that his wife was accepting drinks from another. Apart
from the insult to his manhood, he risked losing his wife altogether, and remaining wifeless for the rest of his life.

Mothers and daughters

Many Lele institutions hinged on men's control over women.
Consistently male and female spheres were clearly separated in
their daily activities and in etiquette. A woman had to learn to
avoid her brothers, not to stay in the same hut with them, not
to speak to them face to face, to place their food respectfully on
the ground near them, not to touch them. She avoided her sons,
and her sons-in-law and, to a less extent, her own father. The
duty of avoiding always went with a right to assistance. The
woman in an avoidance relation was expected to send food to the
man, and in return he owed her help or protection. Avoidance
rules made it certain that she could never be in a position to
command a man. Notions of seniority and minority, while they
hardly entered into the relations of women with women, were
equally irrelevant in another way to the relations of women
with men—the two sexes were estimated on separate and in-
commensurable scales. In one sense, each sex belonged to a
separate world, which only impinged on the other here and there.

Women spent most of their time with other women, and
developed their strong emotional ties with their mothers, sisters
and daughters. It was obvious that their interests did not coin-
cide with those of their menfolk. A woman's confidants were her
own mother and sisters, and if she was obliged to live far from
them she suffered loneliness to say nothing of the hardship of
doing without their help.

Lele considered that, for the survival of a newly born child,
and the health of its mother, the latter should have a complete
rest, *bwali*, for six months if possible. Considering the narrow
margin of their labour resources it was remarkable how nearly
this ideal was attained for young mothers. A woman would
always try to come to the village where her daughter was married,

to stock up a pile of dry firewood before delivery. Then, from the time of birth, she would take over all her daughter's responsibilities, fetching water, pounding grain, collecting relish, and cooking for her and for her son-in-law. After about three months absence from her own husband, she would ask her son-in-law permission to take her daughter and the baby away for another three months of care in her home. For the young mother all this, and especially the visit to the village of her own birth, was so much holiday. For the older woman too, it was welcomed as a break in her routine, a change of air, and source of prestige. The arrangements for feeding men with their age-mates were compatible with periodic absences of their wives. The mother would have anticipated these long visits when plans were laid for her daughter's marriage and therefore use her influence to make sure that the girl's husband would belong to a village congenial to herself, if possible, in her own birthplace, if not in the village of her clansmen.

If the mother was dead, a mother's sister would be expected to come, or an elder sister. A barren woman, or one whose children had all died in infancy, would often hold herself at the disposal of young kinswomen, to do *bwali* for them—proof that the role was much enjoyed and esteemed. Naturally, when a woman reached her fourth or fifth pregnancy, it was more difficult to find a kinswoman to come, and she might be obliged to start working again after only a few weeks' rest.

If mother and daughter supported each other, it was difficult for the men of their clan to marry the girl against her wishes. In the old days, in principle, if a girl refused to go where her father and mother's brothers agreed that she should go, she might be beaten until she complied. But, in practice, the scheme would often be dropped, because, if the girl was not happy with her husband she would soon find some cause for leaving him and coming home to her mother. Her clansmen would be deeply shamed by her breach of the contract they had made and would try to make her return, or failing this they would feel obliged to give another girl. Since girls were betrothed in infancy, if their mothers were set against a proposed union there was less prospect of a happy outcome, consequently, their views carried some weight.

If mother and daughter or two sisters were both married in the same village, their daily co-operation was almost continuous.

They always tried to accompany each other to the forest, to fetch water, wash together, and go fishing. They cut firewood, hoed or harvested and came home together. They pounded grain for each other. Each cooked her food separately in her own hut, and sent basketfuls of food to their respective sons and husbands. Then one would call the other to bring her children, and they would eat together.

A girl was supposed to have no secrets from her mother, and men would express amazement at their lack of reserve. Mother and daughter would go to the river together, see each other naked, scrub each other's backs; one might even ask the other to shave her head, pluck her eyebrows, anoint her, or administer an anal injection, intimate services which men of different generations could not conceive of performing for each other.

A girl confided her extra-marital adventures to her mother. Then, when the girl was in labour her mother would be able to reveal the names of her lovers, so that the delivery would be speedy and safe. If the child was already born when its mother committed adultery, they feared it might die if she touched it before a rite was performed. The young mother coming home from meeting her lover would quickly call her own mother, or a friend and tell her to pick up the baby, and call a diviner to perform the simple rite which would make it safe for the adulterous mother herself to handle it. Inevitably a mother sometimes seemed to be in collusion with her daughter against the latter's husband, but the very strict rules of avoidance and respect prevented her from coming into contact with him.

She also needed to know the names of her daughter's lovers for another reason. She practised avoidance and respect towards them, discreetly, but as strictly as if they had been her sons-in-law. This was only to spare them the shame and embarrassment of meeting their lover's mother.

Apart from the rule against sexual intercourse in another's hut, there was no avoidance and no authority between women. A girl, her elder sister, her mother, were all on terms of the closest intimacy and a girl's mother-in-law was assimilated to the role of mother. Their behaviour to one another seemed a simple and spontaneous expression of their common interests and affection. The informality of their relations, which had an almost instinctive air about it, caused the men to marvel at women comparing them to animals because their behaviour conspicuously lacked the formality shown between men, even men of the same family.

The strict division of labour between the sexes made certain that each needed the services of the other. Whenever the women succeeded in arranging for a girl's marriage within her natal village, they set up a potential focus for their clan section. For, if his sisters as well as his mother lived in the village where he was born, a man might well be tempted to stay there longer, to supervise their affairs and those of their children.

It was an advantage for a man to live near his clanswomen, because they would send cooked food to him whenever his wife was sick or absent. In return he would be expected to send them portions of meat and wine whenever he had any to distribute. When a man settled down in a village in which his own clan was not one of the founding clans, it would generally be because some of his clanswomen were married there. Although men generally phrased their decisions to move in terms of a wish to live near man of their clan, not to be near women, yet women formed the nucleus round which the local clan section would gather in a more important sense than men would admit.

Furthermore, women worked actively to build up the local section of the clan where they were living. They applied the rules of reciprocity to any classificatory kinsman who arrived in their village, however distant or even unknown his actual relationship might be. This is particularly true of women who were not living surrounded by fellow-clansmen. They seized any opportunity to emphasize kin ties in any direction. Towards a distant clansman they behaved as sister or mother, with respectful avoidance and regular portions of cooked food. With a clansman of a sister's husband they would joke, send camwood, even anoint him themselves, as well as sending food. They would enjoy their husband's discomfort at a too demonstrative welcome of a stranger as a classificatory husband. If a clansman of a woman's son-in-law arrived in the village, woe betide him if he did not avoid her punctiliously and perform services for her, even major tasks such as mending her roof, or clearing her fields, for he would be shamed and mocked for not respecting his mother-in-law. Thus the women by working the principle of clan unity to their advantage helped to give it substance.

VII

MARRIAGE

II. THE COMMUNAL VILLAGE-WIFE AND COMMUNAL FAMILY

The village-wife's status

DIVERTING the interests of a large group of bachelors from illicit sexual adventures there were in each village a number of women who as communal wives were licensed to soften the rigours of the marital code. The *hohombe* or village-wife was not an institution peculiar to the Lele. Among the Dinga, Pende and Mbunda something similar was reported. The Reverend Father Hyacynth Vanderyst wrote in 1922 that polyandry was widespread among the Dinga between the Loange and the Kamtsha rivers.

Des hommes libres ou mariés de tout age et d'un même village se réunissent en une société pour exploiter en commune, mais à tour de role, une malheureuse . . . souvent un enfant de 11–12 ans, qui accepte spontanément cette honteuse situation, ou, à défaut de femmes assez dépravées pour se plier aux exigences de ces satyres, on recourt à la force, à la violence, à l'enlevement, aux menaces de mort par empoisonnement . . . les malheureuses portent le nom de *Masusumu*[1]

After repeated representations to the government, the missionaries had succeeded in 1947 in having legislation passed which made the practice of polyandry an indictable offence, for which the punishment was a term of imprisonment.[2] The law

---

[1] *Congo*, 1922, I, pp. 353–4. A letter from the Secretariat General in the Bashilele files of AIMO in Luluabourg referred to 'certaines pratiques immorales telle que l'institution des *Ngobo* chez les Pende, et des *Mobanda* chez les Bambunda . . . une institution analogue, celle de la *masusombe* a été signalée chez les Bashilele.'

[2] 31.1.1947. Ord. Lég. 37. AIMO. Prohibition des pratiques de polyandrie.
Exposé des motifs:
Parmi les formes de la polygamie, dont la Charte Coloniale fait au Gouverneur General un devoir de favoriser l'abandon progressif, la moins compatible avec notre notion de l'ordre public et de bonnes mœurs, la plus désastreuse aussi pour les populations qui s'y adonnent, est incontestablement la polyandrie.

was energetically applied between 1947 and 1949, the beginning
of my fieldwork, so much so that the institution was to some
extent moribund and its functioning distinctly delicate to
investigate.

We have already described the formation of age-sets and the
way in which they dissected the men of the village in a structure
based on seniority and alternation, which counteracted the
alignment of clan sections. The Lele themselves said simply that
the purpose of their age-set system was to enable them to share
communal wives.

To be a village-wife was a great honour. Her prestige figured
in ritual. She would be compared to a chief, and if she died, the
whole village mourned, not in silence, as for a commoner, but
by dancing with special music, as for aristocrats. If a village failed
to honour the deaths of aristocrats or village-wives or their
children in the prescribed way, they believed that all *mituli*,
edible caterpillars and grasshoppers, would disappear. Although
the chest of game was reserved strictly to the Begetters' Cult, on
pain of automatic death, the chest of the harnessed bush-buck,[3]
because of its height, fine marking and stately bearing, was
reserved to the village-wives: in a spirit of gallantry, 'sweets to
the sweet', they said that the most beautiful animal was the proper
privilege of the most beautiful women and no man was allowed
to eat its chest.

The village-wives were sometimes the ambassadors of peace.
If two villages had been fighting, one might send its village-wives
on a diplomatic mission to the other. Their persons were held to
be immune from danger on occasions when a man's life would
have been taken if he had ventured into the enemy village. On
arrival there, they should be welcomed, regaled with wine, fed,
and then they would sleep, each with the man of her choice. Next
morning, they would discuss the outstanding quarrels, and be

Cette forme abusive d'union conjugale coutumière n'est heureusement pas
répandue dans la Colonie. Mais dans les rares tribes on elle sévit elle compromet
irrémédiablement la natalité et réduit à néant les effets de notre action civilisa-
trice.
L'article 3 interdit expressément l'accomplissement de toute cérémonie con-
tumière consacrant cette pratique.

[3] This antelope was held to be a sorcerer's familiar, as it often 'spoke' its gruff
call at night, and this is probably another reason why it was partially avoided
by men.

escorted home, having created the goodwill necessary for peace negotiations to begin in earnest.

To procure a girl, an age-set had two resources. They could ask for a girl to be allotted to them, whose mother had herself been a daughter of a village-wife, of their own village. That is, they could apply the rule of preferred marriage to their case, and ask for a daughter's daughter. For their request to be granted, they were dependent on the good graces of their seniors, for there would be older age-sets, whose claim to an additional wife might be preferred to their first claim. But the fear that their adulteries might disrupt the village if they were not satisfied, and the possibility that they might even fight their seniors, capture a girl, and run away to the forest with her, strengthened their suit. In fact I was told that fighting did take place within the village when a junior set considered that its right to a wife was flouted.

The other resource, which they were encouraged to exploit, was the chance of seducing a girl from abroad. If they abducted her from one of the rivals of their own village, and so made a political score, so much the better for their prestige.

Installation of a village-wife

When a new village-wife was brought into the village, she was conducted ceremonially round to each of the shelters where men were weaving and resting, and there would be given a raffia cloth from every man. In the evening she would be escorted round again, to drink palm wine. For the first few months her only work was to assist in the recreation of her husbands, the age-set to whom she had been allocated. In the day-time she sat with them in their weaving shelter, flirting and gossiping. First thing in the morning, she swept their shelter. If she helped a man with his weaving by snapping off the broken threads, when he had finished the length and cut it free he had to give it to her. If she started to help him again, he would exclaim, 'Ah, no! Please! This time, help my age-mate, I want to keep a few cloths for myself.' Or if she went round to all the looms and made a charcoal mark on every half-woven cloth, they too would all be hers when completed. She could be given camwood to grind into ointment, with which she would anoint all her husbands in turn. She did no cooking, no fetching water, no pounding grain, no chopping firewood. When their mothers sent food to them as usual she would eat with her husbands, in their shelter.

The rule forbidding her to work in the forest was not merely honorific, it was also a precaution against her recapture by men of the village she had left and against unauthorized men of the village lying with her. If she expressed a strong wish to go down to the stream to wash and bring back some water for her hut, one or two of her husbands would gallantly escort her down to the forest and help her ablutions. Then when she started to lift her calabashes, they stepped in and shouldered the water and with many flattering jokes escorted her back to the village. Sometimes she would even accompany them on the hunt. This unusual breach of the custom of sexual segregation was judged a practical necessity if there was a fear that her former husband might be planning to steal her back, when the village was empty of men. She would be taken as far as the first draw, and then, as soon as there had been a kill, one or two of her husbands would be deputed to take her home, at the same time carrying the game. At the village the liver, a delicacy, would be cooked for her by her husbands. During all this time she never wanted for choice food. Her husbands daily brought in squirrels and birds for her to eat, and plied her with palm wine.

At night she received them in turn in her hut, starting scrupulously with the eldest, and going downwards year by year. Each man slept with her in her hut for two nights and when he left he gave her a raffia cloth for her store. In a short while her baskets would be overflowing with at least 100 raffia cloths.

This period, called her *ibenga*, lasted for as long as she wished. Lele recognized that some women were temperamentally more inclined to this role than others, so that some would continue for as much as six months and others for only two or three, before they asked to be allowed to cook. In any event the *ibenga* period would be over before the first baby was born. If a young girl refused absolutely, or made difficulty about receiving her husbands, she would be whipped until she gave in. A father, knowing of his daughter's reluctance, might ask her husbands to be gentle with her, to wait patiently as she was very young. If she stubbornly persisted in refusing them, the age-set had no choice but to allow one of their number to marry her as his own wife.

When she was to be given permission to set up house, and

cook, she went through a ceremony called Bringing out the Wealth. All the village would be present. Her husbands would call on her to enter her hut and bring out the riches they had given her, so that it could be counted. They enjoyed the public display of their generosity. If the cloths already totalled 100, they arranged on the spot for forty to be delivered to her mother, and fifty to her father, with another ten for him in lieu of an axe. If there were not enough cloths to settle the marriage payment at once, then the husbands arranged among themselves to weave the extra necessary amount. Before this they would have performed all the services of sons-in-law towards her parents, going in strength to build a hut for her mother, etc. Now the marriage payments and services would be completed. Notice that her parents received no more for her than parents of a private wife, and no less. When one of them died, however, all the men of the village would turn out for the funeral, and the village treasury provided a suitable mourning gift.

The question of marriage payments being settled, the older men then lectured the girl on her responsibilities. She was told to choose a limited number from her husbands' age-set to live in her house. 'Don't choose two or three,' they would say, 'choose five or six to live in your house and be your husbands. Are our riches used up? Choose a lot of us.' Then they told her to be peaceful, quiet, not a scold and above all not a trouble-maker; not to favour one of her husbands above the others, not to make mischief by telling one what another had given her; not to insult them by letting them see her with other lovers of the village.

If she started compliantly by choosing four or five house-husbands, with the passage of time their number would be reduced to a more manageable household. The wiles of a co-husband contriving to oust the others from her hut were a familiar joke. Although the friendship of age-mates was supposed to be strong enough to resist the temptations of jealousy, yet Lele much admired a woman whose nature was so discreet and just that she could share her favours between two men without breaking their friendship. They sometimes fared less happily, and often one could not forgive the other for supplanting him.

While they were bachelors, the services she performed for her house-husbands were a foretaste of married domesticity. She fetched water, hoed, cooked, swept and kept house for them, exactly as an ordinary wife would, thus mitigating their bachelor's lot in more than one way. If one was allowed to keep his arrows or hatchet in the house, so must the other be. She slept with them in turns with the same impartiality as a polygamous husband.

Once she had been brought out and given the right to keep house, any man of the village was entitled to have sexual intercourse with her in the privacy of the forest. The only condition laid on her was not to flaunt her affairs before her house-husbands. If she was indiscreet, she would be blamed, but the man who went with her too openly might be made to pay twenty raffia cloths to her insulted husbands.

Lele needed to distinguish two kinds of marital status: *numande njua mbulu*, literally, her husband of the house, and *ngalande njua mbulu*, his wife of the house, as distinct from the village-husbands, *ba bola*, and the village-wife, *ngal a ba bola*. Any man could have several private wives, and share a village-wife; that is, a man could be married polyandrously and polygynously at the same time. But a woman was either a village-wife, or a private wife, never both. Therefore, since the two marriages were not perfectly symmetrical in their effect on each sex, in English translation it is easier to refer to the house-husband of the village-wife, and to the private wife of the individual man of the village.

The number of men entitled to have sexual intercourse with a village-wife varied. If she was the first village-wife of a newly formed age-set,[4] there might be only five or six young men who, in the *ibenga* period, could enter her house, and during this time she was not allowed into the forest except under escort. If she was installed at a later stage of the formation of the age-set, as their second, third or fourth wife, she would be obliged to receive all the men of the set into her hut in turn, as many as ten or twelve. In the larger villages of the north they could number as many as twenty.

Incest prohibitions ruled some of them out, of course. A village-wife who, was married in a village where she belonged to one of the founding clans, would be living among many of her clan brothers, who would avoid her as a sister, and similarly men of her father's clan. Men who were married to her classificatory

[4] See Chapter IV.

daughter would avoid her as a mother-in-law, and so on. She could use these classifications to elude attentions which displeased her.

In the subsequent period, after her *ibenga*, they would try to get her to choose as many of them as possible as her house-husbands. At this second stage in the villages south of Yunda any man of the village who wished to have sexual intercourse with her in the privacy of the forest was fully entitled to do so. She, of course, could accept or refuse, or demand gifts as payment, according to her fancy—until she became pregnant. In the northern villages where the men numbered seventy to a hundred, access to the village-wife was restricted to two of the age-sets, which comprised one half of the village. There was no question of a man from another village having access to a village-wife, and one who settled down in a new village had to pay something for the right to sleep with the village-wives. In those large northern villages, the right to count as a husband of the village-wife thereby became part of the definition of full membership of the village.

Sex pollution re-defined

Once she conceived, a village-wife was open to the danger of *hanga*, sex pollution, like other women. But in her case the risks were differently defined. A private wife, if she slept with a man not her husband when she was pregnant, risked death in childbirth. A village-wife, when pregnant, should only sleep with men who had already become her 'husbands' by prior sexual intercourse. If she had for any reason omitted to sleep with one of the men of the age-set to which she was married, then she would have to avoid him until she was safely delivered. She could sleep with any of the men she had known before, but she would certainly die in childbirth if she were to take on a new one. In such a case the man would be sued for a double blood debt, one for her life, one for her unborn child's, and also sued for additional damages if he was a northerner who belonged to another village. The belief which hedged around a polygynous compound that the adultery of a co-wife endangered the others when they were pregnant was said not to be valid for a village-wife. She was not endangered by her husbands' sexual intercourse with their own private wives or (some held, but others were dubious) with other men's wives. On the other hand, a married man would have to leave his polyandrous wife when one of his private wives was pregnant, for contact with her promiscuity was held to endanger the latter.

People were not altogether happy about these adjustments of the ideas concerning *hanga*, sex pollution. Sometimes a parent would refuse to let a daughter join the honoured ranks of village-wives, on the grounds that their husbands tended to be careless about *hanga*, so that the girl would be in greater danger in childbirth. Another common plaint was that the husbands of a village-wife, wishing never to be debarred from her bed, poisoned her (by sorcery) so that she remained barren. This whispered charge would be followed by a survey of barren village-wives. In practice there were always several who had not conceived, but this corresponded to the fact that a girl who failed to bear children in her first or second attempt at private marriage, was an easy prey for an age-set looking for a new wife. The disappointment and dread of childlessness made it likely she would fall for the seducers' usual bait: 'Your husband is not a real man. Come with us. We will give you children.'

The polyandrous household

Even in the early years of housekeeping with four or five husbands, one or other of them would tend to remove his belongings and go. In one case it might be through jealousy; in another because he had acquired a private wife of his own, who resented his other home. In the most usual case, other influences drew the young man away from the village of his childhood and youth. The wife might find one pretext or another for getting rid of those she least liked, so that she could settle down with two or three permanent husbands who got on well together and made a pleasant domestic unit. When she bore a child, those husbands who were permanently resident in her hut were regarded as its social father in a direct, personal sense, though the whole village fully accepted legal paternity.

It was quite possible for an original pair of house-husbands, weeded out in this way, to remain permanently with their village-wife, after they had each married privately. But young men's changes of residence sometimes left the house of the village-wife temporarily without male tenants. In that case, if a man of the right age group arrived in the village he would be offered a place in her hut. Such hospitality was part of her positive contribution to the village campaign for recruitment. If she was quarrelsome or indiscreet, her chances of maintaining her household intact were diminished. She would then find herself in later years being allotted to any men who became wifeless in the village, and in small villages this would be regardless of age grouping. Thus her role made another contribution to public welfare, since it made provision for elderly widowers.

In old age she was in the same position as any other old woman. She need not lack a man in her house. If she had a daughter she might prefer to live with her, counting on her sons rather than on her husbands to do the heavy tasks of a man for her.

In South Homba there were still nine village-wives, four for the two oldest age-sets, four for the set below,[5] and only one for the youngest set.[6] The system had come to a stop since the legislation against it in 1947, but before that it had been slowed down by the baptizing of young men; and the baptizing of young girls had stopped the process of recruitment. There were two young girls living in the village whose grandmothers had been wives of former age-sets, and who, by the rule of preferred marriage, were claimed by the village. But the young Christians had dissuaded their parents from allocating them in this way and they were privately married.

It was difficult to estimate what would in the old days have been the proportion of village-wives in a village. There was no theoretical limit but four or five to each age-set was probably average.

Of the several recurring themes in the records of village-wives the most frequent is the instability of sterile marriages. There was so little joy in the life of a barren woman that some opportunity to try another husband or another style of marriage when one had failed was eagerly grasped. The possibility of becoming a village-wife was open to any woman, and opportunities were constantly being presented. To some extent the risk of losing their private wives in this way softened men's treatment of them.

[5] Including one who had died just before fieldwork. See Appendix A, p. 275.
[6] Who left the village after the official diviner Makaka had made scandalous advances, see Chapter V, p. 107.

But in fact women did not normally envy the lot of a polyandrous wife.

Some of the cases in South Homba include women who had made very many marital changes. It is doubtful whether in the old days such freedom to swop husbands would have been open to them. Since the firm government of the Belgians had ended village warfare, an elopement was a less serious matter than before: it was not likely to end in bloodshed, whereas formerly it was certain to have provoked fighting, and the woman would have been held responsible for the ensuing blood debts. A woman who left her husband to live with a lover in another village, if men were killed on her account, would find life very uncomfortable. Her clansmen would have to bear the blood debts she had brought, and so would blame her. The women, mothers and sisters of the dead men in the village where she had fled, would treat her with every contumely, dancing around her, singing abusive songs, stripping off their skirts, unforgivable in itself, and rubbing her face in the dirty clothes. In the old days women certainly thought twice before running away, but yet they did so. The institution of village-wife was a kind of safety valve which relieved excessive strains of the marital system, for the women as well as for the men. It was an alternative, but for most women not a very attractive alternative to an unhappy marriage with one man.

Status of the children of the village-wife

In the polyandrous family, the house-husbands fathered the children, dandled them, and fed them with meat and wine. Later they taught the boys the necessary manly skills. Their own sisters took the role of father's sister to the boys, and could claim meat and wine from them on the strength of it. Obviously the sisters of all the men of the village, or even of the age-set, would be too many women for the son of the village-wife to honour and supply with the paternal aunt's privileged gifts. Yet, when it came to the financial aspect of fatherhood, the village as a whole was fully concerned and the village treasury the store from which the father's obligations were met.

As the child of the village a son had more advantages than a daughter. He could expect to be materially helped in the many difficulties which beset a young man. For adultery damages, entrance fees, marriage payments and the rest his fathers, the village, could afford to be more generous with him than the one father in the more usual family. A village, as an incorporated kinsman, had sons, daughters and grandchildren, but no matrilineal relatives. So unlike other fathers, it would not be reproached for being too generous to its wife's offspring at the expense of its sister's children.

Even though the institution of village-wife seemed at that time to be dying, and new age-sets were not being formed, yet this aspect of the institutions, the role of the village as father, was not falling into desuetude. Men enjoyed dipping into the common purse to help their jointly begotten son. On these occasions everyone concerned glowed in a favourable light.

As husband, the village appeared virile and aggressive. Unity was often sacrificed when rivals quarrelled over village-wives. But when it acted as father, unity was restored. The village achieved the ideal of fatherhood, lavish and indulgent. If one of their sons grew up graceless and troublesome they were disappointed and lost interest in him. The son they liked was one who brought warmth and dignity to the relationship. On reaching manhood he should present his fathers with twenty raffia cloths, woven by himself, in filial gratitude for the gift of life. As a hunter, he should lay his first big kill before them, with another of the formal gestures dear to Lele. He should be ready to take messages for them, claiming debts in other villages and delivering the wealth again with elegant gestures of respect. Such a man, who performed his role with distinction, could ask for anything and not be refused. By acting the good son, he forced the village into its most pleasing role. They would try to find him a wife (though the incest regulations might make it difficult), and press him to stay with them always. Often the son of the village was put forward as *Capita* for the thankless chores imposed by the Colonial Administration.

In practice, the son of the village did not always grow up so well; the village as father would then be somewhat perfunctory, especially if the boy's mother had died, or run away, or had long since refused them sexual intercourse. In any case, if the boy had no clansmen in the village he tended to go after adolescence to join them. But he would come back to his fathers to ask for raffia cloths at various crises.

When the son of the village died away from home, his death had to be announced to his fathers by a messenger bearing an eagle's feather, and a piece of leopard skin. These were the symbols of aristocracy and also of the unity and sovereignty of the village, which the son's life and death enabled it to express. The immediate kin of the dead man would go at once to his burial. After a few months (time for recalling debts and amassing wealth) his fathers announced their visit to the village where he died, normally that of his mother's clansmen, where they had previously played the role of sons-in-law. They turned out in strength, beating their drum, and carrying rich gifts, camwood and raffia cloths. They paraded through the village, singing and weeping. Then they danced in his honour, held a wrestling match, and finally transferred their gifts to his clansmen. Then, laden with return gifts, they went home. If he died in one of the villages related to that in which he had been born, he would not be held to have died away from home. But if he died elsewhere, all the brother villages should turn out and share the mourning.

Son-in-law of the village

The importance of the daughter of the village lay in the prospects of her marriage. The choice of husband for her was governed by the same rules as for any other girls, except that, if she married in the village, she would have to marry a man who had not been one of her mother's husbands, and one who was not himself like her a child of the village. Her fathers might offer her in marriage to an esteemed new-comer as an inducement to settle in the village. Like other girls, she was pledged from infancy, either as a polyandrous wife, to succeed her grandmother in another village, or as private wife to settle some obligations which her clan or her fathers had incurred. She could not be village-wife in the same village as her mother, for this too would flout the incest prohibitions, though I heard of a case where this was done.

Only a strong and confident young man would offer himself as suitor to the daughter of a village. The services and gifts expected from him were even more than those expected from ordinary sons-in-law. To her mother he had only to give the normal gift of forty raffia cloths, to her fathers he had to give double the normal rate, a hundred instead of fifty. His service was more arduous too. He had to come, with his brothers and age-mates if he could muster them, to live in the village for two or three months. During this time he was at the beck and call of all the men in it. The most insignificant youngster, who could not possibly have begotten his bride, called him son-in-law and peremptorily ordered him about. Anyone might give him raffia to weave, send him out in the rain to draw wine, ask him to make a bench, or mat and so on. In return, he and his companions were lavishly feasted and the women of the village (his future wife's sisters) honoured them by anointing them with camwood. On his return to his home, when he took his wife away, he should be given a handsome present, some said 100 cloths, though I never saw so much figured in outgoings from the village treasury.

He had to work for it, but what he got was a unique position of prestige. On the day of his formal investiture as son-in-law he danced as victorious warrior around the village, and was presented with an eagle's feather and leopard-skin cap. He enjoyed something like diplomatic immunity. If his own village were to fight with his wife's, neither side could strike him, and he could step between combatants and demand truce. He was supposed to be the natural person to send on a dangerous mission for the village, though I never came across an actual case. If anyone killed or harmed him, his in-laws would demand blood-compensation for the insult to themselves.

The daughter of this marriage was granddaughter of the village, and so subject to the rule of preferred marriage. She would be destined to become the wife of a junior age-set, so that the relations between her clan and the village would be renewed indefinitely.

Even more than the son of the village, the son-in-law embodied the village's aspiration towards unity and strength. His insignia symbolized ferocity, because he stood for the proud autonomy of the village. Lele never developed strong chiefship, and we may doubt whether in fact these cherished institutions of village-wife and village son-in-law would have been compatible with centralized control.

VIII

BLOOD DEBTS

BLOOD DEBTS could be pursued by either villages or clans. For a village, this was but one of many other fields of corporate action. For a clan it was the one important context in which the corporate local clan sections were transcended by the idea of the unity of the dispersed clan. This is a paradox, since local clan sections were most active, most corporate, in blood debt negotiations. But certain principles involved potentially the whole clan. The latter admittedly never acted as a unit, but its member sections could not claim blood debts against one another, and any member of the clan had a potential right to accept blood compensation for any other. Thus clanship over-rode residence as the essential criterion of rights and obligations, and the rights were sufficiently valued for clanship to be very much a live principle of alignment.

It took me a long time to realize that the blood debts which I continually heard discussed were rarely caused by acts of violence. They were mainly incurred when a woman died in child-labour after confessing adultery, or when death was attributed to sorcery or sex pollution. Clansmen of anyone definitively convicted of sorcery would have to accept responsibility for his blood debts. The rare killing by violence within a village or cluster of brother villages, would in principle be compensated. But killing a man of another village was a matter of blood vengeance between villages (see Chapter X), and not one to be dealt with between clans.

Payment of blood compensation was essential to the functioning of the village, since men once settled there were expected not to leave it and to live in peace. Jealousy about women was regarded as the main source of friction and adultery was heavily fined when it was known. The idea that adultery could have lethal effects brought secret cases into the open, and gave the injured husband an opportunity to seek blood compensation—a tendency in line with the general insistence that injuries should be made public, and disputes settled. Their method of settling these blood debts caused by adultery or sorcery promoted goodwill within the village.

It was such an elaborate and central institution that it developed a kind of social autonomy of its own. We can pick out a few of its functions, but its full contribution to the pattern of social life is impossible to evaluate. Many subsidiary institutions had grown up round it. Everyone had an interest in making it work. Something of the zest and satisfaction of a competitive game was felt in observing its rules, paying its forfeits, and taking its rewards.

Compensation was based on the principle of equivalence, a life for a life, a person for a person, interpreted in an institution called *bukolomo*, which I translate as pawnship.[1] A pawn, *kolomo*, was a woman who had been paid over in settlement of a blood debt, or one of her matrilineal descendants. Only limited rights over her were transferred; she was not a slave; her own clan shared responsibility for her with her lords.

The rights were transferred in perpetuity. When, about 250 years ago, the Lele came into their present territory, a band of them without canoes wanted to cross a river. A man of the Lumbunji clan bridged it with a tree trunk, and so allowed them all to pass across. From each clan which used his bridge he tried to exact payment of a woman. Descendants of these early pawns are still in the control of the Lumbunji clan to this day.

The story does not say why the clans were prepared to acknowledge the equivalent of a blood debt to the bridge-builder, but it illustrates another important feature of the institution: the extension of the blood compensation principle to other situations. Any man whose life was saved by another considered that he owed a blood debt to his rescuer. I mention below cases of ransoming in war and of restoring health, which were treated as blood debts by those who were saved. Also there was the convention that certain animals were rated symbolically as equivalent to humans for reckoning indebtedness. For instance, a leopard equals a man, since a leopard kills a man; therefore, if a pawn killed a leopard and presented his lord with the

[1] In an earlier publication ('Blood Debts and Clientship among the Lele', *Journal of the Royal Anthropological Institute*, 90, 1, 1960) I called it clientship, but was convinced by Dr. L. P. Mair that this was a misnomer, and now prefer to follow Rattray's term for a similar institution.

entire skin, the lord was in honour bound to release the mother or sister of the slayer from pawnship. There were times when it was a matter of honour to be generous in admitting liability, and to pay up spontaneously. On other occasions it was as honourable to contest claims.

Status of pawn

Pawnship was a semi-servile status, in which the pawn depended for protection on his lord and owed him certain services. Lele vigorously distinguished pawn from slave. As the whole institution of slavery was abolished before my fieldwork, my knowledge of it was based on information, not observation. Pawnship, on the other hand, though it was in process of liquidation in the European-supervised tribunals, was still very much a live concern of Lele of the day, and I was able to observe for myself and check on reports.

A slave was a man without a clan, and therefore without protection. No compensation could be claimed from the owner who killed his own slave. A pawn was a full member of his or her own clan, and doubly protected. For the death of a pawn, double compensation was demanded, one woman for the clan, and one for the lord. This essential distinction between pawnship and slavery was the source of a well-articulated body of rules governing the relations between pawns and lords.

Kumu, lord, is a word of elastic range. It can refer to members of the hereditary clan of Lele chiefs, to the appointed head of a village, to the owner of a dog, to the person in whom rights of pawnship are vested. The lord was always male, never female. He never acted as an individual, but always representing a group, either a section of a matrilineal clan or a village.

Two main rights were transferred when a woman was paid in settlement of a blood debt. The first was the right to dispose in marriage of her and of all her female matrilineal descendants. The second was to use her, or any of her female matrilineal descendants, to settle a further blood debt. This latter right had to be exercised with the consent of the pawn's clan, which should accept a 'mutation fee', called *nghei mwa tet a ponj*, 'wealth of the arrow shaft', twenty raffia cloths and an arrow, to signify their consent to the change of authority.

The first right severely limited the initiative and control of the

mother's brother of the first female pawn, and similarly restricted
the rights of all her male matrilineal descendants. Since competition for wives was one of the key motives inspiring Lele
behaviour, the advantages of pawnship to the receiver of compensation and the disadvantages to the payer seemed to be very
obvious. In effect, a whole future section of the payer's clan was
marked off, and transferred, for these important purposes, to
another clan, for ever.

At first glance it seems as if, to the question 'What does the
lord gain out of his control of pawns?' the answer should be that
he gains wives for himself and for his junior clansmen, and all
the prestige and authority which follow from being in a position
to allocate wives. This reply was never given and the Lele did
not even seem to think of the system as one which gave extrinsic
advantages to the winners, or disadvantages to the losers. They
always spoke as if sufficient explanation of the moves they made
is contained within the rules of the system itself, as if it were a
game played for its own sake.

Ask 'Why do you want to have more pawns?' and they invariably said, 'The advantage of owning pawns is that if you incur a blood debt, you can settle it by paying one of your pawns,
and your own sisters remain free.' Ask 'Why do you wish your
own sisters to remain free?' and they replied, 'Ah! Then if I
incur a blood debt, I can settle it by giving one of them as a
pawn.' Ask them what is the advantage of marrying a woman
who is your own pawn, and they said that if she committed
adultery, instead of the usual damages of fifty raffia cloths, you
could ask for a pawn to be paid, and so then you would have two
pawns where before you had only one. They never seemed to be
able to stand outside the system, and explain it in terms of
social or economic advantages accruing to the lords, or disadvantages falling on the pawns.

The truth is that the ramifications of the system were so
complex, that it is difficult to isolate its effects. There was no
class of hereditary lords distinct from a class of pawns. A man
who was lord of a group of clan X was likely himself to be a pawn
of a man of clan Y, while other members of Y might be pawns of
his own clan. The practical responsibilities of being a lord were
as onerous as the liabilities of being a pawn.

Lele were far more conscious of the pressure (surely increased by the system itself) to pay blood debts, than of other specific patterns of profit and loss arising out of pawnship. Every man was always aware that at any time he might be liable for a blood debt. Ideas of liability were highly developed; even if a woman ran away from her husband, and fighting broke out on her account, the deaths would be laid to her door, and her brother or mother's brother would have to pay up. Since only women were accepted as blood compensation, and since compensation could be demanded for all deaths, of men as well as of women, it is obvious that there could never be enough women to go round. Men fell into arrears in their pawnship obligations, and girls used to be pledged before their birth, even before their mothers were of marriageable age. Pawnship had far-reaching effects on the marriage institutions of the Lele, contributing to the disapproval of divorce and even of adultery.

The rights to dispose of female pawns in marriage, and to transfer these rights to settle blood debts, were primary rights of the lord. They were, of course, exercised as a limitation of the rights of the woman's male clansmen. They could hardly be said to be rights exercised over the women themselves. The latter never had any freedom (which could be said to be restricted by their status as pawns) to marry as they chose. Whether they were free or pawns their personal marital status was exactly the same. For her husband, her co-wives, her children there was no difference between a free woman and a pawn. Pawnship essentially was an arrangement between men, though it concerned the distribution of their rights over women. In recognition of this fact, the relation of the lord to the male descendants of his pawn women was precisely formulated. Unless there was goodwill between them, the whole system broke down.

There was no external machinery of justice which could coerce pawns into honouring their contracts. The interests of the lord could not be enforced against the wishes of his pawns. Consequently, lords were engaged in elaborate manœuvres to keep their pawns sweet, in order that the rights which, *de jure*, according to the conventions of the system, they were entitled to hand down to their heirs in perpetuity should in fact be respected by the pawns. If goodwill were lost, a whole heritage might be lost, for an angry pawn could summon the armed strength of a rival village to support him against an unjust lord.

Any male pawn who thought that his lord was not acting fairly by him could arrange for one of his own sisters to be captured from the lord and installed as village-wife. This sanction accounts for the responsibilities which the lord undertook on behalf of his male pawns. He had full liability for any blood debts which they might incur. He should also help them substantially with raffia cloths and camwood from his stores, when they needed help in paying their entrance fees and fines. He should help them to obtain wives. He usually tried to allot one of his female pawns in marriage to one of his male pawns, hoping that they would continue to live near him. For the death of a pawn, the lord claimed compensation, and this was regarded as an added security. Someone threatened, or bullied, would cry out, '*Wayibu! Ndi mot akana*, Take care! I am someone else's man.' In short, the lord was expected to play a role, both protective and authoritarian, which was very like that of father or mother's brother. The latter did not give up their responsibilities towards a pawn. For him the lord was an additional, not an alternative, source of help.

In recognition of his obligations, and his right to protection from his lord, the male pawn should give one hindleg and the back of any large antelope or any pig that he killed, one foreleg, one hindleg, the back and skin of any leopard, and the whole of any eagle, payments explicitly analagous to tribute to a chief. But a man did not often kill one of these beasts on his own; most big kills were made in the communal hunt, when such private obligations were waived in favour of the hunting team. When he was on good terms with his lord, a man looked forward to killing one of the tribute animals, organizing his younger brothers to help him to carry the meat, and then laying it ceremoniously at his lord's feet. He would go away happily conscious that if he were later to need help in any form, the lord would be under strong moral obligation to give it. Men made these calculations quite explicitly, working it out that if they wanted initiation to a cult group, they would need help with the entrance fees, and that, therefore, the first step was to kill a big beast, so as to lay its back and hindleg at the feet of their lord.

A further sanction upheld the lord's rights. If a female pawn married against his express wishes, he could curse her fertility, and she was expected never to bear children again, unless he lifted the curse. This would be a blow against the girl's clansmen, as much as against herself, and they were thus likely to bring pressure on her to conform to their lord's wishes.

I give here an example of a lord paying blood compensation for one of his pawns, and another case in which the lord was punished for his refusal to do so, by unilateral action on the part of the claimants.

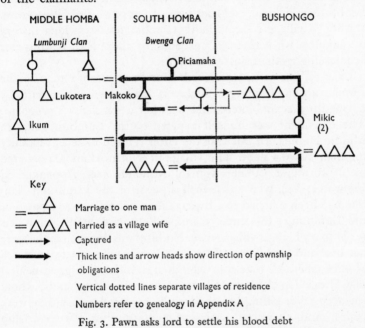

Key

=—△		Marriage to one man
= △△△		Married as a village wife
··········▶		Captured
▬▬▶		Thick lines and arrow heads show direction of pawnship obligations
		Vertical dotted lines separate villages of residence
		Numbers refer to genealogy in Appendix A

Fig. 3. Pawn asks lord to settle his blood debt

Case 1. Makoko, later the head of the village of South Homba, and leader of the local section of the Bwenga clan,[2] was the son of Piciamaha, herself the pawn of the Lumbunji clan, living in Middle Homba, where Lukotera was head of that local clan section. Lukotera had betrothed Makoko's sister's daughter, Mikic (see Appendix A, Figure 13, A2), to his own sister's son, Ikum. Makoko was accused of killing a man who was a pawn of the village of Bushongo. He refused to pay the blood debt, saying that he was a pawn of the Lumbunji clan, and had no free sisters. Bushongo village promptly captured his wife, and held her hostage until Makoko prevailed on his lord, Lukotera, to

[2] Appendix A, Figure 13.

release the child Mikic, who was living with her mother in Bushongo, and pay her over to Bushongo village. Thus his wife was returned to him. Mikic was now pawn of the village of Bushongo and the Lumbunji clan had given up all rights over her. Later the village of Bushongo incurred a blood debt with the village of South Homba, which they at first refused to admit. South Homba simply captured Mikic when she was visiting her brother Makoko, and kept her as their pawn and village-wife. Bushongo village is near South Homba and has a long history of alliance with them. Consequently they had reasons for acquiescing in the transfer of rights.

Case 2. The village of North Homba accused a man of the Lumanya clan of killing with sorcery their pawn village-wife, by having illicit sexual intercourse with her when she was pregnant. The defendant was himself a pawn of the Lumbunji clan in Middle Homba. In this case the latter refused to accept liability for their pawn's debt. The village of North Homba retaliated by capturing a Lubelo woman, Mihondo (see Appendix A, Figure 12, A8), who was herself a pawn of the Lumbunji clan. She had been married to a Bwenga man (who also was a pawn of the Lumbunji) for three years without conceiving, and was ready to try being a village-wife. Nothing was done to compensate her husband for his loss. In eight years as village-wife in North Homba, she bore four sons who died in infancy. A great deal of ill-will developed between her and her village-husbands, whom she accused of killing her children by sorcery because they were males, and therefore useless for continuing the pawnship relation. When the fourth child died she left North Homba, and returned to her original owners, the Lumbunji clan in Middle Homba, who agreed with her that North Homba had had no clear right to capture her in the first place. This happened early in the 1940's, when Belgian administration was well established, but even in the old days fighting would not have been likely to have broken out when she ran away, since North Homba and Middle Homba acknowledged a common origin and were allies.

These two cases show how the lord was expected to pay the blood debts of his pawns, and the kind of reprisals to which he was exposed if he denied the responsibility.

If the arrangements did not work to the profit of both parties, lord and pawn, then goodwill was lost, and there followed a trial of strength, in which pawn was likely to emerge as a free man. The usual way in which a pawn became free was by demanding the release of his mother or sister, when his lord was responsible for a death among his pawns. In the case above, of Mihondo running away from North Homba, if they had tried to follow her, her protectors would certainly have riposted with an accusation that the village had killed one, or all of her children, in which case the village of North Homba would have owed a blood debt to her clan. In such cases, when there was already a basis of goodwill between the parties, it was always honourable to accept the liability and let the woman go free, another reason why North Homba let the matter drop. The following shows what happens when the essential goodwill was lacking.

Case 3. *Ket clan*. A Ket woman, called Mbwengol, died. She was the pawn and wife of a man of Bienge clan, in Mbombe village. Her brother, Pung, in Bushongo, consulting oracles,

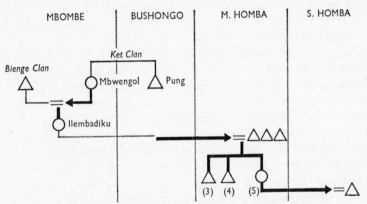

Fig. 4. Case history of pawnship of Ket clan section
(Key as for Fig. 3)

found her husband guilty of killing her by sorcery. His demand for compensation was refused. If it had been admitted, one of his dead sister's daughters should have been released from pawnship. He declared that he would take one of them away, so that her former lords of the Bienge clan should not choose her husband. He carried off the little girl, Ilembadiku, to the village of Bushongo, to be married there. The Bienge clan arranged that the village of Middle Homba, conveniently near Bushongo, should capture her and make her their village-wife, the Bienge receiving compensation from Middle Homba. Then her mother's brother complained of her abduction to the *Nyimi* of the Western Lele, Ngwamakadi, one of the few cases I recorded of appeal to chiefly arbitration. He declared both sides to have been in the wrong, the Bienge clan for not compensating for the death they had caused, and the Ket clan for taking Ilembadiku away from her fathers by force. He proposed that she should now be allowed to remain the village-wife of Middle Homba, and that the Bienge should pay over a pawn to her mother's brother, Pung. The Bienge, stronger and more numerous than the Ket clan, and backed by their own village, agreed with the first part of the settlement, but omitted to carry out the second part. When Pung himself finally died, no compensation had been paid, and his younger clansmen, the sons of the girl in question, felt that they were too isolated, too young and too few to reopen the case.

This part of the case illustrates the disadvantages of belonging to a small local clan section (see below). The second part illustrates the ways in which lords used their rights over pawn women.

While Ilembadiku's children[3] were young, Middle Homba village incurred a blood debt to the clan of Hanja in their own village, which they settled by transferring rights over their communal daughter and pawn, Ihowa. Hanja then settled an outstanding debt they owed to the Bulong clan, and the latter transferred rights over the same girl to a man of the Lubelo clan in South Homba, who had long ago accused one of them of having killed his mother. The girl herself, Ihowa, in the meanwhile, had been baptized (as Modestine) at the mission, and therefore the Lubelo, on acquiring rights over her, had to find her a Christian husband if they were not to lose her altogether. Their own young Christian Lubelo men were mostly married or betrothed. They therefore gave her to Oscar, younger brother of Ngwe of the Ngondu clan, both pawns of the Lubelo. Her two brothers left Middle Homba, and came to settle near their sister in South Homba. They acknowledged their status of pawns to the village of Middle Homba, but nourished a sense of grievance, saying that but for the weakness of their local clan section, they would have been free men, and their sister and her children free to be disposed of in marriage according to their own interests.

When the pawn and lord live in rival villages it was even more

[3] Appendix A, Figure C3, 4, 5, the daughter being Ihowa.

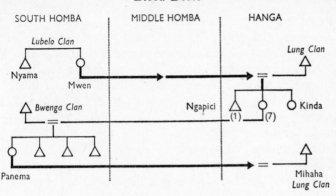

Fig. 5. Pawns declare themselves free
(Key as for Fig. 3)

necessary for the lord to be punctilious in his dealings, as the
following case demonstrates.

Case 4. *Lubelo and Lung clans.* A man of the Lubelo clan in
South Homba was accused, and convicted by poison ordeal, of
killing by sorcery a man of the Hanja clan in Middle Homba
village. Lubelo gave their own sister, Mwen, in compensation.
The Hanja, instead of marrying her themselves, transferred their
pawnship rights to the Lung clan in Hanga village, the hereditary
rival of South Homba village. There she was married to the
official diviner of the village, and bore three children, pawns
of the Lung clan. When her husband died, Mwen was inherited
by another man, but proper purificatory ritual which protects
the widows of official diviners from death by *hanga* was omitted.
Mwen died, and her brother, Nyama, demanded compensation
from the Lung clan. The Lung refused, and the Lubelo forthwith declared their pawnship to be at an end. Mwen's daughters
and her only son became, to all intents and purposes, as free as
if Lung had formally released them. Mandong and Ngapici[4]
went to live in South Homba, and Kinda was married as village-
wife in Bushongo.

Later, Nyama fell ill, and nearly died. Many diviners tried to
cure him, without success. The man who restored him to health
was Mihaha, a diviner of the Lung clan, from Hanga, who went
to endless trouble to get powerful remedies for him.

When he felt his health return, Nyama sent for Mihaha and

[4] Appendix A, Figure 12, C1,7.

declared that, as he owed him his life, he would give to him
Panema, the girl whom Mihaha would have married originally
if the Lubelo had not ceased to be pawns of the Lung clan. As it
happened, Panema had already been married to another man,
and borne him a son. He refused to give her up, and in the old
days the Lubelo would have resorted to force. However, this
happened after the Belgian administration had effectively prevented fighting. Nyama and Mihaha went together to the
tribunal and obtained an order for Panema to leave her husband
and go to be married to Mihaha, as they solemnly but untruth-
fully declared that he was her first betrothed, and that she had
been taken from him by the other by force.

In this case the lord, represented by Mihaha, finally recovered
his pawns, by showing extreme solicitude when their uncle was
ill. Nyama's act of restoring the girl to pawnship as a gesture of
gratitude illustrates the style in which these transactions were
made. The fact that the girl was unhesitatingly taken away from
her first husband shows that the husband who was not his wife's
lord was at some disadvantage in his dealings with his in-laws. In
this sense it is true that it was an advantage to be married to a
pawn-wife.

The clan as lord

When a village owned a group of pawns, there was no difficulty
in recognizing who was their lord, for the village had a corporate
enduring personality, regardless of the fluctuations in its population. This I must describe separately. The clan, on the other
hand, had little or no corporate personality. It was merely an
amorphous collection of individuals, claiming common matrilineal descent.

In spite of this, claims for blood compensation were made in
the name of the clan of the victim, against the clan of the slayer.
But this was largely a manner of speaking. When a claim was
refused, the claimants tended not to capture a distant clans-
woman of the slayer, but a pawn of his, or of his lords.

There are two limited senses in which the whole clan appeared
as a collectivity. First, no claim for blood compensation could
be made between sections of a single clan. If a man killed a fellow-
clansman, this was a shameful act, which would create enmity,
but which could not be compensated by the transfer of a pawn

from one section to another. Second, the fiction of clan unity was validated in so far as its effective sub-units were constituted so that any clansman, born or reared anywhere, related or not related, could become a fully participating member.

This rule, that clan membership was valid anywhere, saved the blood-debt system from breaking down. Wherever a pawn-woman might go, be taken or elope to, her children were still pawns, but her lords could not make good their claims if they could not persuade the woman to come within suitable range. We have seen that women had an interest in living near their mother and sisters, and were often hard to coax into moving, or staying in position. If one of them did move, the others might well try to join her. In short, women were not as compliant as the blood debt system required them to be. Furthermore, a blood debt settled by transfer of rights over one woman might not result in marriage of that woman to her lord, if incest regulations prevented it, or for other reasons the lord might use a pawn to settle a debt he himself had incurred, and the recipient might do the same. The chain of settled debts might run over a large part of the country, and end up only where a suitable man of the lord's clan was in a position to marry a girl of the pawn's clan, without either having to change residence. So the principle of complete parity of status between clansmen, dispersed wherever they might be, gave flexibility to the blood-debt system, and enabled it to overcome certain inflexibilities in residence. Further, the local clan section was often too small a unit to be able to participate fully in blood-debt exchanges with local sections of other clans. The projects would soon be brought to a halt by lack of suitable girls.

The role of lord

We have seen how difficult it is to determine who are the members of a local clan section. Since the Lele themselves tried to avoid making distinctions between new arrivals and established members, let us put aside the attempt to define the local clan section more closely and turn to the problem of how this group acted as lord in relation to pawns. The role of lord needed decision, generosity, and other qualities which are best displayed in one man, not in a leaderless group. Lele themselves said that the senior member of a local clan section acted for the section as a whole. This would imply a degree of authority, which was not warranted by the facts.

The local clan section appeared as a single group at village meetings. It acted as a single unit, under the formal leadership of its elder, in support of any of its members' claims for compensation. It also appeared as a single unit when it had allocated any of its widows or pawn-women in marriage, or when it decided that the claims of a close matrilineal kinsman who had gone to live elsewhere should be considered or not. There were meetings and discussions which made a real thing of the nominal unity. A young boy would say artlessly, 'We gave so-and-so his wife.' But the fine simplicity of the first person plural applied only after there had been considerable shuffling, bargaining and pushing from various points of vantage. It is important to try and discover what these points of initiative were.

For all practical purposes each elementary family of pawns might recognize a different member of the lord's clan as their own particular and immediate representative, whom they referred to as their own *kumu*, lord. If a case of pawnship originated with the action of one man, then he was the lord, nominally acting in the name of his clan, who had most control over the woman who was transferred, and over her children. Ngomabulu, below (Case 5), was an instance. He had provided, single-handed, the wealth in camwood which his village required for two of its wives. In recompense he was given, as his pawns, the daughters of these village-wives. He married them himself, and controlled the marriages of his own daughters himself as if, in this case, he alone represented the clan, though he was by no means the eldest man of his local clan section.

Again, the man in the lord's clan who married one of the pawns of his clan and begot daughters who were in turn pawns, acted as a nearly independent agent in their affairs, for their pawnship had begun with his begetting. Every time a lord-husband died, his successor as husband, if he was a fellow-clansman, took over his role in regard to the children. It follows that, in practice, a descent line of pawns was attached to the local section of its lord's clan through a number of particular allegiances to each of the clansmen who intermarried with the pawn females. No wonder men were keen to be allotted pawn-wives in the gift of their local clan sections. Whatever the other purposes of the act of bestowing a pawn-wife on a junior clansman, the effect on his status was like promotion from an ordinary shareholder to the board of directors, for he could now hope to become one of the founts of authority through which the clan section controlled its heritage of pawns. In short, any originator of pawnship rights for his clan, whether by begetting or by buying, became one of the points of focus in pawn-lord relations.

Case 5. *Ngomabulu's debt.* A Lubelo man was captured in a raid, and would have been killed if a Bwenga man from Mbombe had not intervened and ransomed his life by giving a pawn to his captor. The Lubelo therefore owed a blood debt to the

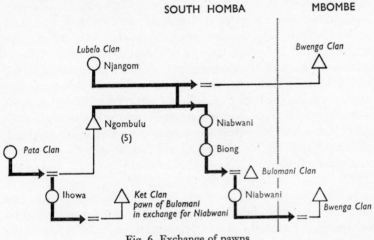

Fig. 6. Exchange of pawns
(Key as for Fig. 3)

Bwenga man, and they paid over Njangom. Her children were born in pawnship, but they went in due course to live with their clansmen in South Homba. Subsequently Njangom died in the poison ordeal, convicted of having killed a Bwenga woman by sorcery. The Lubelo owed therefore another blood debt to the Bwenga.

The debt was never regarded as one concerning the whole of the Lubelo clan, nor even the whole of the section of it living in South Homba, but merely Ngomabulu himself,[5] the eldest male descended from the dead woman who had incurred the debt. Ngomabulu's own sister, Niabwani, had been paid over by the

[5] Appendix A, Figure 12, B5.

Bwenga, his lords, to the Bulomani clan in South Homba, so that he could not give his sister's daughter or her daughter's daughters. He proposed to settle his mother's debt by giving one of his own daughters. Both his wives, Mawoha and Himbu, were his pawns, and he was evidently considered to have the sole right to dispose of their children in marriage, since he had not only begotten them, but himself had been the agent by which his clan could claim them as pawns. But both girls, Biong and Ihowa, he had betrothed from infancy to men in the village.

One of them, Ihowa, had been betrothed to Badiangu,[6] a pawn of the Bulomani clan (the lords of Ngomabulu's sister's children). Ngomabulu now proposed to break off the betrothal, and send Ihowa to Mbombe, as pawn of the Bwenga clan, to make good his mother's debt. However, Ihowa's mother did not want her daughter to go away, and her case was put by her half-brother, Ngwe, of the Ngondu clan, who was a man of influence. Ihowa and her mother were of the Pata clan, hailing from Bushongo. Speaking as a man of Bushongo, Ngwe warned Ngomabulu that Pata girls never did well in Mbombe, and rarely succeeded in rearing their children there. If he wanted to see his daughter's daughters married in their turn, Ngomabulu would have to find some other way of settling his debt.

In the end the solution came from the Bulomani clan, the lords of Ngomabulu's sister, and also of Ihowa's original betrothed. Ngomabulu made a deal with them, transferring rights over Ihowa to the Bulomani, in return for pawnship rights over his own sister's daughter's daughter, Niabwani, whom he then gave to the Bwenga in Mbombe. Ihowa was thus able to stay in the village with her mother, and to marry her original betrothed.

The interest of Ngomabulu's case here is the degree of autonomy with which he exercised his rights as lord of pawns of his own begetting, and the absence of co-operation from the rest of his own clan section. When I knew him, his other daughter Biong had died in childbirth, and so he had no pawns left under his own control, except his two wives. By that time his own sister's sons were all Christians. Since they could only marry once, they could hardly work the pawnship system and enjoy its benefits in the old way.

[6] Appendix A, Figure 16, Ket clan A2.

The proof of whether a man's rights as a lord were vested in him as an individual, or whether the generally accepted theory was valid, that they were distributed evenly through the corporate personality of the local clan section, might be tested by what happened when a man died or left the village. Did he carry his individual right as lord away with him when he went?

The answer depended much on the strength of personal loyalties. The exercise of rights over pawns was always so much a matter of delicacy and compromise that in practice the lord was not likely to have effective authority if he went very far from the normal scene of his pawns' lives. In such a fluid system nothing was easier for pawns left behind than to transfer their individual allegiance to one of his remaining fellow-clansmen. If he tried to make them come with him, he was sure to be withstood by the women, since they regularly tried to resist any proposed changes of residence for themselves and their daughters.

The following is a case in which a new arrival brought with him the right to act as lord in several pawnship cases. One man, Ngwe, was welcomed because he came to where his own pawns, and his lords, were living. By contrast, the young man who joined him later, Makum, gave up any rights he may have hoped to claim in his old clan section in the far north.

Case 6. *Ngondu clan.* We have already described the composition of this local clan section.[7] When he arrived in South Homba, Ngwe brought with him some pawnship rights, which had been vested in the section of the Ngondu clan residing formerly in a little village, Bushongo Bwabwani, which had grown too small to be able to exist independently, and which had now been merged with its brother village, Bushongo Bwankapa. Most of these pawns were now living in South Homba, and on his arrival there, they transferred their allegiance at once to Ngwe instead of to his maternal uncle in Bushongo. Ngwe also carried with him the right to control pawns who had belonged to the vanished village, and not to the Ngondu clan. He said that if the village were ever again restored to separate existence he would hand over the heritage of pawnship rights which he had been administering in its name.

It is understandable that Ngwe as a man of some importance was doubly acceptable as a new-comer to the village of South

[7] See Chapter V, p. 105.

Homba; one of his sisters there was a pawn of the village, he and his brother were pawns of the main clan there, the Lubelo, and several of his own pawns and those of the vanished village, Bushongo bwabwani, were also resident there. He had already been given one of the pawns of the village in marriage. Now, on his arrival there, he was given another, becoming son-in-law of the village twice over. Later he was inducted as junior official diviner of the village. The combination of honours implied that his life was finally committed to being spent in South Homba.

It would be a mistake to think of a man deliberately calculating that a move to village A would give him a better start on the social ladder than, say, village B. When they moved, it was generally under great personal stress, and at any given time the choice of villages where they were welcome would be very small. Whether the move turned out to have been advantageous depended on the numbers, sex, and age of fellow-clansmen and the number of the ties of pawnship, but their personal qualities as good friends would probably weigh more for a man deciding to join a particular group, than a cool reckoning of his own chances of leadership.

The Ngondu case concerns only a very small local section of a clan, four men, three women. Matters were different when the local clan section was larger. First, the complete solidarity and pooling of interests was absent, although clan unity was still invoked on occasion. A large clan section having been settled for some time, factions would have emerged. New-comers to the village attached themselves to one or other of these subgroups, as personal tastes and interests dictated.

Limits of the lord's control of pawns

So much for the question of who, in the local clan section, took the initiative in dealing with pawns. We now should ask how the lords exercised their rights.

Ngwe's case shows that pawns liked to have one of their lords living among them. The fact was that the lord had no possibility of exercising any tyrannous control over his pawns; on the contrary, his role was benignly protective. For this there were at least four reasons.

The first, we have seen, was that, unless the male pawns were satisfied that their lord was good to them, they would seek an opportunity for ending the whole relationship, and this was not difficult since there was no machinery of coercion.

The second was that female pawns who were unhappy tended to be a loss since they could run away.

Third, the rules of incest and exogamy complicated the allocation of pawn-women to husbands. It was impossible for a whole line of pawns to be married to the clan of their lords. Fourthly, the lord was expected to allow his pawn-women to make the traditional preferred marriages.

In other words, the degree to which the lords could derive any personal benefit from their rights over pawns was severely limited. No one might marry into their own clan, or into the clan of their own father. A man might not marry again into his wife's clan, if she was alive. If he was the son of a village-wife, he should not marry a girl whose mother was a village-wife of his village, nor should two women, whose mothers were village-wives in the same village, and who therefore called each other sisters, be married to the same man.

It follows from the first of these regulations that the daughters of pawn-wives had to be married to men who were not of the lord's clan. If a woman of clan B was pawn of her husband in clan A, then her daughters, though they were pawns of clan A, could not marry any man of that clan. Clan A would try to arrange their marriages so that they lived near the village of their lords; when their children were in turn of marriageable age, clan A would again be able to allocate the girls amongst themselves, if they had not in the meantime transferred their rights over them. In short, a lord's clan could intermarry with a pawn in the first generation, and subseqently with her daughters' daughters, and similarly with their daughters' daughters. In each alternate generation the lords got the full benefit of their rights to dispose of their female pawns by marrying them, and in every intervening generation they got the secondary advantage of being able to give away wives to their friends. On how wisely they used their rights in the intervening generation, when the female pawns were debarred from intermarriage with them, depended their prospect of following up their full claims again when these girls' daughters were marriageable.

Long-term planning was required, and some men did not have the energy or ability to succeed. The baptizing of the younger

generation as Christians created a further complication since
Christians are monogamous and intermarry only with one
another. Many of the marriages between young Christians at
the mission, which seemed to be spontaneously arranged, were
in fact a follow-up of old pawnship rights.

Case 7. In the following case, Ngapici had some difficulty
in finding suitable husbands for pawns in his own clan section.
When his sister Kinda died, her husbands, the village of Bushongo, admitted their responsibility, and paid over to her clan
one of their pawns. Whether the girl refused to leave home, or
whether he found the incest regulations debarred his own clan
section, in any case, Ngapici allowed a fellow-clansman living in
Bushongo to marry her.

Earlier, before Kinda had died, he had paid her daughter,
Mwen, as pawn to the aristocratic clan at Tundu, because a
Lubelo man had seduced an aristocrat's wife. Instead of marrying
her himself, the lord gave Mwen to the village of Malembi, and
in return Malembi gave him another woman. The girl's mother,
in Bushongo, protested that Malembi was too far away, and she
asked that Mwen be married in Bushongo. So the Lumanya clan
in Bushongo collected camwood, and bought the rights over her
so that she could marry a Lumanya man in Bushongo.

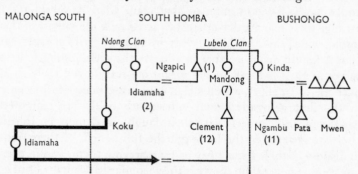

Fig. 7. Claim over pawn postponed
(Key as for Fig. 3)

Later she died in childbirth, naming a man of the Bulomani
clan in her confession of adultery. Both the Lubelo and the
Lumanya clans claimed compensation from the Bulomani for
her death. The Bulomani paid over one of their pawns of the
Ndong clan to the Lubelo, a girl called Koku. Ngapici could not

marry her himself, as her mother's sister was already his wife. The dead woman's full brothers were held to be too young for Koku. By looking among other men of his own local clan section, or beyond it, he could presumably have found her a Lubelo husband, but he let the matter slide, saying that she could marry whom she pleased, so long as the Lubelo could claim her daughters. She went to the far south to be married, and bore three daughters, who, by rights, should have all been pawns of the Lubelo. The distance was too far for easy contact to be maintained, so Clement was lucky to get one of them: Idiamaha was betrothed to him from birth, and at the time of my visit he was waiting for her to finish her instruction for baptism at the mission. This example also illustrates how men tended to apply their rights as lord narrowly within their own clan section.

From the rules of exogamy one would expect that the pawn's line would be intermarried with the lord's clan in every alternate generation. In practice this pattern was apt to be disturbed by transfers of pawnship rights. But it rarely seems to have applied to more than one woman in each generation of pawns which was able to intermarry with their lord's clan. The lords, in fact, sought only to marry one girl in each family of girls, particularly they were circumspect in recognizing other kinship claims, especially the *ikana* (grandchild) obligations.

We have seen that every grandfather had the acknowledged right to claim a granddaughter for his own clan, whether he was a mother's father, or father's father. The main effect of these marriages was to maintain continuity in relations between clan sections, and also between clan sections and certain localities, since a man with a daughter or daughter's daughter to dispose of was likely to choose a man living in the vicinity.

A good example of the way in which a lord used his rights over his own pawns to fulfil his obligations as a son is the case of Ngomabulu's[8] two daughters, one Biong, given to a man of Ngomabulu's own father's clan, the other, Ihowa, destined to succeed her paternal grandmother if her own mother had not intervened (as described above).

Case 8. *Ngomabulu's daughter, Biong.* He had betrothed her to a boy of the Bwenga clan, Polidor, and thus conformed doubly to the conventions of preferred marriages. Bwenga was

[8] Appendix A, Figure 12, B5.

the clan which had fathered Ngomabulu himself and whose pawn he was, so he was giving his daughter to his father's clan. Polidor was further eligible as his son-in-law, since, like Biong's mother, he was the child of a village-wife. If Biong had not become a Christian her father might have been expected to give her as village-wife to the village which had begotten her mother. He came as near as he could to performing his obligations to his wife's fathers by allocating the girl to one of their sons.

It can be seen that if a lord is expected to admit the claims of his pawn's father's fathers and mother's father's clans, his right to dispose freely in marriage of pawn-girls is severely limited. Take the case of a man who has married a pawn. His daughters cannot be married into his own clan, and so he uses the rules of preferred *ikana* marriage as a guide to disposing of them. In the generation of his daughter's daughters, his claim, as their lord, to take one of them is supported by his own claim as mother's father; but he also has to respect the claim of the father's father of the girls, and if a claim has been left outstanding from the previous generation, or in a collateral line, one of the girls may be claimed to succeed a mother's mother's sister or mother's mother's mother as village-wife. He should try to respect all these claims. The result is that, for any marriage, men of at least three clans are likely to say that it was arranged by themselves to fulfil kinship obligations which they respected.

We can now appreciate how very intangible was the actual benefit which the lord derived from his control of pawns. They did not make him, or his clan section, richer in wives. They merely gave him a little additional influence in saying how wives should be distributed among other men. No wonder that, when asked to give a straight answer to a straight question about the advantages of being a lord, the Lele were at a loss to explain.

I give here an example of how the complex interaction of all these kinship ideals and personal interests reduced the initial superior status of the lord, or even inverted it, so that he became a willing agent in the hands of his own pawns.

Case 9. *Ket clan*. The Bulomani clan, who held several pawnship rights in South Homba were represented by two middle-aged men, Bahanga and Yoku, and a distant classificatory sister's son, Lukondo. Yoku died, and Bahanga decided to leave the village, after a quarrel. Lukondo, a young man, was left alone to represent the lord's interests in the village. Amongst other pawns, they counted two brothers of the Ket clan, the elder of whom decided to follow Bahanga to North Homba. The younger, who stayed on, was Badiangu, who, we have already seen (Case 5), owed his wife, Ihowa, to his lord. In that case the lord had married one of his pawns to the other. The two brothers of the Ket clan,[9] Mukwa and Ihaku, came to South Homba to live near their sister, who (as we have seen in Case 3[10]) became a pawn of the Lubelo clan and was given by the Lubelo as wife to one of their pawns. The brothers were wifeless, and in South Homba they had no other male kin than Badiangu. Their lords lived in Middle Homba village. The elder brother, Mukwa, was allowed by Badiangu's lord, Lukondo, to take over one of his (Lukondo's) pawns, Biong of the Lubelo clan. She was the widow of Lukondo's maternal uncle, Yoku, and being of the dominant Lubelo clan, there were few men in the village whom she was not debarred from marrying. She would not consider leaving the village. It seemed suitable that Lukondo should allot her to the brother of his pawn. The younger brother, Ihaku, married the daughter of Ilungu, elder of the Ndong clan (himself another pawn of Lukondo). This was a case of the girl's father giving his own daughter-pawn to a dependant of his own lord. The effect of these givings in marriage to the new arrivals was that when later their sister went away to live in Bushongo with her husband, they stayed on in the village and made it their home.

In this case a man started to build up his local clan section, attract others, and give them wives to settle down with, entirely by using his lord's influence in the village on his own behalf. In helping his pawn thus, Lukondo was felt to be acting as a wise and generous lord. When Badiangu's wife Ihowa lost three babies in succession, shortly after birth, Lukondo arranged for her to have special ritual assistance, and himself paid the cost. By acting thus benignly Lukondo was maintaining the influence of his clan in the village.

The difficulty of arranging wisely the marriages of all his pawn-women explains why a lord tended to cast around widely for suitable husbands. In the cases I have just described, it was expedient to marry the women locally to men not of their lord's

[9] See Appendix A, Figure 16, C, 3, 4, 5.
[10] Pp. 152–3.

12

own clan. In other cases it happened that a pawn-girl was born away from her lord's village, and his plans to bring her nearer might meet with resistance from her and her mother. Then a complicated series of transactions might ensue in which pawnship rights over her were exchanged for rights over a local girl. Alternatively, he might allow her to marry a man of his own clan living in her village, solving the problem by invoking the principle of clan unity. A distantly located fellow-clansman thus fortuitously found himself treated as a member of the matrilineal inheritance group. This was one of the situations in which the Lele found it convenient not to limit the right to inherit to members of the local clan section. Such was the difficulty of reconciling the pawnship system to the waywardness of women that if the dispersed members of the clan were not treated as potential co-heirs of a clan section and allowed to marry pawn-girls who refused to come to their lord's village, then there might be no alternative to losing rights over a girl, allowing her to marry outside both the lord's clan and village.

It can well be imagined that pawnship was not a subject to be investigated by means of rapid surveys. In many cases there were contradictory versions of what had happened. One man would claim to be free, while two clans might claim him as their pawn. My early inquiries were hailed as a means of saving lost causes, and people hastened to have their preferred version of a case recorded. Inevitably, then, I found it most revealing to confine my work to intensive study, since information that I could not follow up with cross-checking was not worth collecting. A detailed chart of the main links of pawnship between members of one village, and those connecting them with lords beyond the village confines, is the clearest way of illustrating the system, and this is impossible to construct accurately on a quick survey.

On my chart of ties of pawnship in South Homba (Figure 8) I have marked local clan sections with squares of a size to indicate their numerical strength in the village, and placed those resident in South Homba within a large circle, representing the village. As several people were pawns of the village itself, I have put arrows to the borders of the village circle to represent this. Clans and villages outside South Homba are shown with squares and circles. The relative position of the clan sections in South Homba in the diagram has nothing to do with residence in the

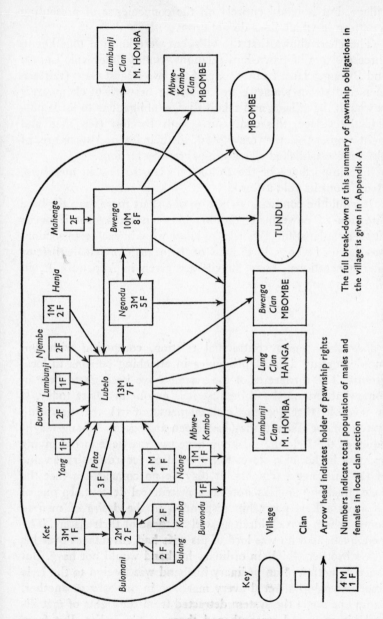

Key

Village

Clan

4 M
1 F

Arrow head indicates holder of pawnship rights

Numbers indicate total population of males and females in local clan section

The full break-down of this summary of pawnship obligations in the village is given in Appendix A

Fig. 8. Pawnship obligations between clan sections in South Homba

village, but is based entirely on the convenience of presenting a pattern in which lines do not cross.

The chart shows that the villagers were knotted together in three clusters of pawn-lord relations, round Bulomani, Lubelo and Bwenga clans. Lubelo, one of the two largest clans (thirteen men and seven women), had a strong network of claims over pawns in the village, and relatively few obligations to lords outside the village, this contrasting with Bwenga (ten men and eight women). Both were typical, in their internal structure, of old, long-established clan sections, reft by factions.

The importance of the Bulomani clan, so few in members, stems from its role as lord.

It would be confusing to put on one chart more than the bare direction of pawn-lord relations between clans. But it needs further explanation. We need to know who, in each clan section, was pawn of whom, how many of them, male or female, first or later generations. These details are given in Appendix A, in Figures 12 to 17.

Conclusion

Pawnship was a contractual relation, competing with and supplementing descent principles in attaching persons to local groups. The intricacies of the system have been given here in somewhat tedious detail because it is unique in Africa today. It is possible that (commercial elements apart) the pawnship system of the Ashanti may have been analogous. Among neighbours of the Lele the Bushong have two marriage forms, giving lower or higher clan status to the children according to the value of the marriage payments. It may be no coincidence that the Lele, Bushong and Ashanti have matrilineal descent. In one of its aspects Lele pawnship responded to the desire of men to control their own children as well as those of their sisters. The Lele husband who was lord of his wife had advantages over his wife's brother which an ordinary husband would not have. But the very notion of an ordinary husband was foreign to the Lele since pawnship affected every marriage in one way or another. From one angle the system detracted from the rights of matrilineal kinsmen and strengthened those of the father. But from another, since the whole thing was played between and in the name of matrilineal clans which had little other field of action, pawnship must have strengthened the matrilineal principle.

Negotiations about pawnship were the field in which the dispersed clan had its function, and that in which members of the local clan section effectively collaborated. The clan sections collaborated for hardly anything else: they did not combine in agriculture, nor in hunting, nor reside compactly together, nor supply the main raffia requirements of their members. Living in a friendly clan section, a man felt more secure knowing that sorcerers would hesitate to make attempts on his life, since his fellow-clansmen would follow up with claims for compensation. More important, joining their group he staked a claim in their pool of rights over pawns: new little pawn girls growing up into marriageable age who had belonged from birth to the clan section, and young widows who would like to go on living in the village. It was with rights to wives, gained largely by administering blood debts, that the local clan section attracted adherents.

IX

THE VILLAGE: AS CREDITOR AND DEBTOR

Now we are ready to discuss the corporate personality of the village. We have given its formal framework in Chapter IV. In Chapter VII we showed how it acted as a husband of polyandrous wives and as father to their children. Until the system of blood compensation between clans had been explained, we could not study the village further. Its full personality emerges from its role as lord of pawns. A village could demand and pay blood compensation. It could use wealth for buying pawnship rights; it could therefore transact with other villages, as well as with clans; and with clans from other villages, as well as with its own constituent clan sections.

We have seen how a lord could claim new pawns, by pursuing his rights with tact and vigour, demanding compensation for specified insults and injuries. The village, as lord, did the same, but there were many more situations in which the village could claim a pawn.

First, offences against the person of village dignitaries or pawns: for hitting or wounding a son-in-law of the village, or the spokesman, or village head; for sexual intercourse by an outsider with a village-wife; for killing (expecially by sorcery and by sex pollution) a pawn of the village, for all these, a woman had to be paid.

Second, for giving sanctuary; if a man in danger of his life took refuge in a village, for protecting him they demanded the equivalent of full blood compensation. If a woman ran away from her husband and took refuge in another village, she was installed as pawn-village-wife and held unless ransomed by her husband by payment of another pawn.

Lastly, for breach of the peace at certain village meetings. If a man quarrelled and showed violence at the smith's forge, at the village cult meetings or when the drum was being played he had to pay a big fine, but if anyone were killed as a result of his provocation the fine was a pawn to the village, as well as to the clan of the dead person.

The list is not complete, nor were the rules so rigid as implied here. Lele liked to be alert to any possibility of claiming a woman. Once I asked what they would say if a stranger from another village came masquerading as an initiate of the Begetters' Cult, and sacriligeously ate a share of their meat. I expected to be told of automatic retribution for violation of the cult and some reaction of horror at the thought of such a breach. Instead, my informants' eyes gleamed and they replied briskly: 'If a man did that, we would say: "Cha! We see a woman," and that man would have to pay a pawn to the village.'

In practice my records show no instance of pawns being paid over for bloodshed at village meetings, or for breach of cult rules. These were presumably rare. But there were many instances of pawns paid for adultery with pregnant village-wives, for killing village pawns, and for the price of sanctuary.

Like the good lord in the preceding chapter, the village would seek to increase its heritage by supervising the marriages of its pawn-daughters, claiming its pawn-daughters' daughters in marriage, demanding a pawn as compensation for the death of any of its pawns.

The differences between a village and a section of a matrilineal clan qualified the village for a different role in the blood debt system. A village, of course, had no matrilineal relatives. It had sons and daughters, who certainly belonged to matrilineal clans, whom it could give in settlement of debts it incurred, but it could never fall into pawnship itself. It settled claims against itself by transferring its pawn-children. This asymmetry between a clan section and a village gave the village a permanent advantage.

Villages dealt with other villages by exchanging pawnship rights, but they never came under the domination one of another. The village, therefore, could play the role of lord in relation to clan sections, but never in relation to other villages. Therefore one whole aspect of inter-clan pawnship, the manipulation of the lord to serve his pawns' interests, did not appear between villages.

Since it had the backing of force, it could afford to be less conciliatory towards the wishes of its pawns and to act more arbitrarily. The village was the only militarily organized unit in Lele society. It had its band of warriors and its junior age-sets for attacking raids, its high palisades and single narrow entry for defence. It had its brother villages for allies. The only way in which a clan section could obtain redress when another clan section refused its claims was by entrusting its case to a village. And villages willingly allowed themselves to be drawn into disputes between clan sections, for this was another method of acquiring pawns. The village naturally exacted a reward for its services.

A village's relation to its members was different from the relation of a clan to its members, and its material resources were greater. One cannot say that clan members were related to something distinct from themselves, their clan, for they were the clan, and it was nothing without them. It had no independent corporate existence apart from them. Within the clan there could be no exchanging of women against goods, and no suing for blood compensation. These rules expressed the unity and solidarity of its members. A man was born into a clan, and never changed it. But a village had a separate legal personality, distinct from the sum of all its members. It could sue them, one and all if need be, for blood compensation. It could give and take from them in marriage. It could exchange pawnship rights with them.

Even when a village was physically extinct, no huts and no inhabitants, all aspects of its personality were not necessarily therefore extinguished: its heritage of pawnship debts and claims could remain.

Since the village treasury dealt in larger sums and had a faster turn-over than clan sections, it could afford a different attitude to the exchange of women for wealth. The village, like any individual, preferred rights to women over rights to material things, and all we have said (in Chapter III) about individuals disliking to give up rights over women for the sake of the equivalent goods, applies to villages too. Yet the village habitually promised pawnship rights in exchange for wealth and gave its constituent members opportunities for converting their camwood and raffia into claims to pawns. Whenever a village needed wealth with which to acquire a woman, one of its constituent clan sections would come forward with the required amount. The village then went into debt to this group of its members, owing them a woman. The village, in these instances, was ready to 'convert down', women into things, not because it was so hard-pressed that it had no option (the only circumstance in which an individual would do so) but because it had so much more opportunity of acquiring women pawns than had individuals, because its life-time had no limits and because of its special relation to its own members. It would be worth while losing a pawn to its own members, if thereby it had contributed something towards attaching them more permanently to itself. Furthermore, in most cases when the village took wealth from a member against a promise of a woman, it expected to use the wealth to get two women, one for itself and one for its creditor.

These differences between villages and clan sections laid the foundation for a peculiar institution by which individuals could transfer their dispute from the inter-clan level to the village level. Sometimes when two clans were disputing a claim to blood compensation, the claimant might see no hope of getting satisfaction from his opponents. The political system offered no direct means for one man (or clan) to use physical coercion or to resort to a superior authority to enforce claims against another. In such a case, rather than abandon his claim to a pawn-woman, he would be ready to take the equivalent in wealth, if he could get it. The usual procedure was to sell his case against the defendants to the only group capable of extorting a pawn by force, that is, to a village. The system, called *ku utera*, to get settlement against someone, was a kind of dispute-brokerage.[1] The man who meant to sell his case to a village asked them for 100 raffia cloths or five bars of camwood. The village raised the amount, either from its treasury, or by loan from one of its members, and thereby adopted as its own his claim to a pawn. Their broker's profit lay in having converted goods into rights over a woman. Now as far as the claimant was concerned, his blood debt was settled. But his adversaries owed a pawn to the village, and the village was prepared to fight to get her, and if they had borrowed the wherewithal for acquiring the claim, they would try to get two women.

[1] A term suggested by Dr. M. Freedman—another instance of 'dispute-brokerage' when a third party was called in to collect compensation with added interest is in New Britain, see Danks, 1888.

At first sight *utera* seems to be a quasi-judicial institution for enabling an individual to apply the armed force of a village to the redress of his just grievances. It could be used in that way. But in itself it was a neutral piece of political machinery. It could just as well be used by the strong against the weak to secure a breach of the conventions of pawnship (see case of Bienge against Ket in previous chapter). Or it could be used in a tangled case, when no one agreed on the rights and wrongs, simply in order to get a final settlement.

The village which bought a private person's case in this way selected two men to present themselves at the defendant's door, to say: 'We come from X . . . village. We have given 100 raffia cloths to Y, and now we come to claim our woman.' The defendant either yielded, in which case one of his pawns or sisters became pawn and village-wife at X . . . village, or he refused, in which case the village of X might attack and take the woman by force. That was the essence of the institution.

It seemed to have been more an instrument of revenge than of adjudication. A village did not consider the rights or wrongs of the case offered to them. The main consideration was their relation to the village in which the defendant lived. If it was friendly, they would refuse the case because they did not want a fracas. If it was hostile, they might welcome a new *casus belli*, and gladly give goods for the right to take a woman from their old rivals.

Correspondingly, the man who wanted to sell his dispute would choose a village which was politically a rival of his opponent. Very frequently the two principals would be members of one and the same village, or village cluster. When the normal pressures for conciliation failed, and A despaired of getting B to yield, A would sell his case to a rival village. New pressures would then be brought to bear on B. There might be fighting. If so, his own village would hold him responsible for every loss they incurred, and make him pay a pawn for each death. In theory this threat was the coercive element in the system, but it usually remained a threat. Case histories show that real fighting rarely broke out in these affairs. If B refused, or delayed, the village which had adopted the case against him would wait, spying out a favourable opportunity to abduct a girl pawn of his. A girl whose own mother lived already in their village would often need little persuading to leave her husband and become their village-wife or to remain with them as temporary hostage. One day, when visiting her mother she would simply remain there. B would hear that his girl pawn had been taken by the village in settlement of their claim against him. There the matter would rest.

Several cases of villages being asked to intervene in clan disputes have already been mentioned in the last chapter, inevitably, since they occur in half the histories of blood compensation. I give here five more cases in detail, which had involved living members of South Homba. Of these, two were brought against members of the claimant's own village, and two against members of brother villages. This suggests that the system acted within a village or group of villages as a safety valve or outlet when all the indirect means of appeasement and control failed. It testifies independently to what we have said about the lack of direct authority in Lele village politics, both internal and external. The system consisted of a manipulation of village rivalries for private ends, and a successfully prosecuted case was one in which these rivalries had been correctly estimated. South Homba could be pitted against Kenge, and Mikope against North Homba, and Kabamba against South Homba, but Bushong could not be used against its close neighbour and ally South Homba. It seems that a man angrily taking what he knew to be a trivial case against his own village would purposely offer it to a village which was not likely to accept it.

1. *A case of revenge*

A man of the village of Kenge, who was born at Tundu, went to visit his father, the chief. While he was away, his own village took his wife, Njilu, and set her up as a village-wife. He came to S. Homba, the traditional enemies of Kenge, to say that he gave them his wife. The men of Kenge had stolen her, but he would never consent to their eating food of her cooking. He told the men of S. Homba to fight Kenge on her account. '*Tola tola miyi.*' If they suffered any casualties, let S. Homba come to him for compensation.

S. Homba accepted the case, gave him five bars of camwood, and waited their chance to capture Njilu. They hoped that she would come near on a visit. But the men of Kenge heard that her first husband had gone to S. Homba for settlement against them, and they forbade her to leave the village. Eventually, S. Homba, who did not intend to fight, grew tired of waiting and ended by capturing her sister, Inangu, together with her daughter, Himbu. Inangu was made village-wife. The five bars of camwood had been supplied to the village by one of its members, of the Lubelo clan. The village therefore owed him a woman. They gave him the child Himbu. This ends the first case.

2. *Settlement against a fellow-clansman*

Himbu, above, was first married to one Nyama, who took her to live with him in N. Homba as his second wife. Then the only wife of his younger brother, Njondu, in S. Homba died. Nyama, as a brotherly gesture of condolence, gave him Himbu. But later, when Nyama's own first wife died, he came to take Himbu back. Njondu was furious with his brother for taking back his gift. He went to the village of Mikope, hereditary rivals of N. Homba, and sold them his case against Nyama. Mikope promised him ten bars of camwood when they should have captured Himbu. But when Njondu arrived home, shame overcame him at the thought of getting a forced settlement against his own brother. He declared that he would not accept the camwood promised to him. The sequel has two versions. On one account, when the men of Mikope went to claim Himbu the Lubelo clan refused to give her up, saying that no camwood had been accepted and that the case had been withdrawn. On the other account, more likely, the Lubelo did not give up Himbu, but another girl, who was still living in Mikope as village-wife at the time of my inquiry. This was obviously a delicate matter to investigate, for when Nyama eventually died, Himbu did not go to Njondu, but to another of his brothers. There is a familiar suggestion that the woman herself was the cause of the trouble, not having wanted to live with Njondu.

3. *A case of adultery*

Ikum, of M. Homba, went to Kabamba to get a forced settlement against Njoku of S. Homba, for committing adultery with his wife. They gave Ikum camwood and took the sister of Njoku, who was still living with them at the time of fieldwork. Adultery was a frequent ground for cases of *utera*. In this case the principals to the dispute were members of brother villages and the claimant very effectively sold his case to a village hostile to his own.

4. *A trivial matter*

Makaka of S. Homba bought a huge hunting dog from the Luba. First time he took it hunting, it killed single-handed a wild boar. Second time, it killed an antelope. The people in the village were jealous and killed the dog by sorcery. When it died, Makaka wept and mourned all night as if for a kinsman. Then at dawn he went straight to Bushongo saying that he wanted revenge on the whole village of S. Homba. He told the diviners of Bushongo to consult their oracles, find out the sorcerer responsible and take a woman from him. But Bushongo refused the case, as they would never fight anyone in S. Homba. As they said: 'S. Homba have married our children, we have married theirs. We have begotten children for each other. When we have been attacked, they have helped us. How can we take up a case against them?'

Discussing this case, the absurdity of claiming a woman for a dog was heartily agreed, but they insisted that any offence, however trivial, could have been avenged in this way, if only the injured party felt angry enough. Even if a man were to climb another's palm tree, and drink its palm wine, he could be made to pay a pawn.

5. *Elopement followed by bloodshed: inconclusive ending*

Piculu married to a man of the Lubelo clan in S. Homba ran away with a man of Makasu village. Her husband asked the village of Bushongo to capture her or another woman in her stead. While Bushongo was looking round for the camwood to give to the Lubelo, two men from S. Homba, novices of the diviners' cult, travelled south in the course of collecting raffia cloths from kinsmen for their initiation dues. It was a grave offence to strike a novice, nor were novices allowed to shed blood. The men of Makasu, hearing that two men from S. Homba were approaching and assuming wrongly that they meant to recapture Piculu, laid an ambush in which one of the novices was killed. The people of S. Homba, outraged, now required two pawns, one for the runaway wife and one for the dead man. They planned to surround and raid the village, but, recognizing that Makasu was too far away they planned for one of their warriors to kill a man from Makasu by stealth. Then the Europeans appeared before the vengeance was complete, and later Makasu withdrew to a site on the other side of the Lumbundji river.

Taking these cases, and those of the previous chapter, we can see how the intervention of villages was an essential part of the blood-debt system. The clan sections so long as they wished to remain on cordial terms transacted with one another in a conciliatory and generous style. They conceded points, following a code of honour rather than bargaining ruthlessly for advantage. But in any contest there may come a point at which the adversary refuses to accept honourable defeat, or a point at which the pressures to insist on one's full profit are irresistible—the conventions are always in danger of being broken. If there had not been a way of drawing in the villages, the system of blood debts between clan sections would probably have broken down. By using the rivalrous villages as middlemen of their disputes, the unarmed clan sections found a means of coercion. The mere possibility of applying this sanction quickened men's readiness to play the game according to the rules.

There is another way in which the blood-debt system depended on intervention at village level. The whole network of blood debts presupposed submissive women, with whose destinies men would be free to settle their obligations. Women were essentially passive objects in the game, transferred hither and thither for the sake of men's needs and ambitions. But in practice, we know that they were not altogether passive, and that their preferences limited, and even reversed, decisions concerning them. There was some flexibility in the system. A dissatisfied wife could try in turn the different men of her original husband's clan section, or she might repudiate a marriage if her children died, thus giving her clansmen a claim for a blood debt against her husbands. Either course was a legitimate means of breaking off a marriage she did not like. But even this amount of flexibility might not have been enough to stop the blood-debt system from cracking in the face of determined female resistance. A female pawn by running away from her clan lords and forcing the intervention of a village on her side, took her own case to the inter-village level. Thus women involved in the mesh of pawnship exchanges had in their own hands a means of redress if the arrangements pressed too hard on them. The existence of two levels of pawnship exchanges, inter-clan, dependent on goodwill, and inter-village, backed by the threat of violence, gave to women who wanted to manipulate the system a very effective area of initiative.

When the Belgian Tribunals were first set up in Basongo territory, Lele flocked to them with their pawnship cases. The Tribunal was treated as a new kind of third party through which a settlement could be enforced against an unwilling debtor. It was just as easy to *utera* a case to the Tribunal as to a village hostile to the defendants. The Tribunal seemed at first exactly to fill the role of an external arbiter with power to enforce payment. The judges listened, questioned both parties, and tried to give a verdict according to Lele custom. The cases from the 1934–5 court records document the account I have given, confirming that the analysis made from the standpoint of one particular village is valid for a much wider area throughout the territory. They are selected to illustrate particular points, and unless too lengthy and confused, they are reproduced word for word as recorded, with only the names changed. Unfortunately, the verdicts or settlements were not usually on record.

1. *Blood debt incurred through sorcery: claim upheld by court and settled by transfer of a pawn* 17.12.34.

'T: Mon frère GG est mort, tué par les gens d'Ibombo. J'ai demandé une femme en paiement. On m'a remis une femme B. Par la suite les gens d'Ibombo ont marié cette femme à N.

Q. Votre frère a été tué comment?

R. C'est un sorcier qui l'a tué.

Q. Pourquoi l'a-t-on tué?

R. Je ne sais pas, mais c'est L. qui m'a dit qu'elle avait mettre quelquechose dans son tabac.

Defendant d'Ibombo déclare: Je veux remettre la femme B à T.'

The case was thus voluntarily settled by restitution of his rights as lord to T. The men of Ibombo reacted as they would have, traditionally, to a transfer of the claim against them from the claimant to a more powerful agent: they yielded.

2. *Blood debt incurred by adultery with pregnant village-wife* 16.11.34.

K of the village of Malembi paid to the men of the village of Tshia one camwood and ten raffia cloths, as a fine for having slept with their village-wife. Later her baby was still-born, and the men of Tshia claimed a pawn from him. The intermediary in the case, a man from Malongo kanjoko, told the men of Tshia that Malembi conceded to them their pawn, X, a girl who then lived in Tshia with her mother. They would have proceeded to install her as a village-wife, but a man, G, asked to marry her himself, and he exchanged with the village his own rights over another girl pawn S, who was then installed as village-wife.

A man in Malembi now reported the case to the Tribunal, saying that he, and not the village of Malembi, was the real lord of the girl X, over whom G had acquired rights from the village of Tshia. Questioned, the village of Tshia protested their ignorance and blamed the intermediary, who had told them to take X for the debt.

The account leaves several points unclear; who was the original offender, K, and what was his relation to the girl X, or to the other man who claimed to be her lord, why was the village of Malembi invoked and not K's clan?

3. *Blood debt for death of a pawn; enticement of a girl pawn; offers to pay with male pawn and child pawn refused* 7.12.34.

A man X of Kayaya charged two men of Malongo.

B homme de Kayaya, frappa M à la jambe avec une os de bête et lui fit une plaie, de laquelle M mourut. Je réclamai réparation, car M est un enfant d'une de nos *Bakolomo*. Les gens de Malongo me donnèrent I, soeur de B, mais elle resta à Malongo, et j'ai appri qu'ils veulent la marier à P. J'allais la réclamée, et P m'offrit une autre femme. Mais je ne voulai pas l'accepter, étant trop jeune.

Q. Pourquoi, après avoir donné I aux gens de Kayaya vous l'avez marié à P?

R. I avait déja été donnée à P quand l'affaire est arrivée. Nous avons voulu donné B (the offender himself) mais X a refusé disant qu'il lui fallait une femme. Alors, nous avons dit que P devrait lui payer une femme.

Q. Pourquoi avez vous voulu faire payer P?

R. Parceque nous lui avons dit que I deviendra son *Bukolomo*.'

In this case the individual P who did not want to break his betrothal to the destined pawn of X was told that if he wanted to keep her, he would have to become her lord and satisfy the pawnship claim against her some other way. His offer of a very young girl in her place was rejected. The refusal to accept a child in lieu of a grown girl was a commonly recurring theme, and reflected the pressure on marriageable girls. The case also illustrates something we have seen in the previous chapter, the tendency to treat a claim for a pawn as affecting only the offender's immediate circle of kin, and not the whole clan section. B himself and his sister were the only persons considered for settling his blood debt.

4. *Indemnity for sanctuary for a woman* 17.12.34.

'M du village d'Ibombo: J'étais allé chercher des vivres au village de Karamishembe, quand les gens d'Iboa sont venus et ont pris ma femme, I, et l'ont enmenée dans leur village.

Q. I est du quel village?

R. D'Iboa.

Q.   Vous seul vous l'avez mariée?

R.   Non. C'est la *nghohombe* du village. Nous avons donné une femme K a Iboa et ils nous ont donné I.

Iboa: N, d'Ibombo, a lancé une flèche sur M à cause de la femme BB parceque M avait eu des rapports avec elle. M reçut la flèche dans la haut de la cuisse. BB se sauva, et vint se refugier à Iboa, mais elle revient au village (Ibombo) un moment après. Les gens d'Iboa réclamèrent une indemnité parceque BB s'était réfugiée chez eux. Les gens d'Ibombo ne payèrent pas; les gens d'Iboa virent la femme I, et en firent leur *Mushishombe*. Les gens d'Ibombo réclamèrent leur femme.'

It was a well-established rule that if a woman took sanctuary for however brief a time in a rival village, she or a substitute should become a pawn of the sheltering village. This is another of the many cases in which a girl allowed herself to be 'abducted' by the men of her own natal village.

5.   *Indemnity for sanctuary for a man*   7.12.34.

'M de Karanenge, déclare que B, femme *Mushishombe*, était aller chercher du maïs à Malongo. Les gens de Malongo s'en emparèrent et en firent leur *mushishumbe*.

Malongo: I, parent de B, est venu chercher chez nous des *madibas*. (raffia cloths). Les gens de Malonga lui donnèrent 100 *madibas*. I leur promit B quand elle serait grande, mais I mourut, et B fut héritée par Bk qui habite Shumba. Là il se battit avec un homme et il le tua avec une flèche. Bk s'enfuit à Karanenge. Les gens de Karanenge exigèrent une femme pour lui donner l'hospitalité. Un jour Buya est venu chez nous, et comme c'était notre femme, nous l'avons gardée.'

In this case a man and his heir disposed of rights over the same girl to settle each his respective blood debt, further evidence of the pressure on the supply of marriageable girls as early as 1934.

6.   *Debt for seduction of village-wife: girl captured as hostage*   4.2.35.

'L de Mobendi déclare: j'ai versé pour le femme N 100 *madibas*, et 1 bois de *tukula*. Elle resta chez moi 3 ans. Les gens de Mobendi avaient une dette, une femme, aux gens de Mapangu. Nous avons envoyé deux femmes, qu'ils ont refusé, disant qu'elles étaient trop jeunes. L'autre jour ma femme N, été allait visiter sa mère au Mapangu: les gens de Mapangu l'ont arêtée, disant que "les gens de Mobendi nous doivent une femme".

Capita de Mapangu déclare: un homme de Mapangu avait couché

13

avec une femme de Mobendi. Les gens de Mobendi nous font payer
et nous avons donné N. l'autre jour I, homme de Mobendi, ainsi
couché avec une femme de notre village de Mapangu; mais le femme
était enceinte; ensuite, elle mourut. Quand nous avons les demandé le
paiement, ils nous ont payé deux femmes et nous n'avons pas les pris,
parcequ'elles étaient trop jeunes. Lorsque nous avons vu N à notre
village, nous l'avons arrêtée. Elle rentrera chez son mari quand nos
deux femmes seront à Mapangu.'

In this case a girl was kept as hostage until her husband's
village settled its blood debt. Although brother villages were
not supposed to capture each other's women or pursue blood
debts with them, at least certainly not in the south, this is not an
isolated case.

These cases were brought to the Tribunal very readily by disputants who saw the Colonial Administration in the role of a third-
party arbiter whose decisions were effective because they were
backed by force. In 1949–50 and 1953 only certain cases were
going to the Tribunal, the kind of case which formerly would
have been sold (*utera*) to a village, cases in which goodwill was
lacking. Apart from these cases, the transfer of pawns went on
unimpaired between men of goodwill.

We are now in a position to consider a village's total budget,
and to see the relation of its debts and holdings in pawns to its
income of goods. All a village's affairs, whether concerning
pawns, children or wealth, were public matters, discussed at open
meetings to which all the men were expected to attend. The
meetings would often be announced the day before, and the
time fixed for first cock crow, or just after dawn, so as to catch
everyone before they went into the forest. Representatives of
other villages coming to make claims or to pay debts would sleep
at the village overnight, so as to be available for the early morning
meeting.

As for a private individual, the main source of revenue for a
village was from the marriages of its daughters—and also from
the payment of cult dues and (less substantial) payment of fines
for offences. In some villages cult dues never reached the village
treasury but went straight into the pockets of initiates, and in
others the practice was variable, the village sometimes taking the
cult dues and at other times the members of the cult sharing
them between themselves, according to the needs of the moment.

Additional funds could be raised *ad hoc* by levies on the constituent clan sections in the village.

In 1949–53 several sources of revenue had dried up. For example, most of the younger generation of men having been baptized and married in church, there were few applications for admission to age-sets, nor for entry into the Begetters' Cult, nor for the Diviners'. Nor, if a young Christian begot twins, did he allow the twin-rites to be performed or pay the entry fees to the twin cult. Formerly five boys forming an age-set would have between them paid about 100 cloths to the village; 100 each when they entered the Begetters', forty more if they begot twins, or twenty if they entered the Pangolin Cult. Not all the wealth would always have reached the village treasury, but a large amount would. None came from these sources in the years between 1949 and 1953 into the village treasury of South Homba. In villages where there was a smaller proportion of Christians, there would have been proportionately larger revenues from cult dues, but not from age-sets, since these had effectively been ended, even before 1948, by missionary exertions.

Consequently, my view of the village treasury was distorted by the fact that its principal source of revenue was now from fees and fines and from the marriage payments of its sons-in-law. This gave the village pawnship system the air of a self-contained institution, the pawns bearing daughters whose suitors would bring in raffia cloths, which could be used to pay *utera* fees to acquire more pawns. But it is obvious that in the old days the village taxed its members much more heavily through the cult associations, and it thereby acquired wealth which it could use to make lavish gifts to its sons-in-law and sons, and to bury its affines with fitting pomp.

The depleted treasury was to some extent a new thing, but not the pile of old debts. No balance sheet was kept, either mentally or by tally. Debts were as pressing as the individual creditors made them be. New obligations, if they offered the chance of acquiring a pawn, were accepted without reference to the state of the budget, for there was no idea of a budget. If a man from a foreign village arrived and offered his claim on a pawn to the village in return for ten bars of camwood, it would be accepted or refused on political grounds. If accepted, he might have to wait for his camwood indefinitely. On his death his heirs of his local clan section would become the creditors and claim the camwood from the village. Old men who could recall past negotiations had an important contribution to make to village life. By remembering details they could produce circumstantial evidence which could confirm a true claim or expose a false one.

In South Homba I learned of debts owed by the village to the amount of 240 raffia cloths, but this was certainly only a small fraction of what could be claimed against it if all creditors arrived simultaneously. The amounts which were received were always paid out almost immediately, but there was no semblance of order in these expenditures. One big debt to a diviner from Middle Homba was paid almost as soon as incurred, another debt to a man who had since died was partially repaid to his heirs; but the next big payment into the treasury by a son-in-law was immediately shared amongst the constituent clan sections, with no regard to outstanding debts. And so on. Each receipt was treated as a separate item; it might be convenient to use it to settle a debt of exactly the same size, or to satisfy the demands of particular creditors at the moment.

Not only were the village revenues much smaller than formerly, but the system was being distorted by the dissolution of pawnship. Formerly, pawns were acquired with wealth, but they also were a steady source of wealth through the marriages of their daughters. Moreover, debts which piled up to an excessive degree, could be cancelled by a transfer of a pawn. The key to the whole system was the fact that a heritage of pawns was self-reproducing. The natural increase of pawns prevented the debts from getting out of hand. But now that pawnship was drawing to an end, many debts had to be written off. This is why goats were so attractive as a substitute for raffia or camwood.[2] As goats also had a natural increase, they were to that extent, a fitting substitute for women, as a bridge between continually expanding claims, and dwindling material means of meeting them.

[2] See p. 64.

Table 13. Village treasury in South Homba

	INCOME		OUTGOING	
Source of payment	Value in Raffia Cloth	Nature of payment	Paid out	Outstanding debts
1. Cult fees	40	2 he-goats	1 goat to man in M. Homba 1 goat to man in Bushongo	
2. Cult fees	40	1 she-goat	she-goat paid to man in S. Homba	
3. Marriage fee from Denis (Bulomani 4)	20	1 he-goat	1 goat & 60 cloths paid on account of a debt of 200 cloths owed to heirs of a man in N. Homba	120 cloths
4. Old debt repaid	60	60 raffia cloths		
5. Marriage fee for 2 daughters	40	2 camwood bars	4 camwood bars to diviner from M. Homba as fees for ritual offices	
6. of the village from Ngwe (Ngondu 3)	40	2 camwood bars		
7. Marriage fee	100	5 bars camwood	5 bars divided among 5 clans in village	
8. Marriage fee	60	60 raffia cloths	40 cloths for girl's own MF leaving 40 still due to him	40 cloths
9. Levy on clans	10	100 francs	20 cloths and 100 francs to head of M. Homba as compensation for false sorcery charge against his wife	
				30 claimed by village head of S. Homba
				30 claimed by another headman of S. Homba
	410 cloths			220 cloths

The table starts with cult fees, paid in the form of goats, each used to settle an old debt of exactly the right size.

Five daughters of village-wives were married within a few years of each other. Three of them married within the village, and their two husbands Ngwe[3] (Appendix A, Figure 17, Ngondu 3) and Denis (Appendix A, Figure 15, Bulomani 4) were therefore only required to pay half the amount that would have been asked if they had come from outside, i.e. two *mihei*[4] instead of four. Denis was blind, and though now married for eight or nine years, he had never been pressed to give more than the first instalment, one he-goat equivalent to one bar of camwood. This the village had put with two other bars raised by getting a debt from another source repaid, and used the total value of eighty raffia cloths to make the first repayment on an old debt of ten bars of camwood (200 raffia cloths) owed to a man of North Homba who had died unpaid and whose heirs were now pressing for payment.

Two other girls were married to Ngwe as a kind of gesture of welcome when he came to settle permanently in the village. Ngwe was subsequently installed as junior official diviner of the village, and as the amount which he paid to the village for both girls exactly covered the fee which the village owed to the outside officiant who had performed the rite of installing him, the latter was paid with unusual promptness.

For the next daughter of the village the bridegroom paid up five bars of camwood. On receiving these, the village ignored outstanding claims against itself *qua* village, and quietly divided them amongst each of its five constituent clan sections.

For the youngest girl the prospective son-in-law paid up three *mihei* or sixty raffia cloths while I was there. The fourth bundle of twenty raffia cloths was still outstanding. Of the sixty cloths paid up, it was agreed that forty should be given at once to the grandfathers of the girl herself as marriage dues for her mother. As the latter had been herself a daughter of a village-wife, four *mihei* or eighty cloths should have been given. At first the representative of the grandfathers refused to accept the half payment, pointing out with justice that it was already overdue. The men of South Homba rallied him by asking why he had not brought the ten chickens with which it is proper for a father-in-law to acknowledge the receipt of marriage dues, and he finally agreed good-humouredly to take what was offered, and to go home to collect the chickens, giving South Homba time to collect the remaining cloths.

South Homba then actually had an additional twenty cloths in hand, as their son-in-law had paid sixty, but it had been decided that this last bundle should be devoted to settling an equally long-overdue debt with the headman of the next village, Middle Homba. He required thirty cloths in damages for a charge of sorcery made against one of his wives, who had been cleared after submission to the poison ordeal. It was agreed at the meeting that 100 francs should be raised by levies on each of the clans of the village, and that these should be added to the twenty cloths, so that this claim of twenty years' standing could be settled outright.

At the same meeting, the old head of the village of South Homba put in a rather hopeless claim for at least thirty cloths as part repayment for the copper bar he had advanced to the village for the marriage dues of one of its (now quite elderly) village-wives. Another old man had a similar claim. The claims were brushed aside, on the grounds that many big debts had to be written off now that it was no longer possible to settle accounts by the transfer of women.

The importance of the village's dealings in pawns and wealth is obvious in the context of village unity and permanence. The Lele village had a strong pull on its members. Their talents for governing by committee were stimulated by the patronage to be distributed, levies to be exacted, and the material assets which had to be administered on behalf of their village.

X

THE ROLE OF THE ARISTOCRATIC CLAN
IN RELATIONS BETWEEN VILLAGES

VILLAGES were to all intents and purposes free and independent. Allies and enemies were treated as equals. Even between brother villages of a single cluster, there was no political sense in which the parent village had authority or leadership. Although they acknowledged the superior religious status of an aristocratic clan, and although its members had pretensions to suzerainty, there was no practical restriction on the independence of the villages.

We shall first discuss the external relations of villages with one another. Then we can try to understand the curious status of the aristocratic clan, who provided neither priests nor rulers, yet who claimed to 'own' the Lele in the same way as a village was 'owned' by its founding clan.

The rivalry of villages was dominated by the idea of wiping out insults and injuries by killing men or capturing women, and of reaching an agreed peace when both sides should have sustained equal losses.

The object of alliances between villages was simply to further these aims. Alliances were based on three principles. One was common origin, when the fission of one village produced dispersed 'brother villages'. The second was propinquity, when the chance of shifting brought former enemies into such dangerous proximity that it was agreed to fight no more. Such a peace was generally sealed with a ritual in which the official diviners of each village brewed a drink for all to share, which would wipe out the memory of their grievances. And third, temporary alliances arose from the very pattern of other existing alliances. If villages of group A were normally hostile to villages of groups B and C, and C to group D, then A and D might combine for a large-scale attack on B who might successfully call C to its aid, since the fight would enable C to work off its old grudges against A. Such large combinations were unusual; sneak raids or small ambushes were the normal way of carrying on hostilities.

Three conventions limited fighting. Women were never killed. If warriors hiding in wait for a member of an enemy village saw women of that village walking unescorted and laden with baskets through the forest, they let them pass unharmed. The rule was explained as needful for the survival of society. 'If our women are not safe, how can life go on? How will we have food and water?'

The second rule was that if attackers arrived to find the village which was their objective had been burnt down, they went home without shooting an arrow. Fire in the dry season was a disaster which might befall any village, and when it happened the victims had to work hard, man, woman and child, to rebuild. They could not defend themselves, nor keep watch for attackers.

Third, it was forbidden to kill a cult-novice, for these were not allowed to strike or wound. They were painted with distinctive white marks so that no mistake should occur. These conventions were not always honoured, and certainly none other restricted the manner of fighting.

The arrows used for fighting differed from hunting arrows, which were heavy and designed to be shot at short range, to inflict a wide, stunning gash. War arrows were very light in the shaft, narrow in the head, and barbed in the fore-shaft. They were designed for shooting in a shower from outside the palisades of a village, and for deep penetration. The person on whom one of these arrows descended was not likely to survive, for it could only be cut out of his flesh by making a much larger wound. Ambushers sure of their target might use hunting arrows.

The warrior embodied one of the ideals of manhood. *Tamo* meant ferocity and courage, and a man who had not proved his *tamo* was not a man. Youths in the junior age-sets vied with one another for a reputation of *tamo*. Each man who had killed a man, or killed a man-slaying animal such as a leopard, and brought back proof of the deed, was formally decorated with an eagle's feather, showered with gifts of raffia by his kinsmen, and allowed to make a triumphal dance round the village (a dance called *waan*) to the beat of a special drum *nkoko*, played only to celebrate man-killing. His age-mates, seeing themselves thus outstripped, would brood, saying: 'My friend has passed me; he has become a man, and here am I, still a boy.' Then they would each go out and seek a chance of killing, and woe to any

benighted stranger who found himself lost in the forest in those
days. If he could not name a clansman or lord in the village, he
would be killed and his head and hand brought back as proof of
the manhood of his killer. I was told that they always mutilated
their dead victims, cutting off the head, genitals, and arm, unless
they found that in error they had killed a fellow-clansman.

The severed arm would be brought home to frighten the
women, and then thrown away with the genitals. The intention
in mutilation was partly to incapacitate the dead enemy in his
future rebirth. The skull would be preserved and made into a
drinking cup, if the warrior had that kind of panache in his make-
up. One old man, whom I knew, renowned for his ferocity in his
prime, was reputed to have decorated his bow with strips of
human skin.

A boy who had proved himself in this way might be considered for initiation as *Ndwi* (plural *Bandwi*), or warrior. Each
village would try to have *Ndwi*, who specialized in acts of
vengeance on their behalf. They did not have authority or
powers to organize defence or attack, but were entrusted with
secret missions of vengeance. The *Bandwi* of several allied
villages regarded one another as professional colleagues, to whom
they extended help when asked, and who celebrated each other's
triumphs together.

The difficulty of interpreting the stories of fighting is that the
villages have since changed their geographical position. The first
history concerns South Homba and Makasu, at the culmination
of a long series of insults, and raids. But it took place at a time
when Makasu was nearer to South Homba, within earshot of
Bushong Bwabwani which still existed as a separate village,
and when a Domaie village was not far from Makasu. None of
these positions correspond to my maps for 1950.

1. *South Homba against Makasu*

Three men from South Homba went to Makuba to claim a debt.
While they were there, a man of Makuba slipped out and went to
Makasu and told them. So when the South Homba men left Makuba
to return home, the men of Makasu were waiting for them. They shot
two of them dead, one escaped (a diviner's novice), but hearing his
companions calling for help, he went back, and shot one of the ambushers. Then he was killed himself. This happened on the path near

Bushongo Bwabwani. The men of Bushongo heard the war-drum, *nkoko*, beating at Makasu, so they went out to pick up the dead. They sent a messenger to South Homba, who came to collect their men. After burying them, they all went to attack Makasu, but a Kenge man saw them hiding in the grass, and warned Makasu, who turned out in force and frightened away the men of South Homba.

In this part of the story, Bushongo helped South Homba, and Makuba and Kenge helped Makasu. In the next part a different alignment appears.

South Homba talked about their dead, but decided that Makasu was too far away for them to be able to go there to fight. Ngwe Njali, *ndwi*, volunteered to do revenge. He went first to Bushong bwan kapa, and learnt there that a man from Makasu was visiting and would soon be going away. He waited in the forest, killed him, took his calabash of wine and his dress, and went back to South Homba. There they beat the war-drum. But Ngwe was not satisfied. Makasu had killed three of their men, and only two of Makasu had died.

So Ngwe Njali went to Ilebo to his kinsman, and said that he had been looking for a Makasu man to settle a village wrong, but couldn't find one. His kinsman took him to Domaie, where he had a friend, Shanga tamo, a famous *ndwi*. The kinsman first hid Ngwe under the raffia palm of Shanga tamo, and went to tell him who was there. Shango tamo had heard of Ngwe as an *ndwi* with a great reputation, equal to his own, and referring to him as *mbai*, promised to help. In the evening he went to the palm, they drank wine together, and discussed the matter. Shanga tamo told Ngwe to hide in the forest in the day, but to come and sleep in his house at night. To enable Ngwe to slip back into the forest unseen, he announced at dawn that, as official diviner, he was going to do rites for the village, and that all were to stay in their houses until he gave the word to come out. Then, while Ngwe was safely hiding, he went to the forest near Makasu, and looked at the palms. He saw one with a wine calabash hanging from it, and waited in hiding until he saw a Makasu man come to draw the wine. Then he went back, and told his friend Ngwe that he had found a place. They went together to the palm of the man of Makasu, and hid near it. At midday they saw him come again, and draw wine. He left the calabash on the ground, by the tree, spilling some wine out as it was overflowing. They waited, till he came back in the evening. While they waited they had a friendly argument as to which of them should shoot first. When the man came back, they shot him, cut off his head and arm, and went home. South Homba beat the war-drum and the affair with Makasu was settled. Both villages had lost three men each.

In this part of the story the other Bushongo village is again
on the side of South Homba, and so are Domaie and Ilebo.
Makasu and the two last-named villages were all on the other
side of the Lumbundji river, so even if they were nearer to
South Homba than they are now, the distance was still considerable, enough for South Homba to have given up the method of
direct attack.

2. *Middle and South Homba against Hanga Ekangu*

Long-standing hostility between the villages broke out some
time between 1926 and 1930.

South Homba captured the village-daughter of Hanga, and set her
up as village-wife. They paid the marriage dues to her father and
mother. One day when she went home for a visit, her own village held
her, and set her up as their own village-wife. South Homba was
astounded at this incestuous act, demanded her return, but was refused.
Later, a woman went mad in Hanga, and one day she ran away to South
Homba. They sent her home, because of her madness, but demanded a
woman to pay for the shelter she had sought. Hanga refused to give
another woman, but said that South Homba was welcome to keep the
mad woman. South Homba sent four of their village-wives to discuss
the matter. Village-wives are like chiefs, it is not allowed to harm them.
But the Hanga men caught them, beat them, and tied them up. One
escaped, and told South Homba how they had been treated. So South
Homba sent Ibonje (*ndwi* living in Middle Homba) to avenge the
insult. He ambushed and killed someone from Hanga, by mistake he
killed a woman. So the men of Hanga, in anger, killed one of the three
hostages.

Hearing of this the Homba villages suggested a truce, since each
village had killed one woman. The matter was left like that for some
time. Then someone in Hanga wanted to avenge the death of the woman
killed by Ibonje. They came and killed two young men of Middle
Homba.

Then the Homba villages were very angry and arranged a fight. They
fought in the open, outside the village. Hanga wounded five men, of
whom two died. This gave Hanga a total of five deaths. But the Homba
villages killed seven men: total for Homba, eight deaths.

After that the matter was dropped. Next time that Hanga
Ekangu moved its site, it moved away from Homba and from
that day there has been practically no intercourse between the
two villages.

In this case, the two southern Homba villages were treated by their enemy as one, they were situated within a mile of each other, and used the services of the one *ndwi*. But North Homba which was farther away, played no part whatever as ally of its brother villages, and Hanga Yulu, which was near, did not help its brother village, Hanga Ekangu. This was because it had moved into the radius of the Homba villages in which enmity was no longer practicable. The only kind of rivalry it permitted itself with Homba was in wrestling matches; real fighting had been laid aside, and there was even a little intermarriage.

Other villages with which South Homba had had fights were Malembi and Bamba to the north, and once, long before living memory, with Mbombe.

3. *Kenge against Bushongo bwan kapa*

About 1920 a long-standing enmity between the two villages flared up. I did not learn the incidents which provoked the final fight, in which the men of Kenge crept up in the night and surrounded Bushongo, shot a hail of arrows into the village at dawn, killed, among others, the maternal uncle of my informant. (The latter was in the village as a child of five at the time.) Kenge set fire to the village, but were put to flight by the arrival of the men of Bushongo's ally, South Homba. We saw (Chapter IX, p. 175) that Bushongo refused to accept a blood compensation case against South Homba on account of their alliance and their intermarriages. Kenge (in Case 1) had helped Makasu against South Homba, so it was right that South Homba should strike a blow against them for Bushongo. These cases show how the pattern of existing alliances and enmities was extended to bring in other villages. When Kenge ringed Bushongo round for a large-scale attack, it got four other villages to send men to help it. They were Mwabe, then situated to the far south near Ibanga, and an ally of Makuba; Hanga Ekangu, the enemy of South Homba; and Kashosh and Koko mikombi, two villages from the other side of the Lumbundji river.

4. *Kenge against Tundu*

When I asked ordinary Lele about the attitude of the head of the aristocratic clan, Tundu, to such a grave breach of the peace, and to such an insult to his own family, since Bushongo

Bwankapa, the attacked village, was a Tundu residence, I was told that even if he had wished to come to the help of his kinsman, or to avenge his village, he would never have attacked Kenge, of all places, because of the way they had once treated a Tundu.

Kenge had been fighting with another village, when a Tundu was killed, possibly by accident. When he died, the *Nyimi*, Pero Mwelu, went in person to remonstrate, but the men of Kenge caught him, tied him hand and foot, and took him into the village. They held him to the fire to scorch him. Some said, 'We have already killed his brother, we won't kill him too.' But others said they would, so they put an arrow in him. After this no Tundu entered the village of Kenge.

Pero Mihondo, senior Tundu, commenting on this ignominious story said first, that neither of the two Tundu who were killed by Kenge was a *Nyimi*, and second, that subsequently the Tundu gathered many supporters, and razed Kenge to the ground, and third, that it all happened a very long time ago. In either version, Tundu and Kenge acted like any other vengeful villages, and it would seem that the outrages followed a long-standing hostility.

It is certain that, for the Western Lele at least, the Tundu clan had neither pretensions to punish bloodshed as an infringement of their own prerogatives, nor powers to avenge insults to themselves.

The spread of brother villages, from south to north, and across the rivers, meant that different members of such a cluster eventually formed different local alliances, and different patterns of intermarriage. To be allied with one set of villages meant to be at enmity with most of their enemies and with the allies of their enemies. In the end the pattern of alliances involved all the villages, so that in the Western Lele no village could be said to be completely neutral, without commitments, either of friendship or hostility, towards any other village, and these commitments also stretched across the Lumbundji, as we have seen. The geographical intermixing meant that the alliances did not alternate in a simple checker-board effect, but something more irregular and shifting.

In practice, people did not often travel far between north and south, as regional dialects testified. But, in principle, however far north a southerner might travel, he could hope to find a village which was allied with villages allied to his own, and equally, he should avoid villages which were hostile to allies of his own village. His presence away from home was a temptation to members of his host's village, who might, following other loyalties, inform on or kill him. When a man travelled, he was a possible object of revenge as a member of his village, and not as a member of his clan. Acts of violence were treated as inter-village offences, not as matters for blood-negotiations between clans.

Individual Lele had much occasion to travel. Their liberty in the choice of residence meant that old friends, from whom old debts or new loans might be collected, were scattered over the country. They travelled to pursue revenge. They travelled to consult famous diviners. They travelled to barter raffia cloth for camwood, copper and iron goods. Aware of possible lurking enemies, they built up protective links wherever they could. One was clanship. Being of the same clan as a stranger, or even better, being of the same clan as one of his in-laws, was a strong claim to hospitality. Another was age-friendship (*bumbai*). If the bond of age-mates was extended to trading partners, and to craft and cult colleagues, it was because anyone who travelled needed friends abroad, because of the hostility between villages.

When we add a summary of the friendly external relations of villages, the giving and claiming of daughter's daughters as village-wives, the honouring of the village-son-in-law, the bespeaking of drums from foreign carvers, and the exchange of ritual services by specialists, and the annual collaboration of firing the grassland, we would seem to have covered the subject of inter-village politics, no scope remaining for the role of chiefs. Politically speaking, this is correct. Nothing restricted the autonomy of the villages. They competed and combined as in a chiefless system.

Ascendancy of the Tundu

In each village we have seen that two or more clans were senior, 'owners' of the village, with mystical powers sanctioning their precedence. For the Lele as a whole the pattern was elaborated: one whole clan was 'owner' of the Lele in much the same way as a local clan section was 'owner' of a village.

All the members, child, male and female of the clan of Tundu were called '*Kumu*'. The word was also applied to other roles in other contexts. It was used for owner of slaves or dogs, for lord of pawns paid in blood compensation, for elder of the local clan section or head of a village, and as a term of respect for Europeans. The latter, mostly familiar with *Kumu* applied to the head of a village, to the Tundu clan and to themselves, translated it simply as 'Chef', a word with even wider connotation than the English 'chief', which, as it designates the person in legitimate control of an autonomous political unit, is unsuitable for translating *Kumu*. The members of the Tundu clan can be called aristocrats, but the *Nyimi*, Tundu holder of a ritual office, has to be left untranslated.

The Tundu clan claimed ascendancy over the inhabitants of the region between the Kasai and the Loange. Some of the latter were autocthones, Bachwa, who at first resisted the Tundu. Others migrated with and stayed with the Tundu, while others again, starting from the same point got separated on the route and rejoined them later. All the immigrants not of the Tundu clan were known as Wongo. Following on disputes now enshrined in myths, Tundu divided into three branches. The main one settled in the eastern area between the Lubudi and Kasai rivers, where to this day they are more numerous than elsewhere. Another branch, known as Shet, went south, the third, known as Yambi, went north and west between the Loange and Lumbundji rivers. The map of Basongo Territory in Chapter I (p. 15) shows the three administrative *secteurs* which correspond to the three regions associated respectively with these three branches of the Tundu clan. A rough sketch map of Tundu residences in the Political Register for 1924 shows seventeen Tundu villages, fourteen in the eastern *secteur*, two in the southern and only one in the western. In actual fact one other Tundu village had been overlooked in the count of the Western Lele, as the sole surviving member of that line was at that time in prison.

A Tundu village was for practical purposes constituted in the same way as other villages. The founding clan section which 'owned' the village and had precedence in it was Tundu, and around it clustered local sections of other clans, recruiting their members and giving them wives in the same way as local clan sections of other villages. The senior male of the local clan section of Tundu was village head. The relations of a Tundu village with other villages, Tundu or Wongo, were not greatly different from those obtaining between Wongo villages. Most of the villages within a limited geographical radius of a Tundu village were its allies just as the neighbours of any village tended to be, but the alliance with Tundu was expressed in the idiom of kinship and marriage.

The head of a Tundu village, making a formal visit to a friendly Wongo village, received gifts of raffia which might be regarded as a form of tribute. The proper procedure was for him to be presented with a raffia cloth by the owner of each of the corner huts, and with one in the middle of the village by the spokesman. There he would sit down and lecture them, reminding them of the dignity of Tundu, the respect due to them, how no one should ever wound an aristocrat, and adjuring the people not to fight. He might be invited to give his opinion in some disputes. At the end of his visit, every man in the village would give him a cloth, say fifty or more in all. Then they would escort him home to his village. There, he should take one of his own daughters, or a granddaughter, anoint her with camwood paste, and present her to the loyal village as their future wife.

Thus in return for their tribute of cloths, the village acquired a wife. Painlessly, without force, the Tundu of the west collected tribute, maintained their privileges, and linked themselves to commoner villages by a special interpretation of the *hohombe* or village-wife institution.

In the first instance, the tribute-paying village became the son-in-law of the aristocrat, for the girl would be set up as a village-wife, the village performing services and making gifts to her parents as usual. But her daughter, according to the rules of preferred marriage, was destined for her grandfather, the aristocrat who had begotten her mother. When she was old enough to be given to him, the village became father-in-law and received gifts from the aristocrat. Thus the relationship of marriage between aristocrat and village was perpetuated. The village lost none of its autonomy, for while it held the subservient status of son-in-law it could anticipate an early future in which the roles would be reversed.

We have seen that the son-in-law of the village was invested with the leopard skin and eagle's feather, insignia of chiefship. The fact that the Wongo village was indeed the father-in-law of the Tundu aristocrat put its commoner son-in-law on the same

14

footing as the aristocrat, and allowed an assimilation of the former
to the noble status of the latter.

In South Homba there were three women whose mothers or
grandmothers had been given by previous aristocrats. Ngomabulu, the predecessor of the current head of the clan in the west,
journeying from Tundu to Malembi, was said to have given two
women to Malembi, three to the Homba villages, one to
Bushongo. Villages north of Malembi he regarded as outside his
range. Kenge and the Domaie villages he did not attempt to
enter, because long ago they had killed a Tundu. The Hanga
group of villages he did not regard as part of his traditional
domain, since they had crossed over from the left bank of the
Loange in relatively recent times.

One final elaboration of the *hohombe* institution knitted the
aristocrats firmly into the fabric of Lele culture, that is the status
of Tundu women. The rule against clan exogamy required them
to marry commoners, yet a female aristocrat could not be
subordinate to her commoner husband in the same way as an
ordinary woman.

Marriage for such women involved a serious contradiction. It
was not a mere problem of protocol, but a conflict of vital
symbols concerning male dominance and clan precedence. The
Lele solution, not uncommon, was to treat the aristocrat woman
as a special case of *hohombe*. She was allowed to behave as a
village-wife, only with greater freedom. A village-wife belonged
to the village which made gifts to her parents, and she could be
transferred to another village or to a private husband, by
appropriate payments. She had to be faithful at least to the men
of her village or group of villages. But nothing limited the whims
of an aristocratic wife. She went where she pleased, and all men
were her husbands. No one could make marriage gifts for rights
over her. When she conceived, the same risks of sex pollution
through *hanga* endangered her as other women, and she restricted herself to the men she had known since her last confinement. To bear her child she returned to the Tundu village.
Once delivered, she was free to circulate again. This institution
naturally put the aristocrats in a popular light, and the whole
Lele people were proud to say of them: 'We begot the Tundu,
all of us.'

Just as the village-wife had house-husbands to father her

children socially, so the female aristocrat had her house-husband. She chose him herself, a life-appointment which he could not refuse. His title paradoxically meant begetter of chiefs, *iboci-la-bakumu*, although his procreative role was devolved largely on his wife's lovers. He had to remain faithful to his wife, lest his adulteries endanger her in childbirth. Therefore, on pain of capital punishment, he might never have sexual intercourse with any other woman.

If there was no adult male of the Tundu clan to head a village in which they were settled, the mother of a young male aristocrat would hold the office until his majority. The female aristocrats whom I knew personally were formidable characters, convincingly capable of making a paradox of ordinary marital relations.

The aristocratic clan had certain prerogatives, which they maintained, not by force, but by lavish reciprocity. The skins of certain animals and the feathers of certain birds, black serval, leopard, and the eagle were their insignia. As such they had other uses, for they were worn by sons-in-law of the village, man-killers, leopard killers, and so on, but aristocrats were able to acquire their share of them and maintain their prerogative by a kind of concealed purchase. Any commoner who formally presented the skin of such a beast to an aristocrat with the correct ceremonial speech created a claim equivalent to a blood debt against the aristocrat. The latter was obliged to accept the gift, and then to take from his treasure-store wealth equivalent to a man's ransom, and give it to the man who had honoured him. Instead, if he wished, and if the man was one of his pawns, he could release one of the man's female relatives, a sister or mother from the bonds of pawnship. Such a generous convention made it certain that no one was likely to deny lightly the skins and feathers due to the rank of aristocrat.

Certain beliefs helped to support the eminence of the Tundu clan. They claimed to be descended directly from Woto, the mythical hero, first ancestor of the tribe. They stood between God and men, they were spirits (*mingehe*) as much as they were men. Therefore the initiations into cults which were necessary for commoners were not necessary for them. Men reached God through the mediation of their cults, but aristocrats spoke with God direct, and when they spoke, God confirmed their word. They spoke for God. They said that they had founded the cults, they upheld them, and were in a sense themselves the source of the benefits which were enjoyed through the cults. Since they were already privileged in their direct access to God, there was no need for them to undergo initiation into a cult group. Indeed, an aristocrat pocketed the entrance fees to the diviners' guild in his own village. In view of their vaunted divinity, it is curious that aristocrats were credited with control over only one small part of natural phenomena: the edible caterpillars and grasshoppers which appear twice yearly, called *mituli*. When a Tundu passed by, the commoners called out to him: 'Grant us *mituli*,' and he would reply: 'I have heard.' If he were angry, or if the rites concerning him were neglected, the caterpillars would not be seen that year.[1]

The aristocratic clan was also said to have been the source of sorcery. At an idyllic early period of their history, Lele lived out the full span of their lives, without knowledge of sorcery. But one man of Tundu, angry with a commoner for seducing his wife, asked God for a means of killing him. God showed him sorcery (*buloki*). At first it was an instrument of aristocratic power only. Then an aristocrat's *mbai* (age-mate) persuaded him to divulge the secret, and from that time, sorcery spread through the tribe, with the disastrous effects every Lele knows: fatal epidemics, chronic illnesses, early deaths, childlessness, hunting failure and all other misfortunes. Aristocrats still kept the strongest sorcery. They were supposed to have been taught it from an early age.

The above applies equally to Tundu in either western or eastern *secteurs*. The eastern *secteur* was distinguished by having developed the office of *Nyimi*, head of the Tundu clan, into a form of sacral, secluded kingship. The *Nyimi* was chosen on the same principle as the head of the village: he was the eldest male member of all the Tundu. Usually he was selected from Tundu of the eastern region, but occasionally from the western or southern branches of the clan. His rites of installation distinguished him from the other aristocrats for the rest of his life.

[1] I could discover no explanation of this association of insect life with the aristocratic clan. Similar beliefs applied to twins and to village-wives; if the proper rites were not performed when they died, *mituli* would disappear, for twins, proof of their relation with spirits, for village-wives of their aristocratic standing in the village.

The ritual included an act of incestuous intercourse with a woman of the aristocratic clan, a classificatory sister. The incest re-enacted the deed of the mythical first ancestor of the Lele, Woto, who committed incest with his sister. The shameful act both sacralized the *Nyimi* and made it impossible for him ever to look his clansmen in the face again. He went into seclusion until his death. An enclosure was built for him and two men deputed to care for him; one, a sister's daughter's son, whose main task was to draw palm wine, and act as his mouthpiece and intermediary; the other, a commoner, whose task was to hunt to provide meat for the *Nyimi*. Each servitor had his wife, and the *Nyimi* also had his wife, called *ngat ambihi mbalu* (the woman after the incest) by whom he could never beget a child . . . (no coherent reason for this was forthcoming). If she died, she could never be replaced, and if the *Nyimi* died first, she could never have sexual intercourse with another man, or both would die. The wives of the two servitors worked for the *Nyimi's* wife. Neither the *Nyimi*, nor his wife ever came out of seclusion.

The ritual incest of the *Nyimi*, related to me in great solemnity by a female aristocrat, I found afterwards to be a well-known secret among all the Lele. Fathers passed it on to their sons, adjuring them never to mention it except to their own sons in like conditions of secrecy. It was regarded as a mysterious and awful subject, which could not be discussed. It was suggested to me that the *Nyimi* at his installation was already an old man, and that both his sister of the *mbalu*, and his wife in seclusion, were too old for child-bearing. The account of the seclusion is worth preserving if only because of its striking resemblance to the chaste chiefs of certain Pende groups neighbouring Lele to the west.[2]

The *Nyimi* was not immune to attacks of sorcery, but was protected by his own superior insight which warned him of evil intentions in time for counter-measures. He was also protected in a practical way, as the man who drew his palm wine and the women who drew his water always had to taste it first: if he fell ill, they would at once be accused of poisoning him by sorcery and be killed.

---

[2] L. de Sousberghe, 'Etruis Péniens ou Gaines de Chasteté chez les Bapende'. *Africa*, July 1954, pp. 214–19. It also helps to fill in the picture of sacral kingship in Central Africa sketched in L. de Heusch's stimulating analysis 'Symbolisme de l'Inceste Royale'.

When a *Nyimi* died, his mourning clansmen lined his coffin with the skins of leopard and black serval and with eagle's and parrot's feathers. They beat the drum and danced, but they did not weep for him. The Wongo ran to hide in fear of their lives. The aristocratic mourners took a live cock, and cutting off its head sprinkled the breasts of his surviving kinsmen, then they went to surrounding villages, slaughtering any living things they saw, chickens, dogs, goats, and commoners. Before the Belgian administration, no Wongo felt safe until after the burial. When the grave was dug, two men were caught, Wongo of course, and one, with his head cut off, was left unburied, the other buried alive under the royal coffin.

When the *Nyimi* died in 1949, and until his successor was installed, the administration policed the region carefully to prevent the untoward disappearance of any Wongo in the course of the obsequies.

Whether the slaughter was as great as I was told remains unproven. On the death of any commoner of note, it was expected that his angry kinsmen should descend on the village where he had died, and shoot the chickens and dogs, threatening and abusing the villagers. Often fighting would follow and people might get killed in the confusion. However, I never saw or heard of an actual case of mourning for commoners being expressed thus destructively.

Apart from his special rituals of accession and death, the *Nyimi* was said to claim the sole right to take human life, a right acquired from his ancestor Woto, the child of God, because of his defiance of the prohibition on incest. Aristocrats exercised this right on his behalf and with his permission. If news came of any killing by commoners, the *Nyimi* gave his permission for the Tundu aristocrats to punish it with an indiscriminate massacre.[3] I learned of no instances of this practice which was so much at variance with the realities of the Lele political scene. It could be that the Lele *Nyimi's* power had once been effective politically and had withered to the shadow it was in this century, or it could be that the whole notion of a *Nyimi* holding the lives

[3] The ascendancy of the Tundu over the Lele has something in common with the ascendancy of the Alur chiefly dynasty over Lendu (Southall), but its political development on similar lines was obviously inhibited by the Lele attaching value to the village-wife institution which supported village autonomy.

of his subjects in his hands could have been derived from the *Nyimi* of the Bushong, who had become a very effective ruler. The above applies to the *Nyimi* of the eastern *secteur*, but each of the three branches of the Tundu clan installed one of its members as a *Nyimi*. I know nothing of the *Nyimi* of the southern *secteur*, but in the west, where the line had dwindled to no more than two adult men, his office did not require him to be secluded.

The Europeans, translating *Kumu* as *chef*, and *Nyimi* as *grand chef*, took the *Nyimi* of the eastern *secteur* to be a paramount ruler over the whole tribe, comparable to the *Nyimi* of the Bushong. When the holder of the office died in 1922 they went to great pains to ascertain the rightful successor, and invested him forthwith as Chief of the Lele, District of Basongo. Difficulties followed thick and fast on their attempt to use him as an instrument of indirect rule. The administration complained that the Chief abused his powers and tyrannized his subjects. The other Tundu refused the Chief their support, some denied him access to their villages, some were outright rebellious and were exiled by the Colonial Administration. After ten years of frustration a new administrator, Monsieur Wautier, making ethnographic researches, discovered that there had never been any authority in the traditional Lele political system, and that Tundu had never had power to intervene in disputes (Pol. Reg. II. Basongo). The administration then decided to give up indirect rule, to abolish the 'Chiefdom' they had created, and to administer direct through sub-districts called *secteurs*, in each of which the senior Tundu would be the nominal head, while administration was in the hands of paid, appointed government officials.

In the western *secteur* even the nominal position of the senior Tundu as *chef de secteur* had to be given up in favour of a more efficient Wongo clerk. The ex-chief became head of a small village, Tundu, but his deposition from chiefship made him, politically speaking, no worse off than his own ancestors seem to have been. For the Tundu of the Western Lele to have filled any authoritative and responsible role outside their own village would have been incompatible with the constitution of Lele villages and their normal relations with one another.

To hear Tundu speak haughtily of their pre-eminence, and then to hear commoners discuss village politics was confusing. The two worlds of discourse seemed to have no point of contact.

Villages warred with one another as autonomous units in a political system which admitted no external control whatever. The Tundu vaunted their power and prestige, but in a political vacuum. In effect, the impression of two distinct planes seems to have been correct. Whenever I tried to bring them into relation by asking what the aristocrats' role had been, or why they had not intervened in particular village disputes, I found that they were not expected to intervene. Sometimes they might be invited to arbitrate between two contending parties (as in the case of Ket *v.* Bieng, Chapter VIII above) but this role of mediator might fall to any respected third party outside the dispute who happened to be visiting. The aristocrat's opinion was not necessarily followed, and he had no sanctions or even pretensions to enforce his judgement.

I conclude that the role of the Lele aristocratic clan, whether or not the atrophied relics of a former power, was somewhat like the theatrical function which Bagehot insisted was a great part of the role of British monarchy. One might say that, at the cost of some life at the funeral of a *Nyimi*, the Tundu clan enriched and sacralized the culture of the Lele. They embodied in their persons a physical link between mankind and the creative power of God, through Woto, the mythical hero from whom they claimed descent. They enacted at the succession of each *Nyimi* the incestuous act of Woto with which Lele history began, whose punishment was leprosy and whose reward was god-like command of life. Above all the Tundu were the fount and guarantee of the efficacy of the cults, and living proof of the dangers of sorcery.

Tundu killed commoners for seducing their wives, and killed commoners for their funeral rites. Commoners for their own part repeated the pattern, in a lower key. They claimed blood compensation for the seduction of their pawn-wives, and killed slaves for their own funeral celebrations.

We need not expect above the village level a pattern of authority strikingly different from that applied within the village and within its component units. The most characteristic feature of organization within the village was the attempt to live in community without defined authority. The precedence of the founding clan in the village was an intangible thing, giving subtle satisfaction to its members, but, politically speaking, null. The pre-eminence of the aristocratic clan might be seen as a larger-scale model of the same kind. The aristocrats certainly enjoyed prestige, but they had to manipulate (not dominate) the existing political structure in order to maintain their prestige.

XI

RELIGIOUS SANCTIONS ON VILLAGE UNITY AND THE ORGANIZATION OF VILLAGE CULTS

WE have seen that though the Lele valued peace in the village, they instituted no direct authority for enforcing it. We must therefore study their cults which brought religious sanctions to bear on breaches of the peace.

God was to men as an owner to his slaves. He ordered them, protected them, set their affairs straight, and avenged injustice. The word *Njambi* was often on their lips. They invoked him in oaths, as well as in profane remarks such as our 'God only knows' or 'God willing'. Each man's individual make-up of talents and frailties was ascribed to *Njambi*. However, there was no direct cult of *Njambi*. His interventions in human affairs were mediated by a subordinate order of spiritual beings, *mingehe* (sing. *ngehe*).

If a human were to set eyes on a spirit, he would be struck blind and die of sores. Spirits, neither named nor numbered, were said to be associated with particular streams, and named stretches of grassland or forest, but the association was very vague. They were never addressed individually in rites or prayers.

According to popular belief spirits were not, and never had been men, but in some practical contexts *mingehe* (spirits) seemed to be identified with *baotale* (ancestors) and *miendo* (ghosts). However, though the dead were often thought to intervene in human affairs, no cult was paid to them either and their names were not recalled in ritual. The belief that they could be reborn at any time they chose may perhaps have been inconsistent with a cult of individual dead.

Spirits had to be known and understood, as part of man's environment, and they should not be angered. If they made friends with men, they might reveal to them secrets about the use of herbs and teach efficacious rites. They inhabited the deep forest, especially the sources of streams, sleeping in the day, but roaming around at night.

They controlled the fertility of women and prospered men's hunting, or they might withhold the game, turn aside the hunter's arrow, prevent women from conceiving, or strike a village with sickness. The study of their ways was the diviner's secret lore.

Nearly all important rites were associated with the practice of healing. The idiom of medicine so dominated their religious forms that it was often hard to distinguish two separate spheres of action. Such power of healing and curing barrenness as might be exercised by humans was derived only from God. Hence, healers were at the same time religious experts. Whether they were trying to cure a fever, or to set right the relation of a village to spiritual powers, they first used divination: then they prescribed and applied some herbal remedy with the proper formula, and imposed a number of restrictions on the patient.

Verbally the two categories of moral and physical disorder were distinguished: a sick man would be feverish, but a village bad (*bube*) or spoilt (*wonyi*). If the man was cured he was strong (*bunono*) or (*manyin*), but a good village was soft (*bolabolu*) or peaceful, quiet (*polo*). The word for curing a sick man was *belu*; for setting right a disordered village, *ponga*, to mend, set straight, arrange in order.

On the other hand *nengu*, the word for rites and medicines, applied equally to healing and to village ritual. As individuals, diviners had each their own practice for healing. As a body they had a public responsibility towards their village, administering *nengu* for it. For translating into English idiom it is better sometimes to use 'medicine' and sometimes 'rite' for *nengu*.

All sacred medicines, to be effective, required prohibitions to be imposed on the patient. Their power was not strictly *ex opere operato*, but depended on whether the diviner had undergone the correct initiation, paid for the power to apply them, followed the proper restrictions himself, and also on the goodwill between himself and his client.

A man under medical treatment had to accept restrictions on his way of living. He might be forbidden to drink palm wine, to eat certain kinds of fish, to enter the forest, etc. A village undergoing a course of ritual was similarly put under restrictions.

The character of these gives us some further insight into Lele
religious ideas. The favourite themes which were used over and
over again were the separation of the two spheres, forest and
village, the separation of the sexes, women's exclusion from the
forest, the association of the forest with spiritual power, the
neutrality of the grassland.[1]

The place of women in Lele ritual deserves a note. It is likely
that male-female symbolism would be developed in their
religion. Women were treated as objects of men's political
action. Rights over them were the media in which male competition for status was expressed. We have seen that women,
in secular contexts, were thought of as immeasurably precious
creatures, worth waiting and fighting for, at the same time as
being despicably weak, inferior beings, needing authority and
protection. Some of these themes were developed in the concept
of *hanga*, sex pollution, which provided an automatic sanction
on marital fidelity and which appropriately punished female
trespasses more directly and severely than male ones. At the same
time, it emphasized female fragility and vulnerability. These
two ideas, sex pollution and the vulnerability of women, were
further developed in the ritual segregation of the sexes.

The sphere of the forest, for all the work the women did in it,
was treated as a male sphere, to be protected from female
contamination at marginal periods. Women were prohibited
from entering the forest on every third day and on all religious
occasions, such as mourning, birth of twins, appearance of the
new moon, departure of a chief, in menstruation and childbirth.

The appropriation of the forest by the men was balanced by
treatment of the grassland as the exclusive sphere of women.
The grassland had no prestige like the forest. It was dry and
barren. The one crop which thrived there, the ground-nut, was
exclusively cultivated by the women. Ritual sanctions forbade
a woman who had lifted the first sod of grass on her ground-nut
plot to have sexual intercourse until a month or six weeks later,
when the seedlings were well established.

Most other activities which custom allocated entirely to one
or the other sex were similarly protected by sexual taboos, some
lasting even longer than this example. No hunting expedition

[1] This has been described in more detail in *African Worlds*, Chapter 1, 'The
Lele of the Kasai'.

was undertaken without one night of continence being imposed first on the whole village. A man making pit traps might have to abstain from sexual relations for several months until certain specified animals had been caught. Most situations of ritual danger affecting the village as a whole were treated in the same way. The refrain 'Tonight each woman her mat alone, each man his mat alone' was a regular announcement preceding important rites.

To segregate and exclude women from the forest makes sense in the full ritual pattern. It is not merely that sexual intercourse and menstruation were thought to be dangerous to men, but that in their most vital function, child-bearing, women themselves were highly vulnerable. On the one hand, they were liable to frustration of their function in barrenness, miscarriage and stillbirth. On the other, they were liable to die in labour. Child-birth was a matter for fear, and for all the more anxiety since every man's career depended on his becoming a father and grand-father and on the increase of his matrilineal clan—a triplicated focus on child-bearing. Hence the emphasis on fertility in Lele ritual. The spirits in the forest controlled both child-bearing and hunting. They could make all the women or individual women barren, all the men or individual hunters fail, as punishment for individual or collective transgressions.

In the first place, the spirits upheld the observance of the day of rest, of food-privileges of cult groups, of the distinction of the sexes and of the forest from village. In the second place, they required all persons living in a village to be at peace with each other. The village faced its own forest and through it the spiritual world as a single whole. In this the ritual corresponded to the political situation, in which each village was autonomous and potentially at war with other villages. In religion the soli-darity of each village was such that an offence by one member affected adversely the whole village, and the barrenness of a woman or the failure of an individual hunter might be attributed to the general condition of the village in which they lived.

In a small village changes in the fertility of women are not easily observed. By watching the hunt, in the way that the Lele did, we can see what kind of harmony between its members was rewarded by the spirits, and what dissensions were punished by hunting failure.

The success of the hunt required that internal solidarity be real in the fullest sense. Bloodshed and striking of blows spoilt the village, but so also did hard words and insults. Whether the offender was a resident or a temporary visitor made no difference, but within the village itself the higher the ritual status of the persons quarrelling, the more fatal their ill-will might be. The officially appointed diviner of the village might spoil it by a rebuke to his wife, whereas a more open show of anger from an ordinary man might escape notice. The villages seemed to be specially sensitive to any breach of marital peace. A wife who ran away in anger, even if she returned penitent the same evening, had spoilt the village, and both she and her husband owed a fine before hunting could be resumed. The anger of an old man, whether just or unprovoked, was highly dangerous. A simple rite performed usually before any hunt illustrates their interpretation of ritual peace. Each man, as he set out, took the matchet or knife from his girdle and gave it silently to his neighbour, who completed the exchange with his own knife. The meaning of this action was explained as if one were saying: 'My age-mate, you take the matchet with which I may have been hitting my wife,' and the other replying: 'And you take my knife, in case I have struck my children with it.' At the end of the hunt the weapons were returned to their owners.

Cults were organized primarily on a village-basis. Each village had its own cult groups, but these were uniform in their objectives and rules over the country. Initiations into a cult were often on a wider basis, two or more brother villages might combine for an initiation ceremony, or a diviner from a brother village might be called in to restart a cult whose membership had died out. Only brother villages combined for ritual because a diviner from an enemy or even a neutral village might be tempted to abuse his intimate position of trust. He might make his ritual efficacious for the first few weeks, so that his fees and reputation were secure, and then cancel it by a secret act of sorcery timed to take effect after his departure. Furthermore, it was cheaper to employ diviners from a brother village, as foreigners charged more for their services.

With one exception the cults were all directed towards fertility, good hunting and the defeat of sorcery. The exception was the group of Begetters, whose *raison d'être* was little more than to honour fatherhood and to accentuate the social gulf between married men and bachelors. The cults seem to fall into two series. One was based on male begetting, and consisted of two grades. The first was the *Baboci*, Begetters (into which all men were normally initiated after begetting a child in wedlock). For the second, the Pangolin Men, *Bina Luwawa*, the qualification was the begetting in wedlock of both a male and female child. This last was a fertility cult, whose ritual was held to be extremely powerful for enabling women to conceive and for good hunting.

The Begetters performed no special ritual, either for healing, or for fertility or hunting. At the initiation ceremony, the candidate had red pepper rubbed into his eyes, was led to the stream to wash, while women sang: 'Now you are a man, now you will see, you will kill many animals.' On his return there was a triumphal march of initiates round the village, during which women and uninitiated men hid for embarrassment while ribald songs were sung at the expense of *nkolokol*, any man who was not a Begetter. The initiate provided a large feast, and a fee of 100 cloths. Once initiated, men were able to eat with impunity young of animals, and the chest of big game: anyone else doing so would risk death from coughing. The only healing rite possessed exclusively by the Begetters was one to save a confessed transgressor from the effects of infringing their privilege.

We should note that begetting out of wedlock was not a qualification for entry, nor was fathering the child of a village-wife. Since entry to this cult was the first step to entering the powerful Pangolin Cult, and since the age of marriage was late, roles in this series of cults were reserved to mature men.

Entry to the Pangolin Cult was restricted on other grounds. The candidate had to have begotten a male and a female child by the same wife; he himself had to be a member of one of the founding clans of the village, and his father also; the wife through whom he qualified had herself to be a member of a founding clan. The result of such stipulations was that very few men were ever eligible for initiation, even when the rules were relaxed to include the founding clans of brother villages. The implicit intention in these regulations was to honour the members of the founding clans, to encourage their intermarriage, and thus to sustain the continuity of the clan population in the villages. It is difficult to say whether the specific rewards of cult membership had any effect in promoting these marriages, or whether the hope of entering the cult ever decided an individual to reside in a village in which he would be qualified for it. But certainly the cult helped to emphasize the prestige of the founding clans, and supported the belief that a member of a founding clan was an 'owner' of the village in a sense that his anger, or his leaving it in anger, would be harmful.

The Pangolin Men could only hold an initiation when they killed a pangolin, for the ritual feast on pangolin flesh was part of the ceremony. They were then invested with power over hunting and over fertility of women, and over a wide related range of human ills and misfortunes. Their special responsibility was the ritual for the removal of the village to a new site, when a Pangolin Man, with his wife, had to be the first to sleep on the new ground. They had to set up the fertility emblem for the new village and to make it efficacious with their ritual power.

No one would wish not to join the Begetters, if he had the necessary qualifications, but entry was theoretically voluntary. The same for the Pangolin Men, there was no obligation to join. Qualified men did in fact refuse the honour of Pangolin initiation, if they feared the consequences of ritual eminence.

The other series of cults were not voluntary in this sense. They were held to be vocations which a man could not refuse on pain of death. These cults were directed to communication with the spirits, and if the spirits made known their intention of calling a man, they would kill him if he refused their friendship. Each of the three cults was called *Bukang*, and its members, *ngang* (plural *bangang*), which I translate diviner. Three different paths led men to joining the diviners, and each had accordingly its own initiation feast, fees, and its own special powers. But it was clear that all the diviners were fundamentally the same, they all received their powers from the spirits, and all could perform one another's rites if need be.

The first, and largest group were the diviners who were supposed to be called by a direct spirit summons, in the form of a dream, or a possession frenzy. If a man claimed to have had a dream summons to join the diviners, the other diviners questioned him closely to test the authenticity of his claim. Those who were spirit possessed came in from the forest, or woke the village in the early morning with wild shouting, rolling their eyes and throwing themselves on the ground. Eventually, when the candidate lay quiet and still, the other diviners would carry him into the village, lay him in a hut in which sexual intercourse had never yet taken place, and then make preparations for his noviceship.

I was told secretly that the visible symptoms of spirit summons could be faked, if necessary, and indeed, the regular discussion about individual cases of initiation, which revolved always around the practical politics of sponsorship, was at variance with the notion of divinely inspired vocation. In spite of the theory that a spirit vocation should never be obstructed, admission seemed to depend entirely on sponsorship. Any boy of any age might be initiated, if his father or mother's brother sponsored him. A middle-aged man, who was not a member, explained that he had never had a chance, as he had been orphaned young; another, that he had been brought up away from his home, so that no one was available to promote his case. Or again, it was said that a young man who had quarrelled with his brother, and taken the latter's wife off to live in the next village, would never get the necessary support for his candidature, as the elders of his clan were angry with him for making trouble and going away. Another man explained that he would like initiation, but that he had not so far been able to afford it, but one day he certainly intended to find the necessary fees.

A long noviceship followed the first initiation, one or two years, according to the diviners' esteem for the candidate. This was a period of hardship, with severe restrictions on personal behaviour, including sexual abstinence. The novice should hunt for game with which to give his coming-out feast, and weave raffia for his fees. Once through the final initiation ceremony, the diviners would teach him the rudiments of their skills. He was then allowed to practise, and to collect techniques and formulae wherever he could buy them. Diviners had certain food privileges, and abstained from others.

Every local clan section liked to have one of its members a diviner, for they could claim free professional treatment from him, and they liked to see him amass fees from consultations with other clients. A father liked to have his son initiated, so that his daughter would have a closely interested specialist for her fertility rites and for caring for her infants.

A proof of vocation more imperative and unmistakable than the dream summons was begetting twins. Twin-parents, *bina mayehe*, were not allowed out of their hut for nine days after the birth, special foods were procured for them, and special rites performed by the other twin diviners, *bangang bamayehe*. The rites were followed by a feast, fees were due, but no noviceship was necessary. If the rites were not performed, the parents and the twin babies were thought to be gravely endangered, and the whole village too would suffer.

Both parents, man and wife, became diviners on an equal footing. This was the only instance of ritual office being open to women, and in itself is significant of the importance the Lele attached to this manifestation of the spirits. The special rites of the twin diviners concerned hunting and fertility. Power was attributed to them over other multiple births in the village. A dog-owner, for example, had to seek out a twin diviner to bless a new litter of pups. After initiation, twin diviners had to avoid certain meats and parts of animals.

The third way to become a diviner was by a special vocation called *nga 'njambi*, diviner of God. The spirits were said to make a direct approach to a man they selected to be their close friend, *mbai*. One man told me that he had experienced this summons, but had kept it secret, for fear of the restrictions on his sexual life which it would involve. The spirits were very angry with him, and inflicted him with abscesses all over his body before they left him alone.

Not every village had a diviner of God, and if there was one, he was usually alone. He might be called at any age. The one I knew best started communing with the spirits from the age of eleven or so. As part of his pact with the spirits, the diviner of God had to abstain from nearly all meats, a real sacrifice. He was also forbidden to have sexual intercourse in the forest. In the night his spirit friends would come to him, chat and tell him where the game was hidden, and reveal secrets for healing his friends. Their intercourse took the form of singing, he to them, and they secretly to him. If he stopped the conversation before they were ready, they pinched and buffeted him until he went on. Sometimes he had to sing all night, and in the morning he would call the village, and tell them where to go hunting. The diviner of God could not be asked to spit a blessing,[2] because of his direct contact with the spirits.

The different diviners of God in different villages, when they met, would discuss matters of common concern. They tended to observe the same dietary restrictions. Since there was no initiation, no fee, no feast, no instructions, the diviner of God was a solitary, ascetic figure. But he was held to be a diviner with at least as much power over spirits as the Pangolin Man.

This completes the list of normal cults in any Lele village. At intervals they would be superseded or suspended by anti-sorcery cults. But I was assured that these five approaches to God and the spirits ante-dated any of the successive foreign cults that informants had ever heard of, and that after the latter had been discredited, these original elements of Lele culture were always restored. How much syncretism of foreign elements really went on is difficult to assess.

In each village two diviners were installed as official diviners of the village (*ilumbi*, plural *bilumbi*). Their position was very important, and their ritual power reckoned to equal that of the Pangolin Men. Since their role was largely to combat sorcery it can best be described in the next chapter.

There were many incentives to join the cult groups. The diviner worked hard. He might have to travel far to get a particular kind of remedy or oracle, and would give high fees for them. He never had peace from the solicitations of sick kinsfolk and neighbours, but he obviously enjoyed the praise of clients, and the periodic feasts and food privileges. A more effective inducement was the profit flowing from membership of a cult group. Fees were charged for every transfer of knowledge. Entrance fees were also a source of profit, so initiation fees were a kind of investment, producing long-term dividends.

It follows from the principles of recruitment that the cult groups were distributed over the population of a village in a largely haphazard manner. Those for which a candidate had to qualify by begetting children of each sex, or twins, had an implicit lower limit set by the age of marriage, but a young boy might become a diviner of God. Entry into the diviners depended on sponsorship, but a man might equally be sponsored by his

[2] See p. 70.

father as by his mother's brother, and so there was no correlation between membership of the most important clans of the village and of the corps of diviners. There was no control over entry into the twin diviners' group. Although each of the main clan sections of the village would like to have had its own representative in the Pangolin group, it was not always easy to find a man who had made the right marriage, and begotten children of both sexes, and who had also the approved temperament.

It was also held that it was wrong for one clan section in a village to hold too many cult positions: both dangerous to others lest they try to eliminate their rivals and dangerous to themselves lest they provoke jealousy. Although it was theoretically possible for the official diviner to belong to all the other cult groups, in practice it was most unlikely that a Pangolin Man should be installed as official diviner. Although clan sections put forward their own members for the diviners' guild, and rules limited candidature for the Pangolin Cult, anyone might beget twins, or come forward with the *nga 'njambi* vocation. In short, cult-group membership corresponded only roughly to positions of power based on clan, kin or age-set interests.

The following table shows the distribution of cult statuses between the six clans inhabiting South Homba village.

Table 14. *Distribution of Cult Status between Clans*

Clan	Total men[3]	Begetters	Diviners	Twin Diviners	Diviner of God	Pangolin	Official Diviner
Lubelo	11	6	6	–	1	2	1
Bwenga	10	6	5	1	–	–	–
Ndong	4	3	2	1	–	2	–
Ngondu	3	3	2	2	–	–	1
Ket	3	2	–	–	–	–	–
Bulomani	2	1	1	–	–	–	–

Senior positions in the clans were not necessarily validated by senior cult positions. It was a matter of chance whether a clan senior could play his role in the clan with the aid of wealth and influence accruing from membership of several cults, or not. A closer congruence between cult and clan status would obviously have strengthened the authority of the senior men in the clan sections.

[3] Excluding Christians.

Generally men in the different cult groups were able to collaborate quite smoothly in the day-to-day business of providing ritual for the village hunts and for fertility in general. Occasionally there was friction and frustration. But the strong moral pressures causing diviners to control their passions were so effective that disagreements about ritual hardly ruffled the surface of village life. A sequence of hunting rites in South Homba in the dry season of 1953 will illustrate their collaboration. In the course of this one month, the twin diviners, the Pangolin Men and the official diviner were all called in; the junior official diviner colluded with the twin diviners to pretend that twin-rites demanded by the Pangolin Men had been performed, though they had not; the senior Pangolin Man refused to perform rites until he had been compensated for adultery; the senior official diviner was suspected of sorcery, but they still collaborated.

At the time, tension was running high in the village. Hunting failures, personal or communal, were attributed to sorcery; so also was sickness, but diviners offered alternative explanations. The senior Pangolin Man said that after a woman from abroad had entered the village recently, it was discovered that she had borne twins but no twin-rites had been performed to prevent her entry from spoiling the village; he urged the twin-parents to perform the necessary rites.

6 August. The twin-parents duly consulted together. One of them drew attention to her ulcerated leg, protesting that, in spite of the callous disregard of others, she held no grudge against them for their neglect. If she had been heard to complain, it was in pain, not in anger. She performed the ritual of blessing. Instructions were given for a hunt for the next day.

7 August. The hunt was moderately successful; although four duikers escaped, two small 'blue duikers', one water chevrotain, and one young bay duiker were killed. The success was consequently attributed to the performance of the twin-ritual.

There was no more communal hunting until 12 August. Individual hunters complained of their lack of success, and considered the village to be 'bad'. The senior official diviner of the village, Makaka,[4] was informally approached and asked to do his rites for the next hunt. On the eve of the hunt, he ordered those who had quarrelled to pay fines and announced that he would do ritual. Before the hunt one of the Pangolin Men spoke a blessing, in case his grief at the obstinate and rude

[4] See p. 106 and Appendix A, Figure 12, E6.

behaviour of the young Christians should spoil the hunt. The hunt was a failure. They drew three covers, saw little game, killed only one adult and one young 'blue duiker'—a quite negligible bag. Makaka felt discredited. He announced that the animals which he had seen by divination had been escaping behind the hunters; next time he would do different rites.

13 August. During the day it transpired that the twin-ritual was still outstanding. The village had been tricked into believing that the successful hunt on 7 August had been the result of twin-rituals whereas, in fact, the junior official diviner, Ngwe, himself a twin-parent, had persuaded the others to let him try a 'spirit rite' which had been highly successful a month earlier. Everyone was angry at the deception. The senior Pangolin Man, who had originally diagnosed that a breach of twin-ritual had 'spoilt the village', declared that if only the twin-parents had been frank, the diviners themselves would have stepped in to perform the necessary twin-rites. Twins (*mayehe*) and spirits (*mingehe*) are all the same, he said, and initiated diviners do not need to beget twins in order to do twin-rites. Angriest of all was Makaka. More serious than being made to look a fool, he had looked like a sorcerer chasing away the game. His opposite number in the next village had recently been hounded out for failure to produce game, and in the old days he would have been made to take the poison ordeal.

In the next week men refused to go on a communal hunt as the village seemed obviously 'bad', i.e. infected with sorcery. Individual hunters had some success; a duiker was caught in a trap, a man chancing on a wild sow just after she had farrowed easily shot her and killed her young; a large harnessed bush-buck was shot. In spite of these successes, there was an atmosphere of frustration and acrimony in the village.

24 and 27 August. The women went on two long fishing expeditions. While they were away there was little food, and the village just ticked over till their return. On 28th two Pangolins were killed. When the women came back the atmosphere had changed overnight to one of general rejoicing. Middle Homba asked to send a candidate for initiation into the Pangolin Cult. Among the ritual specialists annoyance about the overdue twin-rite still rankled, but the Pangolin rites had to take precedence now.

The junior Pangolin Man announced on behalf of the initiates that the village was 'tied' (*kanda*), that is that sexual intercourse was banned until after the eating of the pangolin and the shedding of animal blood in the hunt that should follow the feast. Etiquette appropriate to the presence of a Tundu in the village was to be observed. Unfortunately a quarrel between children broke out, adults took sides, and blows were struck. A fine had to be paid to the Pangolin Men.

29 August. A meeting was called. The village was in a ferment because a man had been caught seducing the wife of the senior Pangolin Man.[5] The latter, Ngomabulu, refused to carry on with the Pangolin initiation and feast.

30 August. There was a spate of early-morning speeches. Ngomabulu was reproached for turning household affairs into village affairs, and for making the village suffer for his private wrong. Someone pointed out that if the pangolins were left to rot, the people of Middle Homba, who wanted their candidate vested with Pangolin power, would think we had refused to eat the pangolin to spite them. All those who had quarrelled were roundly taken to task in public speeches. All were convinced that to go hunting while the senior Pangolin Man was feeling angry would be useless.

31 August. Village opinion, originally sympathetic to the injured husband, Ngomabulu, now turned against him as he insisted that full adultery damages should be paid before he proceeded with the Pangolin rites. The pangolins had already been dead five days. If they were to go bad without being eaten with proper ritual, the whole village would go 'hard' and suffer for a long time, until Pangolin ritual had been done again. Repeated injunctions were made to keep the peace until the pangolin hunt. Two more cases of fighting occurred.

2 September. Fines for fighting were all paid up, and the major part of the adultery damages given. Ritual was performed to make the way clear for hunting the next day. The two official diviners, the four Pangolin Men, and the twin-parents met and agreed to do two rites, twin-ritual and Pangolin ritual, for the hunt.

3 September. Before the hunt, two twin-parents aired their grievances; one again on account of her ulcerated leg, which she felt no one took trouble to diagnose and cure; the other complained that her husband had abandoned her for a new young wife. Her husband's colleagues replied for him that it was nonsense to suppose that a man would leave a woman through whom he had attained three of God's callings or vocations (*mapok manjambi*); through her, he was an initiate of the Begetters, Twins and the Pangolin. She was reminded of the danger to the village if a woman who was in these three senses one of its 'owners' nursed her anger.

The hunt that followed this concerted ritual effort was a failure. Seven animals in all were seen, but only two small duikers were killed. There was great anger, and agreement that the village was bad. However, blood had been shed and the Pangolin feast could proceed. After the Pangolin rites had been performed, people assured each other, we should all see great quantities of game being brought back. The pangolin

[5] See Chapter V, p. 110.

would draw animals to the village. The next day was fixed for the feast.

That very afternoon a third pangolin was killed. There was great satisfaction. 'Just as we were saying "Tomorrow we shall eat pangolin and invest new members" . . . behold, another pangolin comes into the village!' They spoke as if the pangolin had died voluntarily, as if it had elected to be the object of Pangolin ritual and to offer itself for the feast of initiates; as if it had honoured this village by choosing it.

At night a junior Pangolin Man announced that no one was to fight, above all no one was to fight secretly. 'If you must fight, do it openly and pay up. He who fights tonight, let him be rich. The fine will be twenty raffia cloths.'

5 September. The Pangolin feast and initiation rite were eventually held. All were confident that the hunt of the following day would be successful.

6 September. The hunt went off in good heart, twenty men and eight dogs. It was an abject failure. Powerful sorcery was evidently at work, since all ritual had been duly performed. People discussed a leopard's bark that had been heard in the precincts of the village that night, and of leopard tracks seen on the way to the hunt.

The village was still 'tied'; the ban on sexual intercourse had not been lifted since 28 August, and could not be until blood had been shed in a hunt following the feast of Pangolin initiates.

9 September. A hunt took place in which one small duiker was killed. The ritual requirement was fulfilled, and the ban on sexual intercourse lifted, but from every other point of view it was a failure.

It was very remarkable that for the space of about ten days the village was closed to visitors, and sexual intercourse banned. During the month the senior official diviner, Makaka, was deceived on a professional matter by his junior colleague, and the senior Pangolin Man, Ngomabulu, was deceived by his wife. The latter was allowed by custom to give vent to his anger by insisting on damages. It was considered very natural that he should sit about in silent thunderous gloom. Even when he held up the Pangolin rites in order to enforce payment on the adulterer, some criticized him for exaggerating, but it was clear that his was still an approved form of reaction.

The senior official diviner, Makaka, by contrast, was not allowed to show the least resentment, though in many ways his status was more dangerously attainted than that of the injured husband. Realize that, by his office as *ilumbi*, he was reckoned a *de facto* sorcerer, and that many people in the village, even his friends, seriously thought that the recent hunting had been poor because he had 'tied' it, that the leopard was none other than himself, personally warning off the game, and add to this that the man who had initiated him had recently been chased away from Middle Homba as a convicted sorcerer, it is clear that things looked black for him. Though a volatile and easily roused temperament he controlled any anger he may have felt, because an *ilumbi* must never show anger on any subject.

In the case of adultery, a man was allowed to express anger, but he was obliged to accept compensation, and this paid, the matter was closed. There was no compensation for breach of trust or deception between fellow-diviners. Pressure was brought so that such quarrels did not come to the point of open anger. First, the belief that a diviner's ill-will inevitably harmed his village gave his friends their cue to beg him to be calm. Second, the belief that he controlled the means of sorcery meant that, if he showed ill-temper, all the misfortunes of the village would soon be laid to his charge, and he would risk acquiring the unpleasant reputation of a generally acknowledged sorcerer. These beliefs certainly contributed to the amicable functioning of the cult groups. The risk of being accused of sorcery was a sanction forcing diviners to co-operate amiably.

XII

SORCERY

LELE had no doubt that in their midst were sorcerers, whose
extraordinary powers enabled them to move invisibly, or in
animal form, and to strike people with illness and misfortune.
Their powers were supposed to be based on the same source as
the beneficent powers of diviners, and to work in much the same
way. Like the techniques of healing, sorcery[1] required materials,
actions and a formula of words. Some contact with the intended
victim was necessary, even if it were only the scraped-up dust of
their footprints, or the bench on which they habitually sat.
Diviner's art had to be acquired by payment and by consent, or
it would not work. Similarly, sorcery had to be bought, and used
with the consent of the vendor.

Presumably there were Lele who practised sorcery. It would
be more than human if men were never tempted to try it, and the
same sequence of events which confirms delusions of persecution
in the case of supposed victims, equally would confirm delusions
of power in the case of would-be sorcerers. Sometimes people
confessed to sorcery. One man, caught by native police in 1950
for his alleged responsibility for a thunderstorm in which five
were killed, pleaded that though he had sent the lightning he had
only meant to kill his runaway wife and not to injure anyone else.

The Lele idea of the sorcerer

The picture of the sorcerer which a people holds in common
should reflect the strains and rubs in their social system, but not
necessarily very directly. From Lele descriptions, one would
expect the accusations to fall mainly on neglected old men, unfortunates who faced old age without the support of wives and
children, venting their grudge against society by recourse to
occult powers.

They said that anyone might commit sorcery, if actuated by

[1] I use the term according to the convention of anthropologists to distinguish
belief in visible, intentionally harmful actions from 'witchcraft', belief in in-
visible, not necessarily intentional, psychic power to harm.

bubih (spite). They either paid a sorcerer to do their revenge for them, or they bought sorcery techniques from him. The price in either case was a life. It was not clear how a man transferred rights over the life of his mother or sister, or other relative for the power of sorcery, since no one admitted to having done it. But it was thought that if he merely withdrew his protection, merely consented to the death of one of his own clansmen, a sorcerer could then kill with impunity the person thus exposed. 'If no clansman gives leave for you to be killed, the weapons of the sorcerer fly by you, harmless. You cannot be killed if your clan all want you to live—except by God.'

Whereas they thought that anyone with a powerful motive might commit sorcery once or twice, the person whom the Lele feared and abhorred was the fully committed sorcerer, given over entirely to his lusts. His victims were withdrawn from the normal cycle of reincarnation, and made his familiars (*nkadi*, *mikadi*), in the form of carnivorous animals. They carried his messages, spread illness for him, hid the game, turned aside hunters' arrows. They ate no wild food, but snatched chickens and goats from villages, and craved for human flesh. If not regularly supplied with this by their master, they would one day turn and kill him. In this way the Lele saw the once-committed sorcerer pressed on to kill more and more. He became utterly depraved, denatured. He had broken kinship with mankind, and made it with the wild beasts. He ate no animal meat, only the putrefying flesh of human victims. While he existed in a village no enterprise could prosper. For jealousy of their happiness he killed small children. He envied the young and the strong, and blighted them too. He polluted the water-supply. He 'poisoned' the hunters' whetstones, blunted their arrows, in animal form he ran before them and saved their quarry.

The sorcerer was thus one who acted essentially from irrational motives. He belonged to a realm of discourse which had its own logic, contrary to that which ruled other people. There was no need to seek in social relations for motive, when a particular person was suspected. The more unlikely and outrageous the crime he was thought to have committed, the more typical a sorcerer he was thought to be. It was enough for him to have acquired an initial reputation for sorcery for the most far-fetched accusations to stick.

This is very unlike the witchcraft beliefs described in other parts of Central Africa, where jealousy of office and possessions are thought to motivate witches.[2] We need to ask how the Lele could live with such corrosive beliefs and whether there were any checks and balances which operated to limit the scope of accusations. At first glance one would suppose that their beliefs in sorcery would destroy any hope of corporate unity in the village.

First, to complete the description of the Lele image of the sorcerer, the type of person who was thought to give himself up to sorcery in this total sense was not a woman, not a young man, but an old man, usually a diviner. Barren or unfaithful women were occasionally accused of sorcery against their husbands. But they were not cited as the usual type from which sorcerers were drawn. The lack of status competition in their lives and their ignorance of divination made it implausible that they should be accused: 'A woman! What would she know of rites (*nengu*)? How could she get sorcery?'

Young men, also accused individually in practice, were in principle excluded from suspicion, because of their ignorance of ritual matters. The unity of knowledge indicated diviners as the most obvious group of people since they had professional access to sorcery techniques. Among them, some were old, ill, neglected. They were thought to resent the happiness of others, and to take no interest in the success of the communal hunt or in the yield of palms if their junior kinsmen forgot to bring them a share of the meat or to give them wine. They gradually slipped into sorcery as human pleasures slipped out of their grasp. The normative effect of these beliefs was easily seen. People tried to meet adversity with a brave face, uncomplaining and undemanding.

In practice, accusations of sorcery did not generally fall on lonely unfortunates. Lele were noticeably punctilious about not making allegations which would make the life of a sick, old person more difficult for him. In fact, the most generally accused types were stronger characters, persistent adulterers, irascible temperaments, intriguers, the men who had got their fingers burned one way or another by not conforming to the Lele ideal of unassuming kindliness, control and tact. They were not necessarily very old, not necessarily neglected, but self-regarding, hot-tempered types.

[2] Marwick (1952), and Mitchell (1957).

If accused witches or sorcerers are punished, accusations become a technique of social control. In the Cewa-Nyanja-Yao group of peoples in Nyasaland it was either the envious heirs, younger brothers or uncles, who were suspected of attempting witchcraft to usurp the status of their seniors, or the older men who were accused by their ambitious juniors.[3] Among the Lele it was the old men, the powerful diviners, who were thought to be jealous of the young men. The significance of this lies in the barely veiled hostility which marked the relations between generations of men, and in the massive, but precarious privileges which the older men had an interest in protecting.

I could cite many examples of hostility against young men, expressed in the general terms of conflict between *baotale* and *babilenge*, old and young men. Quarrels between initiates and non-initiates, Christians and pagans, and between age-sets, were spoken of indiscriminately as disputes between *baotale* and *babilenge*.

Although the material and technical conditions of the economy were weighted against the older men, they were able to pre-empt the young girls and to practise polygyny, while forcing the active young men to remain as bachelors. In the pre-colonial days the hostility between old and young was likely to have been as strong as at the time of fieldwork, since the discrepancy between their privileges was greater, but in those days the old held the system more tightly in their grasp, and so the hostility was more controlled. Remember too that an old man was not easily able to change his residence.

In this delicate equilibrium between old and young men, a plausible accusation of sorcery against a particular old man was undoubtedly a weapon which could redress the balance, if individual old men were to push their claims too far.

Accusations of sorcery must inevitably reflect the real distribution of power. For all their privilege in cult and in marriage, the old men, and the whole economy, depended on the brawn and muscle of the young. To protest that they feared sorcery or to propose leaving the village as the victims of sorcery, was an effective way for the young to spike the guns of a senior antagonist. Old men tended to wear a deprecatory and self-effacing manner, possibly a defence against the general belief that they

[3] Marwick (1952), and Mitchell (1957).

were potential dangerous characters. Certainly, their failure to exert authority in all their relations with the young men is consistent with the use of sorcery beliefs against them as a counter-weapon of control.

Given that no rational motives were thought to direct the sorcerer, and also that old men and especially old diviners were thought to be sorcerers, we need to ask whether there were any countervailing beliefs to check a build-up of accusations at every point of tension. Otherwise, sorcery beliefs by widening rifts and undermining all authority would destroy village unity. In fact, there were many checks.

For one, people were afraid to accuse a sorcerer by name. So for the most part, sorcery remained an uncharted dimension of social life. People whispered, used hints and euphemisms, and rarely voiced precise suspicions openly. They feared the sorcerer's quick retaliation if he were to hear his name discussed. If sorcery were to be revealed by an oracle as causing a person's sickness, his kin did not try to identify the sorcerer. They had their suspicions, based on the enmities of the sick one. But they directed all their efforts to placating the unnamed sorcerer, or frightening or shaming him by public speeches extolling the victim, or begging and commanding him to be left alone. One family, which tried to find the name of the sorceror who was making their child sick, was held to blame when the child shortly afterwards died. They were sued for blood compensation by its lords, since it was agreed that they had gone out of their way to invite trouble by getting the name of the sorcerer while the child was still ill.

Divination

The most effective check of all on a build-up of sorcery accusations lay in the fact that the men whom popular accord was most ready to accuse were those who operated the oracles. It is not surprising that they tried to use their authority to turn suspicions away. When death occurred, the deceased's kin consulted diviners in the hope of pinning responsibility on to someone capable of paying a blood debt. There were various divinatory techniques. The rubbing oracle, *Itumbwa*, was the commonest, but there was also a whistling oracle, *Kapulu* (worked by a feat of ventriloquism), a horn oracle, *Kahei*, a sniffing bag oracle, and others more mysterious, said to involve use of skulls of sorcerers' victims. Consultations took place in private, the diviner announcing afterwards to his clients the results of his seance. None of these techniques was regarded as incontrovertible by all the parties. The first consultation would be held by, or at the expense of the kinsmen of the deceased, but the killer thus denounced invariably rejected the verdict. The second consultation would be held at an oracle agreed by both parties.

The verdict of divination which was not accepted by both parties risked reversal by another oracle. If every verdict were regularly contested, the credit of divination in general, and the diviner's prowess in particular, were likely to be impaired. This may further account for the tendency of diviners to place responsibility for deaths in quarters where the charge would not

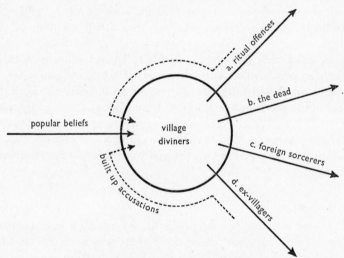

Fig. 9. Incidence of sorcery accusations

Popular beliefs inculpated elderly diviners of village, but these operated oracles which exculpated themselves by attributing sickness and misfortune to:

(a) ritual offences: sexual pollution or breach of cult rules
(b) the dead: clansmen punishing former neglect by cursing descendants or dead executing vengeance on sorcers who caused their own deaths or dead victims of sorcery turned familiars
(c) foreign sorcerers: official diviners from enemy village using lightning and sandstorm for political ends or foreign diviners who killed a sick person they had once treated
(d) ex-members of the village.

But in spite of this diversion of popular beliefs away from local diviners, some accusations tended to build up against one or two of them.

be disputed. Friends of the deceased might whisper the names
of suspected sorcerers, but when the case was finally submitted
to divination, the diviner was likely to blame the dead or someone who had already quarrelled and left the place. It was in the
interests of diviners as a profession, and consistent with much
else in Lele culture that they should seek to avoid verdicts which
would disrupt the village.

Diviners formally consulted tended to divert suspicions of
sorcery away from fellow-villagers. The work of spirits, or
automatic sanctions for sexual pollution or breach of cult rules
were favoured kinds of explanation. Another was the power of
the dead to harm the living. If sorcery was blamed at all, diviners
were more likely to indicate sorcerers living at a distance, unnamed sorcerers from enemy villages, or foreign sorcerers who
had just visited the village and left. When they indicated a
resident as a sorcerer, responsible for a death in the village, it
was likely to be someone who was not a full member of the
village.

The dead were thought to be able to harm the living in three
ways; by posthumous sorcery prepared while still alive, by a
curse or by ghostly familiars of living or dead sorcerers. Both the
curse and posthumous sorcery were thought to rectify past
injustice. The former avenged past neglect, and the latter avenged
killing by sorcery. God would not allow a sorcerer to avenge
his own death, therefore only the just were able to do posthumous
vengeance.

Posthumous sorcery

Nghongo was the rite or medicine, by which a man ensured
vengeance for his own future death. One who made *nghongo* for
himself would publicize it widely, thus indicating his own innocence, and hoping to deter sorcerers from killing him. It was
equally common for a man to arrange such a vengeance for the
life of his wife, or a child, as a kind of insurance.

One man, Pung, told me about his brother's death. The dying man
told him not to consult oracles to find his killer: 'When I am dead, don't
mourn for me, don't follow my corpse to the grave. Wait and watch in
the village, and you will see a man die. My *nghongo* will get him.' Sure
enough, as he waited while others buried his brother, he saw a man die,

then, knowing that vengeance was done, he went off to mourn and weep.

When it was known that a man had done *nghongo*, there was no need to consult oracles to discover the cause of his death, nor that of the next person to die. The two consecutive deaths cancelled one another, so no compensation was required for either. Sometimes a dead man would be made to take the blame for more than one death. It was then said that the vengeance rite had been excessively strong, so that it claimed too many victims, or that more than one sorcerer had conspired to kill the one dead man.

For example, old Nyama,[4] who in the course of his lingering last illness expressed much bitterness against his neighbours, warned his clansmen that even while they were burying him, the first of the sorcerers who had killed him would die, and that while they were burying that one, they would find the next dying, and that even when he had finished killing his own murderers, he would still go on killing. An epidemic followed his death, and so many dead were attributed to his ghostly vengeance that the village moved its site to escape him, the Christians persuaded the mission priest to say a Mass of exorcism, and his younger brother tried to break his power by exhuming the corpse, gouging out the eyes and cutting off the hands. (See death of Ngapici, below.)

One man assured me that the posthumous vengeance which he had arranged for himself was not the kind that was likely thus to get out of control.

The village of Potambishi had a recent history of ghostly vengeance that became famous among the other Lele. It was told that their *ilumbi* had prepared vengeance so terrible that at his burial people saw a python go before, and a leopard follow the coffin. That very night, when they got back to the village, they heard his voice announcing: 'Now that I am dead, look out, all of you. What are you going to drink? Will you drink trees? Will you drink earth? Look out!'

For weeks the people stayed in their huts until broad daylight. If a man went too early to the forest, he would meet the ghost in the path to the stream. No one who saw him survived. They died in numbers. Finally, they decided to break away and hide from him. Orders were given that next day everyone was to hide in their huts until the sun was high. Then they were to come out, leaving everything behind. Not one

[4] Lubelo clan, see p. 151.

thing was to be taken, clothes they had worn, baskets, knives, matchets, tools. They went and hid in the forest, then they built a new village, from new materials, with new tools. They shook him off, and everything was peaceful and good. They didn't see the ghost again. Then one man couldn't resist going back to the deserted village to get a dog bell. Next day they saw the ghost again and people died. So they did the same again, hid in their huts, abandoned their village in full daylight and started afresh. After this, the ghost lost contact with them for good.

These vividly recounted stories of posthumous vengeance were important in confirming belief in a favourite verdict of diviners which could not be refuted and which no one had a direct personal interest in trying to refute.[5]

The curse of the dead

The curse of the dead was called *mimbera*. If a woman's babies died, or if she miscarried several times, the diviner might diagnose *mimbera*, the harm from her own dead clansfolk. The remedy was a series of potions accompanied by rules which put her out of contact with any members of her clan. She could not even taste food nor touch water brought by her own mother, or speak to her, or let her breasts be seen by any one of them, until her next baby was safely born. *Mimbera* was thought to be caused by angry dead, who had died suffering an injustice, for instance a false accusation of sorcery.

Familiars (*Mikadi*)

The last of the three types of divinatory verdict which contradicted the belief that a death had been caused by living sorcerers, was that it had been caused by a sorcerer's ghostly familiars. These were believed capable of causing a whole string of deaths, even after their master's own death.

The father of Bukoko was killed like that. He was ill, and they got a diviner from abroad to treat him. He did, and he went away. But

[5] That posthumous sorcery was a widespread belief in the Congo, see Verhulpen, *Baluba et Balubaisés*, p. 173 . . . 'Lorsque le divination révèlent que les manes des ancêtres ou des membres défunts de la communauté sont trop turbulents et causent des malheurs, la famille s'addresse aux Bakasandji. Le soir le défunt est déterré, décapité et brûlé . . .' See also R. de Beaucorps for similar beliefs among the Bayansi.

when he went he *homene* the sick man, so that only his body was left. His body stayed there, and wasted away. He died. But the real man (father of Bukoko) was his *nkadi* (familiar), in the power of the man who killed him. The owner gives his familiars food to eat, and uses them to scare the game away from the hunters. But the familiar will be full of anger at having been made to leave his home and family; he will ask his owner: 'Give me a man to kill.' So the owner tells him who of his clan first gave permission for him to be killed. So the familiar at once kills whoever it was, his mother or mother's brother. That one also becomes the familiar of the sorcerer. In time the band of familiars may swell to ten! A familiar cannot be deceived, he is full of anger, and very strong to kill. If their owner dies, the familiars are never reborn. They wander about for ever. They chase game, come to the village for chickens, occasionally they kill a man. If the sorcerer is killed by his own familiars—if he doesn't give them enough to eat, or enough people to kill—then he will be reborn, because familiars cannot make a man into a familiar, they are just ordinary people (i.e. not sorcerers).

If it was not the dead, or breach of ritual, then foreign sorcery was frequently indicated by diviners as the source of trouble. Sorcery was not entirely restricted by geographical range. True, a man who was consistently ill in one village would suspect its members to be working against him, and might be advised to leave to escape their machinations. But sorcerors could work at long range from another village, even from a distant one, using lightning or sand-storms. Long-range sorcery was less able to discriminate its targets. Hence it was that foreign sorcery was thought to represent political action taken by enemy villages when the identity of the victim was of no importance, while local sorcery expressed personal conflicts within a village.

Official diviner

The official diviner or *ilumbi* had to protect the village from these enemy attacks of sorcery. All diviners learnt something about sorcery in acquiring techniques to combat it, but the official diviner had to be himself a very powerful sorcerer. He had to be able to hurl back lightning against other villages, be able to assume leopard form to fight leopards sent by enemy villages, and to be able to use the ghosts (*miendo*) of his own victims as familiars for divination. Above all, he had to be capable of joining other sorcerers at their night-time dances.

There he should bargain with them, for the lives of his friends, and outwit them with double-dealing on behalf of his village.

Torday[6] described a conversation with the *ilumbi* of Mushenge, interrupted by a storm and a flash of lightning which shivered a palm tree near them. Instantly the *ilumbi* struck an attitude of command, pointing a finger at the charred stump, and thereafter claimed credit for saving the village by having diverted the lightning into the palm tree. Among the Lele, too, control of lightning was in the special province of the *ilumbi*. Several defences against it were known. One village had small basket fish-traps strung on high poles around it, another had something buried in the centre. Men sometimes wore a special green leaf pinned in their hair as a personal safeguard while they travelled.

Apart from lightning, the second main danger from foreign sorcerers was from sand-storms. The enemy was thought to enter the village in the dry season in the guise of a whirl of wind, striking illness right and left. Defence against this too was the prime responsibility of the *ilumbi*. At the beginning of the dry season, he should call all the village together, and administer potions and anal injections to them, to protect them from the illness which generally characterized the season.[7]

When inter-village fighting was suppressed, the scope of his office was more than halved. In the old days, before a raid was to take place, he was supposed to meet the sorcerers of the enemy village by night, and plan with them the course of the fighting. They agreed on the casualties by a process of hard bargaining, each trying to satisfy his own grudges, save his friends, and give away only the lives of those he had no interest in preserving. Next morning the official diviner, waking his own village, called out the men in a file and administered protective rites to those who were going to fight. Double-crossing the sorcerers he had bargained with, he tipped off those whom he knew would be going to their prearranged deaths. It must have been reassuring for the warriors to be told before the fight, by a friendly *ilumbi*: 'You can go, you can go, you can go!' All the more reassuring since he would stop others, saying, 'Not you today! You stay at home.'

After the fight, he treated the wounded. If his village scored

6 1925.
7 See Chapter I, p. 20.

less deaths than the enemy, he was expected to use sorcery to equalize the losses. When his village wished to make a lasting truce with a former enemy, the *ilumbi* had to brew a peace-cup for them all to drink, to obliterate memory of their past hostility.

Since his main role was to defend the village from foreign sorcery, the *ilumbi's* existence had the incidental effect of diverting people's suspicions away from the sorcerers within the village, and focusing them on outsiders. Every thunder-storm and dry season epidemic reminded people of the external, anonymous enemy. In relieving some of the pressure of suspicion against the enemies at home, his role would help to revive the feeling of village solidarity which was always liable to disintegrate under mutual suspicions of sorcery. At a ritual level, the *ilumbi* complemented the role of the village head, and also that of the *Ndwi* or warrior.

As an arch-sorcerer himself, he was at any time likely to be under suspicion. If hunting failed too often he would be given the poison ordeal. Because of his necessary control of sorcery, people tried to eliminate occasions of conflict between himself and his village. Adultery with one of his wives was condemned as an offence against the village, and the fine was correspondingly heavy. On his part he was not allowed to have sexual intercourse with village-wives and could be fined for doing so. These rules, setting him out of the range of normal quarrels about women, were supported by the belief that his ritual would kill instead of curing any with whom he mixed his sexual affairs. When tending the wounded after a raid, he would ask them first if they had gone with his wives: if they said no, he treated them, and they would soon be cured. If they admitted yes, then he passed them over. If they were to conceal their adultery, and take his healing potion, then they would automatically die. Similarly, if he went with a village-wife, and then did rites for the village, all his patients who had had sexual contact with that woman would die. This sanction was thought to work automatically, and without any intervention or even knowledge on his part, the condition of the efficacy of his treatment. But his jealousy was also feared because of his sorcery. Ritual separation of the widow from the dead husband, a minor rite in an ordinary case, was very important for the widow of the *ilumbi*. If she died soon after him, full blood-compensation was claimed from the clan of the *ilumbi* for if they had neglected the ritual, it was held certain that the dead *ilumbi* had killed her in jealousy.

This is a consistent adaptation to Lele values. All men were expected to be vengeful if their wives were tampered with. The *ilumbi's* revenge would be too deadly to bear. Consequently the *ilumbi's* wives were set apart from all other women, and he himself excluded from intercourse with the common wives of the village, so that situations calling for such revenge should not arise.

The ideal candidate for the post of *ilumbi* was a gentle, soft-spoken, trustworthy character, not likely to rouse antipathies against himself. He was referred to as *ngal a babola*, the village-wife, a comment on his role as a dedicated public servant. Usually there were two official diviners in each village, the senior choosing and initiating the junior. If an *ilumbi* acquired a good reputation for hunting or healing rites, he might be invited to other villages, where he would stay for two or three months, to set them right and then be escorted home with drums and much wealth in camwood and raffia. He handed the fees to the village treasury, whence some portion would be returned to him.

When the oracular verdicts of sorcery pointed to living persons, they generally fell on people who were absent or to whom odium of one kind or another was already attached. For example, it was common to blame a foreign diviner who had recently been called in to save the patient. Several people told me that oracles had revealed that their parent had died at the hands of the ritual expert who had been brought from abroad to cure him. The motive of this unprofessional conduct was the well-known desire of sorcerers to use a dead man's spirit as a familiar. Suspicion of outsiders was thus reinforced.

In spite of all these alternatives suggested in divination, laymen still nursed their private suspicions that their misfortunes were caused by local sorcerers. To test these suspicions it was often necessary to consult an outside oracle. I noticed that fellow-villagers were less likely to be denounced by oracles consulted in the village than by distant oracles. The latter, partly because they were more likely to confirm the consulter's worst fears, were held in very high esteem. Hence too the disapproval voiced by local diviners against villagers who took their custom else-where. In general, the tendency of local oracles, if they indicated the living at all, was to name someone who had recently left the village following a quarrel, or persons who had arrived as guests after suspicions of sorcery had made their own village too hot for them, and who were likely to remain marginal to village society.

For example, in 1950, a young woman, whose adultery had caused her husband to quarrel with another man, ran away from the village when her husband died. In one quarter it was held that he had died as a result of ritual vengeance, himself a convicted sorcerer (see *Melu*, below). But his close kinsmen did not admit his guilt, and their consultations revealed his runaway wife as having poisoned him (with sorcery) in order to marry a lover. No member of her clan was present to rebut the charge, and the matter remained inconclusive.

For a woman to commit sorcery was contrary to most of the common beliefs about it, but if she was childless, had left the village, and was also unsupported by a strong local clan section, her guilt seemed not to be incredible.

It is important to appreciate the inconclusiveness of these oracular findings, and the impossibility of shifting partisans from their preconvictions about guilt. However much confidence Lele had in the validity of their oracles as such, they were equally convinced of the guile of their fellow-men. If they had not personally been present at a consultation, if its verdict was unpalatable they would doubt whether it had ever taken place, or whether it had been truthfully reported, or correctly performed.

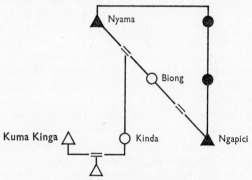

Fig. 10. Nyama's widow

We have already described the redoubtable vengeance accredited to the dead Nyama. At one stage before his death his wife, Biong, was accused of trying to kill him. As she survived his ghostly vengeance, one would have thought her innocence was proved, but the subsequent deaths of her next husband, Ngapici,[8] and of her grandchildren, were by some attributed to her, and by others to Nyama's ghost.

Ngapici, while he lived, divined that Kinda's child was dying from the sorcery of its dead grandfather. He took Kinda with him to Nyama's grave, and after mutilating the corpse, performed a rite to protect her and her child. To allow a woman to see a diviner's grave was an offence against diviners in general but he took the risk of retribution knowingly, for the sake of the cure he hoped to do. According to one body of opinion in the village his rash act brought down Nyama's final vengeance on himself and on the sick child. Some time later, finding a jackal in one of his traps, he understood that Nyama had caught up with him. He returned to the village very faint and ill, saying: 'Today I have seen my death!' After that, his strength ebbed, and he died. The child's subsequent death was divined as due to the same cause, and Kinda was advised to leave the village, for her own sake. She accepted the invitation to become a village-wife in the next village.

Her only remaining kinswoman in the village she had left, her widowed mother, Biong, quarrelled with young men of Ngapici's clan about palm wine, and was accused by them of putting human faeces in the disputed palm tree. The fact that it was far too high a palm for an old woman to climb, and a physically impossible place for anyone to defecate in, only lent verisimilitude to the idea that she must be a very dangerous sorcerer. Later she was found by divination to have attempted sorcery to kill the boys with whom she had disputed the rights to the palm wine, and to have earlier killed her first and second husband. On one version she was chased out of the village, on another she left voluntarily to go to stay with clansmen. When she was gone, her son-in-law, Kumaking, consulted an oracle in the village about the death of his child. The diviner indicated Biong as guilty of this too, and Kumaking, anxious to get his wife back, not to offend his mother-in-law, and at the same time anxious to know if he had a case for compensation, was planning to raise funds to consult another diviner, distant, and with a weightier reputation.

No one who believed the story of Nyama's powers of vengeance could also believe that his widow was the sorcerer who had killed him and his brother, Ngapici, and her own grandchild. But certainly, not every one subscribed to the theory that Ngapici was a victim of posthumous vengeance. For one thing, his death took place several years after that of Nyama. His clansmen suspected his widow, but his son suspected his clansmen, and thought it sinister that they had never consulted a famous diviner about his death.

[8] Appendix A, Figure 12, C1.

I could cite other instances of conflicting theories about the causes of any particular death, and of the inconclusiveness of divinatory methods. But, understandably, each time that a divination turned up a name which had been turned up before, the suggestion that so-and-so was a sorcerer, incredible at first, gained weight. There was a tendency for sorcery accusations from diverse sources to accumulate at one point once the mud-slinging had begun. If the object of these accusations left the village, it was as good as offering himself as target for more miscellaneous accusations. Diviners seemed to have less inhibitions about naming an absent and widely suspected person.

It is essential to distinguish popular suspicions from diviners' findings. The former regularly inclined towards sorcery, and everyone had their own theories about guilt. Professional diviners, on the other hand, as a body and individually, were very cautious. They frequently asked people to be careful, lest death by natural causes should start up a hunt for sorcerors. For example, when some children ate the rotting flesh of a hyena, which no adult would have dreamed of touching, an old diviner spoke in the village, reproaching the person who had given the children the unwholesome meat: 'If they die of bad food, their mothers will start blaming sorcery.' On another occasion, young Christians defied their seniors and ate meats which were reserved to the pagan cults. In the ensuing quarrel, a diviner from the north who happened to be visiting, told the cult members to restrain their anger: 'Supposing one of these boys is ill to-morrow, and supposing he dies? Who will be accused of having killed him? Does any of you want to be called the sorcerer?' It was common ground with older men that women, when trouble fell, tended to rush about accusing everyone of sorcery, without any evidence. Diviners at least were aware of the danger to the community of indiscriminate accusations.

The image of the sorcerer as, first and foremost, a senior diviner, would appear to be another of those devices[9] which control frivolous and disruptive accusations. The diviners acted as a brake on public opinion, and diverted suspicions from members of the village to outsiders, or to marginal persons whose downfall would not split the village into opposed camps.

The very inconclusiveness of divination favoured the splitting

[9] See Mayer.

of opinion. Every local clan section tended to have its own diviner, whom they expected to divine, and if need be to commit sorcery on their behalf, and whom they also would be ready to suspect of sacrificing their lives as the price of sorcery powers. Some in each large clan section would be ready to disown any one of its diviners, and others ready to stand by him. At the level of sorcery and divination the beliefs corresponded to the covert competition between senior men in such secular matters as wife-getting or raffia-giving. Each diviner was expected to protect his own friends and relatives from the sorcery of his colleagues, and to build up a personal following from among them. In practice they showed considerably more *esprit de corps*.

In the old days the conflicting views would have been sustained by both parties, until resolved by the poison ordeal.[10] Since killing by sorcery gave a case for blood compensation, all the clansmen of the accused would have been in the habit of defending his innocence (unless the victim was one of themselves). In most of the cases described in Chapter VIII in which a blood debt incurred by living sorcerers was settled, the girl was captured by wile or force from a rival village, and the enforced settlement acquiesced in by her owners if she herself consented to it. I have no records of a living person, accused of killing by sorcery, consenting to his responsibility and paying compensation.

When a serious accusation of sorcery was made within a village, if resentment was not to fester indefinitely a conclusive verdict of guilt or acquittal was needed. This the poison ordeal used to give. Its role was so central to the working of their system of beliefs that it is surprising if any intelligibility remains after its suppression. However, we must try to interpret what place it may have filled, by examining what happened in its absence.

At the time of fieldwork, after accusations started to fall on a particular person, the sequel moved into four main phases. First, not one but several accusations would reach the same target, so that one individual found himself bearing much of the acrimony of other people's disputes, or rather, found that his own quarrels and the deaths of people near him acquired for him a new sinister significance. Second, the pressure of public hostility (which might formerly have sent him to the ordeal) would force

[10] Prohibited by Décret, 24.12.1923. Bulletin Official, 1924, p. 54.

him to leave his village. It was not necessarily because diviners had found him guilty of killing. Bwato, for example, left Middle Homba because he could not stand being cold-shouldered and refused drinks. Makut (below) did not leave in the first place because of diviners officially finding him guilty, but because of the intervention of a European in response to popular opinion, but in his absence divination did convict him. When he was finally sent away, his hut was torn down by a shouting, angry mob. Biong, above, was sent away after a Chokwe diviner found her guilty.

Third, the eviction was found to do nothing to soothe the animosities in the village. His supporters, still protesting his innocence, nursed their own convictions as to the true culprit

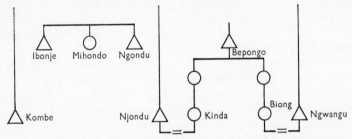

Fig. 11. The three senior men of Hanja clan section in Middle Homba

sheltering behind him. If anything, tension was aggravated. Illness and death still occurred, so that those ills which were not fastened on him were attributed to others in the village. Unity was as unattained as ever, and blood compensation could not be collected, though it would be claimed.

Fourth, wherever the rejected individual went for asylum, his reputation went with him and he tended to attract more convictions, and be thrust out again.

In 1949–50, Ibonje, the eldest male of the Hanja clan section, was living in the north, having been forced to leave because of sorcery accusations, and particularly after having quarrelled with his full brother, Ngondu. He had been the famous warrior mentioned on p. 188, Ch. X. Bepongo was the next eldest, a Pangolin Man, and Ngondu was *Ilumbi* for the village. By 1953 Ngondu had been driven out of the village, accused of spoiling the hunting by his sorcery. Ibonje, lame and half-blind, took the opportunity to come home, to be cared for by his old sister, Mihondo, saying he had been unjustly accused by

Ngondu. He proceeded to dispute with Bepongo about the allocation of the two girls, Kinda and Biong. One had been given in marriage to Njondu, and the other was promised to Ngwangu. Kombe was living as house-husband of a village-wife with no wife of his own.

Planning to get Biong for himself, Kombe brought palm wine and meat to Ibonje, built him a hut, and succeeding in making him his advocate with Bepongo. Invoking the principle that daughters' daughters of clansmen should be allocated according to the view of the senior member of the clan section rather than according to the whims of the girl's own mother's father, Ibonje told Bepongo that Biong should be given to Kombe. But Bepongo refused to break his promise to Ngwangu, whom he personally favoured. Then Ibonje changed his tack, and pointed out that Kinda was not happy with Njondu, and was childless. It was only a matter of time before she would leave him, so it would be better to transfer her now to a more virile clan member, such as Kombe, rather than lose her altogether. Njondu, whose wife admittedly did not get on well with him, saw that he stood in the way of the plans of Kombe and Ibonje. He publicly accused Ibonje of sorcery against him, and left the village, protesting that his life was not safe there. Later he was accepted as a candidate to the diviners' noviceship.

What other wheels within wheels were turning in that village, I do not know, as I was not living in it. There was probably a rivalry between the founding clans (Hanja, Lumbunji and Bucwa). At all events, by 1953, all three of the old men of the Hanja clan had been discredited and exiled. First Ngondu was driven out. Then Ibonje was rumoured to have died in the poison ordeal administered to him on the other bank of the Loange. Bepongo, having been driven away on sorcery charges, had gone to stay in the village of his birth, Bwawa, with the wife whom he had married there. His other two wives, his daughters and sons were convinced of his innocence. In Bwawa it was not long before he was accused of sorcery afresh. Ill, and losing his eye-sight, he seemed to be in danger of the same fate that overtook Makut of Ngoie, being out-lawed from human society altogether.

I only heard of Makut's case when he had already been sent away from the village of Ngoie, his name having become a by-word for the most depraved and bestial sorcery. He had been sent to prison for manslaughter after a young Flemish doctor, fresh from Europe, had happened to be in the village when they were wailing over the corpse of Makut's alleged latest victim. Before that date, Makut, though he had his detractors, had been a respected diviner following his calling. He belonged to the large founding clan of Bulumbu, which was split into several factions. Called to the sick bed of one of his clansmen, he was trying to save him and squeezed some liquid into his eyes, when the sick man died. Shown the body, the European doctor confirmed that death had taken place, and was told (through interpreters) that the dead man had been poisoned (the usual expression for committing sorcery), and that the poisoner was old Makut. On being asked, Makut readily produced the bottle which held the remains of the concoction he had used, which the doctor judged to be noxious. On this evidence, backed by his own admission of other 'poisonings', Makut was sent to prison to Luebo for manslaughter. In his absence, his reputation for evil grew to such wild proportions that, when the term of his sentence was shortened because of his ill-health, and the village heard he was to return home, a general exodus was threatened. There was no mistaking the panic and dismay at news of his return. Visitors left precipitately. Wives carried off their children to visit their mothers. At all the weaving looms and pounding places people were discussing the danger of letting him return. I was begged to intervene, to get him sent elsewhere, and was asked how I would do my work in a deserted village and how I would eat meat if no game were killed. The clamour against him was so violent, and seemed so universal, that I was astonished to learn that Makut was being met and carried home by two of his clansmen, one, his full brother. Later, when he was expelled from the village and when no other place would receive him, his brother never left him and the two men were said to be living in the forest, the younger caring for the older. It was obvious that friends from the village were sending food to them, for they survived there for a long time.

Bwato of Mbombe[11] was the fifth example of an exile. For quarrels, indiscretion and adultery he had earned the rancour of his own clansmen and women and been turned out of two villages. Each new accusation of sorcery stuck, because of previous ones. But he too was not without his supporters in his clan, who would have favoured an alternative explanation of the deaths which were, by others, being attributed to him.

In S. Homba, he and Makaka were poised, one against the other, as alternatives for those who sought to blame sorcery within the village. Makaka had never been expelled from his village, but he had taken the poison ordeal before. Now, not old, but a leper, like Bwato, and like him, embroiled in many quarrels about women, and like Bwato again, suspected by his own clansmen of killing them off for spite, he was in an even more exposed position, because of his office as *Ilumbi*.

All six of these accused sorcerers, who aroused popular suspicion, were diviners, all were in the second oldest age-set, all were members of one of the founding clans of their own village. Each was one of the senior men of a large local clan section, including at least seven men. For Bepongo, Bwato and Makaka, at least, the quarrels they were involved

[11] See Chapter V, p. 108.

in concerned rights over women, either claimed for themselves, or on behalf of younger men of the clan. They had each lost some of the support of their junior clansmen, who accused them of sorcery, but each had adherents who declared them innocent. Without some definitive verdict, therefore, the village would remain in conflict with itself. Expulsion of the suspected man did not produce the harmony which the Lele tried so hard to achieve. In the old days, recourse to the poison ordeal would have had a different result, and it is likely that men who had become notorious as sorcerers would have welcomed the ordeal as a final answer to their problems.

XIII

CONTROL OF SORCERY

IT WAS impossible to learn how often they resorted to the poison ordeal, *ipome*, or how many people it killed.[1] Lele said they frequently used it and that many succumbed. Verdicts of *ipome* figure in histories of blood compensation, but not very often and not always as convictions. It was forbidden by law in 1924, and by 1950 the institution seemed to have disappeared from Lele life. It was said to be still administered in secret in the border areas of Lele country. I was not able to identify the tree whose bark was used in the potion. One diviner showed me a small piece of bark, which he said he kept to test his private suspicions. A few scrapings in a man's drink, he said, would cause him to vomit if he was innocent, and to die if guilty of sorcery. *Ipome* could not lie. It was God's medicine (*nengu*), and above any question. The same old man had had to pay blood compensation for a death attributed to his own mother, who had succumbed in the ordeal. He shrugged his shoulders laconically on the subject of her guilt: 'If people kill, they must die. *Ipome* is God's thing, it cannot deceive us.'

Another man, whose innocence had twice been vindicated by the poison ordeal, described it to me. The village of Bwawa used to have an *ipome* tree, and the men of Makasu used to go there and pay to take away large quantities of bark. When South Homba had a single case to settle, they took the suspect to Makasu. The clan of the accused bore the costs if he proved guilty, his accusers, if he survived, forty raffia cloths for Makasu. Another *ipome* tree was said to grow near Mikope, and others on the right bank of the Lumbundji river. They were evidently scarce, and a source of profit for those living near them, or those who specialized in collecting the bark.

If there were several candidates for the ordeal, the village would send its men to buy *ipome* from one of the villages which

[1] In a good account of poison ordeal in a neighbouring tribe, Weekx (1937) says it was almost a daily occurrence.

241

kept a store. The accused were ordered to sleep outside the
village, in an enclosure built for them among the palms. They
were not allowed to eat cooked food, only bananas, which gave
them the best chance of survival. Their numbers were increased
by volunteers, friends or relatives, who, as a gesture of faith in
their innocence, would take the ordeal with the accused. The
bahaka (officials of the ordeal) returned with the bark, and
pounded it, singing as they worked. When the concoction was
ready, the *bahaka* each drank it first, to prove their own innocence
and fitness to officiate. Then they administered it, singing and
dancing, to the accused in turn. As each accused sorcerer came
up, his friend or loyal clansman would step in front of him, forbidding him to drink first. Since his heart was clean he had
nothing to fear. 'If you die, we die together,' he would say. Such
volunteers did not necessarily always survive the ordeal. *Ipome*
would catch them if their goodness had been a sham. Some of the
accused would vomit, and thus proved innocent, joined the
dancers. Then, when everyone had drunk, those who had not
yet vomited were made to dance and run. Movement was
supposed to help the stomach to reject the poison. So, chased
with sticks and whips by the *bahaka*, they ran until they collapsed
and died. The survivors triumphantly re-entered the village,
singing and dancing; their clansmen and wives welcomed them
with gifts of raffia cloth. Their false accusers were made to pay
a full blood compensation for the injury to their name. My
informant, Makaka, graphically described his sensations on the
two occasions he underwent the ordeal; his triumphant vomiting,
and his dances and songs of defiance against his enemies. He was
obviously ready to take it again if need be. Since he was again
widely suspected of sorcery, he felt the difficulty of silencing his
accusers without that recourse.

Ipome was a delicate subject. It would have been impossible to
expect a trustworthy answer to the questions which spring to
mind. Could the ordeal be rigged? Or were the officiants in the
dark about how the poison worked? All I can say is that its disappearance left a big gap in the village institutions.

First, accusations were made more freely than they would have
been before, since an accuser who could not be proved wrong
could not be made to pay compensation for blackening another's
name. Second, explicit threats of sorcery were heard. It had been

common before to make oblique warnings, for example: 'Youths have died for this before now—take care,' or 'Next time it rains—watch out' (a reference to lightning). But these vague remarks were made in defence of the privileges of a cult group or an age-group. To threaten sorcery to defend an individual right was not likely in the days of the poison ordeal, but it was occasionally done in the 1950's. As the memory of the poison ordeal faded, sorcery loomed larger and nearer. It became cumulatively more oppressive as means of dealing with it were more effectively forbidden.

The custom of administering the ordeal to a group of suspects, some of whom died and others survived, vindicated the survivors' innocence in several ways. In one sense, the survivor had literally faced and overcome death itself. His false accusers owed him full blood compensation, as if for having wished him dead. The same people would not accuse him again lightly. A new series of oracular consultations concerning the killings of which he had been previously accused would soon bring the social forces into a new alignment. I have little doubt that those who had succumbed under the ordeal would soon have been carrying the onus of deaths originally attributed to the survivors. Relations of the dead had no choice but to pay compensation for the killings now laid to their door. Finally, transfers of rights over women settled the long tangle of quarrels which first provoked the ordeal. The poison ordeal divined who were guilty, executed capital punishment upon them and indicated that restitution should be made by their clansmen. Pawnship was the means of settling the disputes finally. The friendly relations which the pawnship system needed if it was to work at all made of the settlement a real and lasting one.

In the period in which recourse to the poison ordeal was forbidden, individuals who were widely suspected of sorcery might be exiled—an unsatisfactory solution for all concerned. The exile became a target for new accusations. His village was divided between his supporters and his accusers. Without a final verdict, one way or the other, no compensations could be claimed, and every new death increased the tension.

On the other hand, no one could say that the poison ordeal was an ideal solution to conflict in the village. It freed some from hate and suspicion, but at the cost of the lives of others. Though

17

it was final in any particular case, it was never final in the long run. The very next death might be attributed to fresh sorcery and the whole process would have to start again. It is likely that Lele themselves should have cast around for another less drastic solution.

Whatever their functions in the other tribes through which they swept in turn, the anti-sorcery cults adopted by the Lele gave them an alternative to the poison ordeal. In the last fifty years they could recall five cults for controlling sorcery. It seems that at ten-year intervals Lele villages turned away from both poison ordeals and from sorcery beliefs, and made concerted efforts to live in peace without them.

A cult movement starting in one Congo tribe quickly spread through many others, changing as it went from tribe to tribe. Some may have originated with the Lele, as de Jonghe (1936) has said. For the most part Lele claimed that their successive cults originated in other parts. De Jonghe[2] gives the following sequence in the Sankuru area:

1904–5	Epikili pikili and Tonga Tonga (a remedy against sickness).
undated	Lukoshi or Lukusu, protection against sorcery.
undated	Lukusu replaced by new remedy invoking ancestors.
undated	Lukusu replaced by a snake oracle; object: to chase away the whites.
1933	Lukusu in new form, announced return of ancestors, and eclipse of the sun. On the model of cargo cults elsewhere, fields were left uncultivated, as the ancestors were expected to bring ample new riches with them.
1934	Eclipse of the sun took place, but no ancestors appeared, discredit and collapse of the movement.

Lele evidently adopted some of these cults, though they did not call them by the same names. A rough estimate of dates of Lele cults gives the following sequence:

1900–10	Mambwi, an anti-sorcery cult, but the sorcerers eventually found a way round it.
1925	Ngendu, from the east, a cult to kill sorcerers and game animals; lasted four years.
1930	Lukwoh, from the east, same objects as Ngendu.

[2] 1936. See also Struyf, 1933.

1932   Imbwanga, or Manduund, from the north, announced
        return of ancestors; found to be a hoax, discredited in
        one year.
1933   Ngwato, cult from the west; object, to chase away the
        whites. Encouraged by the promises of the cult, the men
        of Mbombe made an armed ambush against the district
        administrator, were routed and the cult was firmly
        suppressed.
1943   Melu, a cult to kill sorcerers.
1952   Kabenga-benga, to kill sorcerers.

Each cult passed through the country by purchase from one
village by the next; each had its set of rules and prohibitions on
food and behaviour, whose breach accounted for any failure of
the cult to fulfil its promises. Each of the anti-sorcery cults was
supposed to kill the first person who committed sorcery after its
adoption. In each case men could recall one or two victims of the
cult convicted by their own deaths of attempted sorcery.

At the time of my first visit, in 1949, Melu was petering out.
Its rules had been broken so often that it was losing its efficacy.
Even so, one man's death was attributed to it, while I was living
in South Homba. No one had previously thought of him as a
sorcerer but as he had died while the cult was in operation, it
was supposed he must have tried to commit sorcery. His friends
blamed his wife, whose infidelity had driven him to sorcery
against her lover, and thus to his own death.

At the time of my second visit, in 1953, Melu was forgotten,
and a new cult, Kabenga-benga was replacing it. Kabenga-benga
came to the Lele from the Bushong, where it was known as
Mikom iyool, after the legendary being who founded the cult,
and who was thought to be an emissary of God. From Professor
Vansina's account of Miko mi yool[3] among the Bushong it seems
that the Lele had transformed the cult almost out of recognition
when they brought it to their side of the Kasai, just as the
Bushong had previously done in adopting it from Luba culture.

A village in the north of Lele country had sent its men to buy
the power to install the cult in their village, some time in 1952.
They paid 100 raffia cloths and four bars of camwood, received
insignia, and instruction which they passed on to other villages in

[3] 'Miko mi yool, une association religieuse Kuba', *Aequatoria*, XXII—1959,
Vol. 2.

return for a similar payment. Working down from north to south it had just about reached South Homba, Hanga and Bushongo by the time of my visit in 1953. Whether to adopt or not was being hotly debated.

Colonial policy was always alert to the subversive effects of messianic movements, and at this time they were being suppressed the more energetically because of reports of Mau-Mau from Kenya. The administration was therefore ready to back the missionaries by putting down Kabenga-benga. The latter, counting adherence to a pagan cult as a breach of the First Commandment, refused the sacraments to Christians who adhered to Kabenga-benga. Reasonable though this seems, the Christians found themselves in a hard predicament. The cult had to be adopted by a village, acting as a single unit. It was made impossible for anyone living in an initiated village not to adhere to it. Therefore the Christians tried to use their influence to stop the spread of Kabenga-benga, and where they were numerous and convinced, they succeeded at least in delaying it. I found myself earnestly wishing they were less strong in South Homba, where they vigorously threatened to leave the village *en masse* if Kabenga-benga were adopted, and I naturally considered staying in another village for the sake of witnessing the introduction of the cult. However, it was not worth moving for the few weeks that were left to me, since my presence would have acted as a deterrent against adoption wherever I went. The suspicion and hostility my inquiries met in villages which had already adopted it persuaded me to stay where I was welcome, and to record the argument as it was being waged in that village.

Of those who spoke in favour of the new cult, some hoped merely to frighten sorcerers; some hoped it would be introduced so that sorcerers would be really killed; others proclaimed themselves in favour in order to show that they themselves were not sorcerers. A man who spoke against its introduction had to be very confident that he himself was above suspicion and in fact the two men most widely suspected did not speak against Kabenga-benga. Those who did were the Christians, or men responsible to the administration, who feared they would go to prison if their village was reported for adopting the cult, or men who were afraid that conflicts would come to a head, and that the Christians would carry out their threat to run away.

The pressures to adopt will appear more clearly when we see how the cult was supposed to work. In the first place it superseded all existing ritual offices and rites. It was supposed to cancel completely the existing ritual order. Even the Lele day of rest, enjoined by the spirits every third day, was abrogated, and a new seven-day week, with a Friday sabbath, introduced. All diviners and cult members of the old order voluntarily laid down their powers, and handed in the instruments of divination and healing. The only valid prohibitions and rules were those promulgated by the new experts, the men who had first gone for initiation to the village from which the cult insignia were bought. They had the power to initiate others.

If this was the only way in which the movement was staffed, one might look for a rigid adherence to the original rules of the cult. But once the cult had been adopted in a village, the spirit of Miko mi yool might move any member, male or female, to come forward as a prophet, inspired in dreams to make new rules and interpretations. Hence the changes in the form of the cult from one tribe to the next.

The Kabenga-benga experts took over full responsibility for health in the village, and no alternative form of divination was allowed. Complete abrogation of the earlier techniques of divination gave to the verdicts of Kabenga-benga the finality which under the displaced system belonged to the poison ordeal. The principal tenet of the new creed was that after a village had adopted it, any initiate who then attempted sorcery would not only be thwarted, but he himself would be the only victim. Following from this, it implied that no one else would die, until their due time. That meant that they would go old and white-haired to their graves. An end of sorcery would automatically usher in the millennium. Hunting would prosper; barren women would conceive; the sick would recover; there would be no illness or death. Even more important, as a corollary, there was no reason why exiled sorcerers should not be allowed to return home. This underlines the comparison with the poison ordeal. To submit to Kabenga-benga was like submitting to the ordeal; survival was proof of innocence. If a convicted, dyed-in-the-wool sorcerer was prepared to risk Kabenga-benga, he could come home, because after initiation he would be harmless. If he so much as tried to commit the least act of sorcery, he would die at once.

By 1953 Makut, the sorcerer so much feared in Ngoie in 1949, had been allowed to return to the village which had driven him out; Bepongo, turned out of Middle Homba the year before, was allowed to return there when the village had adopted Kabenga-benga. All this, without the expense of hate and life which accompanied the poison ordeal. The whole of my second visit was dominated by talk of Kabenga-benga. All the explanations of illness and hunting failure, and suggested remedies on traditional lines were given against the background of the argument whether or not to adopt the new cult. Our village felt humiliated when hunting failed, and culpable when illness spread, in the eyes of other villages which had at least done all in their power to check sorcery. Sorcerers were constantly ordered and begged to desist. One person was the unnamed butt of most of the charges, Makaka, the official diviner. The quarrels and rivalries of his life were being exacerbated and blown up to an alarming scale.

The argument focused on two main subjects. One was the pride of the village, its sense of being observed by its rivals, so that every sickness and death, and every hunt was occasion for self-congratulation or reproach. They spoke as if they were living under arc-lights of foreign scrutiny. Extremely sceptical about the claims made for Kabenga-benga, they were as ready to ridicule the villages which had adopted it as they were to be ashamed of their own shortcomings.

The second was the usual disagreement about the cause of death, on which the poison ordeal still seemed to give the only definitive ruling. If someone died in a village which had taken Kabenga-benga, then the members of that village were *prima-facie* committed to belief in his sorcery; even his close kinsmen and friends. The cult required the dead to be buried like a dog, unanointed and unclothed, without coffin or funeral gifts, in a rough grave in the grassland. But the kinsmen of the dead, in the villages which had not adopted Kabenga-benga, were by no means committed to believing this. If they had any interest in an inheritance, either of raffia or of rights to women, they would come to the burial, insist that the corpse should be honoured, accuse the village in which he had died of having killed him by sorcery and run amok in it, killing dogs and chickens in their grief, and threatening to fight. This was the usual form of mourning display, but in a Kabenga-benga village it created terrible chaos. Such a breach of the rules of the cult endangered their lives; the strength of the medicines would be turned away from the sorcerers and against the initiates. So the women of the village beseeched the visiting mourners to respect the rules of the cult.

This in itself gave each initiated village a further good reason for spreading the cult. Since each villager had close relatives in neighbouring villages, a cult of this sort could not be practiced in isolation. Common adherence throughout Lele country was necessary if it was to get a chance to work at all. There were many pressures they could use to persuade their neighbours to join them. In the first place, they put their oracles at the disposal of any who cared to consult them for a small fee. The prestige of Kabenga-benga was so great that if their diviners cleared a man of charges of sorcery he was for the time effectively cleared. A stream of men and women came up from the south to consult the *bina-cilumbi*, as Kabenga-benga experts were called, to get their own innocence proved and to get clues as to sorcerers in their own villages. I noticed that volunteers who submitted thus their own names to the oracle, as to an ordeal, were generally comforted with proof of their innocence, and warned against sorcerers at home. They returned to speak in favour of adoption of the movement in their own villages. Second, any sickness or misfortune in a village which had not adopted it, was played upon by relatives in Kabenga-benga villages as a reason for adoption. Third, most people found the restrictions on social intercourse between initiates and others very irksome. The check on visiting between villages hampered women particularly. Initiates and non-initiates should not eat together, should not set eyes on one another before working in the forest or hunting (or the day would be wasted); could not draw water for one another, and so on. Visiting could only take place on the day of rest, when no forest work was to be done. The day after an initiate had left an uninitiated village, a compulsory day of rest was imposed on all its members. No wonder that people, especially the women, were impatient to end these restrictions.

These considerations were much more important in helping to spread the cult, than the financial question. True, those who had paid for the cult counted on recouping their outlay from selling the power to others, and this sharpened their interest. But I never heard the problem of cost being mentioned in any of the arguments that raged. We have seen that budgeting problems never worried Lele villages unduly. Credit was always available, so cost was a minor point altogether.

When I arrived in South Homba in the middle of June 1953, Middle Homba had just 'drunk the medicine', and expected South Homba to follow suit. Its other neighbours, Hanga and Bushongo, had sent envoys to obtain the power to install the cult. A series of hunting successes led South Homba to boast that they could hunt without Kabenga-benga, while Middle Homba, in spite of having drunk it, was unsuccessful still. The gossip centred on three women who were reported dead or dying of snake-bite in Kabenga-benga villages. None believed these women to have been sorcerers, indeed, they were happily married with children. It was agreed that Kabenga-benga was powerful, but regrettably inaccurate. Only the most revealing events concerning the cult are recorded below; details of the avoidances practised between South Homba villagers and visitors from Kabenga-benga villages, of complaints about ill-health attributed to sorcery, and details of traditional remedies applied are omitted. The period is much the same as that covered in Chapter XI (in which mention of Kabenga-benga was left out).

On the 13th of July Lukondo broke the quiet of the evening by complaining in a voice choking with rage that his new-born baby was ill; others blamed it on sex pollution, but he knew it was not that. It was widely understood that he was attacking Makaka, whom he already thought guilty of having killed his wife's mother and her previous babies. On the 15th of July, Ngwe, the junior *ilumbi*, lectured the village at length: 'Let no one fight secretly; tomorrow we cut palm fruit; the next day we go hunting. If you have to hit your wife, do it openly, so that we know, and can do something about it. If you fight in secret, the hunt will fail, and people will start looking for sorcerers to blame for bewitching the animals. Then they will start asking for Kabenga-benga. When we go hunting, let it be a good hunt.' Then he started to inveigh against people's credulity, recalling the wisdom of his old father's sister, who used to be very sceptical about the power of medicines to stop sorcerers from striking women with barrenness. She used to say that it was all very well to count the number of pregnancies following a new cult, but she would only be impressed when barren women started to conceive.

The following hunt was not successful, but people were even more concerned with sickness. There was much talk about sorcery, particularly from Bikwak, who made a public complaint about dysentery and coughing among his small children. In the night of the 19th a leopard was heard speaking near the village, and someone heard the gruff barking call of *mbadi* (*Tragelaphus Scriptus*). Both animals being classed as sorcerers' familiars, it was agreed that it was pointless to plan any hunting. Next day there was a spate of speeches. They all made the same points: 'The villages to the north have drunk Kabenga-benga, and so they have no sorcerers. If we hunt less well than they, they will say we have a sorcerer in our midst; the villages to the south are all watching us to make up their minds about taking Kabenga-benga or not; if they hear that leopards speak near our village, we will be shamed: we will drink Kabenga-benga too.' They all ended in glowing phrases about how good it was for a village to be *polo*, peaceful, for men to hunt and bring home meat, and for women to conceive. It was seriously suggested that I should frighten sorcerers by announcing that if they did not behave I would report the village to the Tribunal for its bad hunting.

A few days later Makaka suggested to the other diviners that it might be worth getting a Kabenga-benga expert over for a day just to sniff round the village, to frighten sorcerers. Then later Bikwak, who was still worried about his children, visited his wife's father, a *cilumbi* or specialist of Kabenga-benga in Hanga village. He came home saying that he had learnt that our village was bad, it had a sorcerer. At night he harangued the unnamed sorcerer to be quiet, to leave them alone, let the children alone and let the men go hunting. Details of his consultation circulated through the village privately: the *cilumbi* had actually named four sorcerers of S. Homba, the three oldest people, whom no one in the village would have thought of accusing, and Mikic, classificatory 'mother' of Bikwak, whom he had never forgiven for neglecting him as an orphaned child. Hanga was not a village which had close or regular contacts with S. Homba, and so the lack of subtlety in selecting names may be understood, but many thought that Bikwak had made up the whole story.

Bushongo, having taken Kabenga-benga, went hunting for the first time. There was jubilation in S. Homba on learning that the hunt was an unqualified failure. On the 27th Ilungu, a diviner, made a speech. He said, 'All the villages to the north and our brothers in M. Homba and Bushongo, have now drunk Kabenga-benga. Only we have refused it. Don't listen to what they say. Don't go consulting their diviners. The men who were sick are now recovered. Sorcery was not at work killing them.' He continued in this vein for a full quarter of an hour, and then the junior *ilumbi* took up the same theme. They were reproaching

Bikwak for having taken the affairs of their village to be judged in
Hanga.

In the next week, since hunting was still not good, Bikwak tried
making a direct personal appeal to Makaka. With Ngomabulu present
to encourage him, he raised the matter tactfully over a drink of palm
wine. He described the conversation thus. Calling Makaka 'father',
he reminded him that he was the foremost person in the village; as
capita the Europeans had made him responsible for everything that
happened and the villagers had made him their *ilumbi*; therefore he
had a double duty to look after the hunting; moreover, there was now
a visitor in the village (the ethnographer) and it was not good that
she should go to bed hungry; everyone looked to him to do good
hunting rites for them. Makaka listened, then said: 'Ngila', (the name
he liked to give Bikwak). Bikwak said: 'Eh?' Makaka replied emphatically: 'You're right, quite right; I see your point. Now the twin
diviners are doing their rites. We'll hunt tomorrow. Then, after the
new moon has appeared, I'll do my best. We'll go hunting, and we'll
kill much game.' At this point, Ngomabulu made signs to Bikwak to
drop the subject. Makaka had agreed. We have seen that in practice
Makaka's hunt was another failure (Chapter XII, p. 217).

On the 13th in the early morning Kombe, the village head, made a
speech against the sorcerers. 'Now the dark has lightened. We have just
been hunting. When we went hunting before, the other villages used
to say: The men of South Homba, they always kill game, without
having taken Kabenga-benga. And when we went hunting, we did kill
game, two wild pigs at once! It was a fine thing. The news went to the
other villages; they used to hear: When the men of S. Homba went
hunting yesterday, they killed game. Well, that was good, wasn't it?
Without their having drunk Kabenga-benga. But now, when we went
yesterday—one little duiker. That was very bad. We are not pleased.
Who is he, the man who has said, "I'll chase away the game," who is he?
When you have chased off the game, what do you eat then? Do you eat
dogs? or people? We are grieved. There is great anger in our hearts. As
we have said, "We won't drink Kabenga-benga," don't go in Kabenga-
benga villages. Don't consult their oracles again. If you do, when you
tell us their findings, we will refuse to believe you.'

Then he broke into song, reproaching those who had sulked without
joining the dancing recently; and continued, still addressing the unknown sorcerer: 'You have done wrong; those children they shall stay
with us; we don't consent that a single child shall fall ill. If one child
sickens we shall be very angry.'

The same day news came of the death of a prominent man of
the Bwenga clan, in Mikope, a Kabenga-benga village. He was automatically regarded there as a sorcerer, and as automatically as a victim

of sorcery by his mourning kinsmen in S. Homba. The latter made
a collection and prepared to go to Mikope to see to his decent burial.
News came that they were too late, he was already buried. They went,
breathing threats of violence against the murderers of Mikope. When
they got there they found that his son, also from another village, had
insisted on his being honourably buried. The people of Mikope were
full of fear about the consequences to themselves of the breach of cult
rules: 'You are killing us, killing us,' they protested as the Bwenga
performed extravagant songs and dances in mourning for the dead,
and the Bwenga retorted: 'Good. Die, then; Kapala is dead. It doesn't
matter if we kill you,' and resumed their singing.

On the 15th a man from Yunda, visiting his sister in S. Homba, gave
the official explanation of the deaths of two women from snake-bite
which had earlier been a stumbling-block to faith in Kabenga-benga.
Women who worked in the forest without avoiding sexual intercourse
the day before always risked snake-bite, the punishment inflicted by the
spirits. In this case the *cilumbi* had dreamed of danger from snakes, and
had actually warned the women not to go. They had gone to the forest
in defiance of instructions, and therefore had died. As to hunting, he
said that people still fought in secret in Kabenga-benga villages, and
so brought the cult into disrepute.

Next day Makaka's wife, Manda, fell dramatically ill, fainting over
her cooking. Her son ran to M. Homba to fetch her sister, who came
within half an hour, shouting furious abuse against the sorcerers in
S. Homba. Women crowded into her compound, offering suggestions,
sympathy, and promises to consult the *cilumbi* the very next day. The
cilumbi himself, Makaka's brother-in-law, came in to see if he could
help, but he was much more sympathetic to Makaka, remarking that
women only had one idea when things went wrong, to seek out sorcerers.
The sick women was eventually carried off to M. Homba for treatment
and rest in her sister's house.

Some laid her illness to Makaka's door, but he himself regarded it
as part of a village-wide plot against him. In the last year each of his
three wives had been overcome by fainting and he himself was ill. The
village was against him. He also knew well what grounds for complaint
against him they had. His third wife, Whahela, had been a village-wife,
but he had been so violently jealous of any man she so much as spoke
to that the village had given her up to be his private wife. He had
manufactured a pretext to send his chief rival, Ilungu, to prison on
account of her. Then, when his illness had reached a climax, Whahela
had packed her things and left him. Now that he was better she returned, but his other wives were not on speaking terms with her; he
was too hurt by her desertion to make any advances to her, and no one
else in the village dared to approach her. He had been heard to say that

anyone could have her who liked to take her, but let him look out—
Makaka would accuse him of wife-stealing at the Tribunal. Her very
presence in the village made trouble now for everyone.

On the 30th of August, a visitor from Bwawa, also on his way north to
consult the *cilumbi*, stayed a few days with Makaka, helped him in the
fields, ate and drank palm wine with him. When grievances were being
aired right and left, he took the traditional privilege of a visitor to try to
soothe the disputants. Taking Makaka to task publicly for his quarrels,
he begged him not to nurse his grievances. 'Remember, the village lies
in your head,' meaning that Makaka, as *ilumbi*, was responsible for peace.
He also surveyed the current quarrel between the Bwenga and Lubelo
clans. Ilungu followed him, addressing Makaka directly.

He first reminded Makaka of their old quarrel about Whahela, and
of how Makaka had sent him to prison, and of how now they had not
been on speaking terms since. Implying that he himself had no rancour
left, he ended: 'Why must you always be finding things to be angry
about, day after day?' and reproached Makaka for not having attended
a diviners' meeting the week before. Considering that an *ilumbi* is
supposed never to be angry, and never to go after village-wives, this was
a serious complaint against Makaka.

A few days later, in a hunt, Bikwak shot an arrow which stuck in the
ground at his feet. When this happened to a grown man, an experienced
shot, it was no use going on with the hunt. He wanted to go home, but
the others dissuaded him. Yet, if two men had misfired like that they
would have all come home together. It proved that the village was bad.
This was the time at which a pangolin had been killed, and the proper rites
were being held up by the senior Pangolin Man (Chapter XI). Anxiety
about the state of the village was assuaged for the time by the killing of
a third pangolin. Disappointment was all the stronger when the hunting
failed to improve after the Pangolin ritual.

Ilungu, on the 8th of September, made another speech attacking the
unnamed sorcerer. 'Those who pass on the path or the road, as they
hear sounds of dancing and music, they say: "Listen, they are dancing.
That is what their village is like . . . dancing and songs!" Good! But
what about that other matter? That disgrace, who did it? Was it a woman?
Or a man? The gossip in those villages, they will say, "When they
wanted to hunt . . ." listen! "they refused the medicine". This is the
bad thing, listen all of you: "From the village, footprints of leopard, all
the way to the forest!" Ah! Men of Homba, are you not ashamed?
Whoever it was, who forbade the hunt, let him feel ashamed. We feel
deeply ashamed in our hearts. The *bulumbi* and the Pangolin, it has
always been the same, they stand in one place together from the time
of our forefathers, they are the same thing. When the Pangolin Men
did rites, along with the *ilumbi* shouts of joy filled the village. In the

old days, when they fought their wars, as they did rites for the fighters, disbelief was quelled. In the village which we fought, they found no strength. We pushed them right through the other side of the village! Men of Homba! Who is doing this to us? No game is killed. That is disgraceful. Tomorrow to the hunt. Sleep now.' He further suggested that a foreign expert should be brought in, to put the village right. And added that in the old days, if the *ilumbi* did hunting rites, and the hunt was a failure, rival villages hearing of it would make up mocking songs about them. Then, they would certainly go and kill someone of that village. Men had died before now for matters like this. He added more warnings to sorcerers, and criticism of those who thought the situation called for Kabenga-benga. If we heard of a village in which, after Kabenga-benga had been taken, barren women were starting to bear children, and the hunting was really successful, then we would grant it was a genuine, good remedy.

The next hunt was again a failure, and the next night Ilungu again returned to the charge, two nights running, blaming, cajoling and shaming the sorcerers. 'Another useless hunt, again we come home with empty hands. One bay duiker is scarcely more than one dwarf duiker.[4] What can we rear our children on? Must we feed them with earth? In the old days there were sorcerers, but we still managed to kill game. Now, you bewitch but you never put it right again! Well, it's your affair, I have spoken.' And next morning again: 'The day has lightened. Men of Homba! What I said last night, I say again today. This is shameful. The news will go round that the men of Homba, who wouldn't drink Kabenga-benga, went hunting and came home with nothing. Shame! Now all those villages are laughing at us. Now today is a rest day. Tomorrow work hard. Next week we will see about the hunt. Leave it to us, old men. Those of you who fight, if you feel angry, fight out loud! If you were asleep through this, ask what I said. If you were awake, listen. Peace.' After a pause, he continued: 'In the old days, when old Makoko did Pangolin rites for the hunt he would sit in the village, until midday. Then he cut sticks, and built a stand for them to put the game on. Then, while he pulled out benches for them all to sit on, shouts were heard from over the hill. They were bringing home the game! Peace!'

On the 11th of September, as Ngwe was announcing the next hunt, he was interrupted by furious shouting from Lukondo. What was the point of calling the men out to hunt every day, while all the time *you* (diviners) were preventing the game, sending leopards to chase it away. Coming from Lukondo, it was interpreted as an attack on Makaka. Bikwak remarked that no more game would be killed in the village until

---

[4] *Cephalophus dorsalis castaneus* and *Guevi monticola*.

Ngomabulu (supposed to have influence over Makaka) had given him a severe scolding, and forced him to change his ways. The case against Makaka looked blacker when people recalled that he had learnt his *bulumbi* from the *ilumbi* (see p. 237) who had recently been chased out of M. Homba for exactly the same behaviour.

At this stage Makaka began to talk about leaving the village. He had no other village he could go to, as he had been born in South Homba, but he suggested that he might build his compound on the edge of the village, like the catechist, so that people would leave him in peace. He felt in danger of sorcery, he and his wives were being killed by the ill-will of the village.

Soon after this, I had to leave. It was hard to say whether they would take Kabenga-benga or not. It had already swept past them to the south and started to be discredited. My presence, of which they were so conscious all the time, no doubt helped to deter them at the moment of greatest enthusiasm, when the villages around them were just taking the plunge. If they continued to reject it, Makaka's personal tragedy may have been deepened. His quarrels were magnified by the sorcery beliefs affecting his position. The village found itself with completely the wrong kind of man as *ilumbi*. They were moving towards an impasse which would only be resolved by one of three ways: exile, ordeal, or anti-sorcery cult. Makaka would have played a prominent role in a new cult; he would expect the ordeal to vindicate him again, as it had done before. As a sick man, exile would have been a tragedy for him.

The experience of this village suggests an approach not only to the anti-sorcery cults of the Lele but also to the anti-witchcraft movements which have swept through Central Africa, including Mcape and Bwanali-mpulumutsi,[5] which also have some of the characteristics of an ordeal substituting its final verdict for that of the poison ordeal. Certainly the Lele were not brought to adopt their cults from a childish, irrational credulity which swallowed the most wildly unlikely claims. They found themselves tempted to adopt it, in spite of a lively scepticism, from strong practical motives. Kabenga-benga may have had another form, and made other promises, on the other side of the Kasai,

[5] Richards, 1935; Marwick, 1950. My interpretation of the latter's material based on Lele experience will appear in the symposium on witchcraft edited by Dr. J. Middleton.

but its interest to the Lele was its solution to pressing internal problems. Its appeal was on the political and moral rather than on the religious plane. It gave its adepts a chance to live together without belief in sorcery. While the cult lasted, there could be no sorcery. Small quarrels could not be fanned into great ones by the aggravating effect of accusations and rebuttals. Adoption was like a cool decision to bring in the millennium by acting as if it had come. It was a confidence trick to allow the lamb to lie down with the lion.

Conclusion

Poison ordeals and anti-sorcery cults were alternative techniques for resolving the conflicts which sorcery beliefs exacerbated. If proof be needed, the events of 1959 give it. Poison ordeals had been prohibited by then for nearly thirty years. The Lele had evidently grown tired of the succession of cults, each discrediting its predecessor. After Belgian Colonial Administration had become ineffective in 1959 and before Congolese independence had been officially proclaimed, a crop of poison ordeals was reported from Bushong and Lele territories.[6] They had evidently taken the first possible opportunity of settling their suspicions and solving the conflicts on which the cults had merely called a moratorium.

According to my interpretation, the persons most likely to have been forced to undergo the poison ordeal were men like Makaka and Bwato, members of large, established clan sections, who did not fit their expected roles. Both ran too flagrantly after other men's wives, both had lost the support of their own clan sections. Their presence disturbed the peace of the village. As they were senior men, there was no smooth way of evicting them.

Professor Vansina was in Ruanda in 1959 and according to his information from the Kuba area the poison ordeals were not applied merely to the social misfits, but indiscriminately to anyone who had provoked charges of sorcery in a wholesale attempt to purge society of malefactors.

At first I had been inclined to regard anti-sorcery cults as a modern response to the abolition of the poison ordeal. But inquiry soon showed that the cults and the ordeal had existed side by side long before the law of 1924 prohibiting ordeals and

[6] Communications from Professor D. Biebuyck and Professor Vansina.

therefore much longer before that law was effective in Lele
country. Professor Vansina cites evidence that Miko mi yool
among the Kuba was one of a series of cults extending back into
the past.[7]

It is interesting to find that the so-called cargo cults of
Melanesia are also thought to be not merely a response to the
strains of European impact, but expressions of a tendency rooted
deep in the traditional cultures.[8] It is also argued by Dr. Burridge that Melanesian cargo cults express primarily a longing
for moral regeneration, to put on the new man, to make a new
world free of contradictions. Certainly in the Lele case too, there
was every sign that the adoption of a new cult was a regular
occurrence. People knew what to expect and what to argue
about. There was a well-known history of cults which had worked
for a little and then been abandoned for a return to traditional
rites . . . probably something was lost and something gained each
time. The desire for moral renewal, a clean start and an end of
conflict and passion, was also there. We have seen something of
the contradictions in Lele society. Its machinery was so set that
it could only stumble along towards its ideals; every now and
again it ground to a standstill, sabotaged, as they thought, by
sorcery, and blocked indeed by suspicions of sorcery. Poison
ordeals failed to remove the obstacles. When a new cult appeared
on the horizon, whatever its objectives in its place of origin, the
Lele hailed it as a new technique for surmounting the difficulties
of living together, young and old, men and women, in a spontaneously ordered peace.

[7] op. cit., p. 87.
[8] K. Burridge, *Mambu*, 1960, p. 25.

XIV

EUROPEAN IMPACT ON LELE SOCIETY

LELE had little direct contact with Europeans. Luba and Chokwe servants were preferred for domestic work. Lele were regarded as more simple and honest, but too inexperienced to employ in the house. They sometimes got jobs as gardeners. One Lele woman thanked me for coming to live with them, 'So that we can see for ourselves that what they say about the Europeans is true.' She added that many Lele doubted whether Europeans had teeth or eyebrows, since they usually received only a blurred impression of pale, featureless faces. In spite of this lack of personal contact the Europeans made a tremendous impact which shook the society to its roots.

The influence came through three agencies, the administration, industry and the mission. We can distinguish their effects, but to the Lele they were as one. The administration ensured security of life and property, transport and communications. Without it neither commerce nor missionary development would have been possible. The commercial interests subsidized the missions, who trained their staff in schools, and gave extensive medical services. The state supported the missionaries in the course of their normal enforcement of the laws of the colony, some of which were framed in response to missionary demands.

Administration

Providing roads through the length of the country was the first and most essential step. Until 1917 Basongo was a military post. The first fourteen years of civil administration made very little difference to the Lele until the building of the road system. Begun in the western chiefdom in 1931, its main arteries were completed between 1934 and 1935. Under a system of forced labour each village was made responsible for building the road near its own site, all the men and women being mustered until it was done. Then a lump sum of money was paid to the village.

When the road was finished, all the villages were ordered to

259

change their sites to within easy access from the road. From then the traditional way of life was virtually ended. The administration could use motor transport for its work, could swiftly punish raiders and homicides and armed resistance to its officers. The last occasion in which an administrative officer with armed escort was forced to fire on Lele was in 1933 when the men of Mbombe laid an ambush. From this date the country was fully pacified and native political life had no more free play.

Although they often hankered for a chance to snipe at their enemies, Lele were spontaneously grateful for the security which followed the making of the roads. They would exclaim that it was a marvellous thing for women and children to travel from one village to the next unescorted, and for men to be able to go without fear to their fields.

The second major source of change was through the Tribunals set up by the administration. From the first the Lele seem to have welcomed these as impartial arbiters in their disputes. The idea that they might be a fount of justice was slow to develop and even at the time of fieldwork contenders confidently used to threaten revenge by 'writing up' their enemies on false charges at the Tribunal. Since they had never had law or courts affecting a wider unit than the village, and since most of their own codes were upheld by religious sanctions, the punishments imposed by the Tribunals struck them as arbitrary exactions. Now all violence was punished, recourse to ordeals of any kind, rape or seduction of non-nubile girls, and even polyandry after 1948. So ended warfare between villages and the rest of their traditional life. Punishments ranged from small fines to prison; long sentences were served in Luebo, short ones in Basongo where the prisoners drew water, hewed wood and cleared latrines for the European residents.

Lastly, an energetic programme of agricultural development was followed to end the occasional famines which used to afflict the area. Every able-bodied man was registered as a cultivator,[1] unless exempted by some other approved occupation such as wage-labour, and was required to clear and plant a given area, whose harvest he could keep or sell. They were encouraged to sell the surplus because by native methods of storage the grain did not resist well the ravages of insects and damp. In the hungry

[1] 1942. See below.

season they could buy it back at the same prices, without regard to the expense incurred in preserving it. New crops were introduced, rice, beans, ground-nuts and improved strains of manioc. The people were encouraged to clear more land, and to plant maize twice yearly instead of once. The cleared fields were inspected to make sure they would be ready for firing before the rains started. Laggards were threatened with imprisonment or fine. None of these benevolent activities was valued by the Lele. The administration also tried to control erosion by restricting grass-burning and enforced the colony's laws for the protection of rare animals. To this restriction of their freedom to hunt the Lele objected vehemently. But the positive achievement was an end of recurrent famines and now a surplus of grain and ground-nuts could be exported from the district.

On all heads the administration was astonishingly effective. It reflected a determination to raise these poor and backward people willy-nilly into a better life. Solicitude for their well-being took account of hygiene. If their huts were dirty and falling into disrepair, they were prodded into rebuilding, and might be fined for failure to do so. If a village wanted to move to a new site to escape from sorcery, telling the administrator that the old site was infected with disease secured permission at once. Malaria control measures were put in hand, also smallpox and sleeping sickness innoculation. In provision of medical services the state worked hand in hand with the Huileries du Congo Belge,[2] the big company of the area.

The only criticism of the administration is the mild one that it never made the tribe share its own enthusiasm for economic betterment. Consequently the many laws appeared as a multitude of arbitrary infringements of liberty. The risk of going to prison for not planting enough ground, not keeping their homes repaired, not paying taxes and so on loomed oppressively.

Industry

In any enterprise if the parties are not agreed on the need for haste, there will be conflict. The Lele were labelled lazy and thriftless by employers not less than by their administrators. The most important commercial venture in their region was the

[2] Known then to Europeans as HCB and to Lele as 'Companie', its name since independence has been changed to Plantations Léver au Congo.

Huileries du Congo Belge which in 1920 obtained a concession of
land near Brabanta. It made its first oil-palm plantation in 1923,
and started a factory for extracting palm-oil in 1925. Initially
Lele provided manpower for none of these undertakings. Under
the head *Main d'Oeuvre* the *Rapport Economique* 1924 states:

Encore aucun Bashilele fournit un travail manuel dans un centre
Européen. Les 1,428 travailleurs du territoire sont des étrangers.

In the same year an agent of the administration reported in like
strain from the south of the territory:

Travailleurs . . . néant.
Portage . . . nul. Les indigènes refusent de porter.
Les Bashilele refusent de faire du commerce et ne produisent rien.
(Lettre du Gérant à L'administrateur, Basongo, 8.11.1924, Charles-
ville.)

By 1948 the figure for foreign immigrant labour had risen to
5,000. By 1953 the plantations numbered 500,000 oil palms and
the factory had installed electric equipment. But the Lele did
not begin to get drawn into wage-earning until the middle of the
Second World War. When Belgium was occupied by the German
army, the Congo administration adhering to its exiled leaders in
London turned the economic effort of the Congo to help the
Allied cause. In 1942 the Colonial Administration took emergency
powers to combat the labour shortage.[3] From that date able-
bodied Lele were obliged to undertake wage-earning either as
plantation labourers with HCB, or as agricultural workers in the
administration's programme for increased food production, or as
palm-fruit cutters working in their own villages. Agricultural
workers were rewarded when they sold their crops. The palm
cutters were paid monthly according to the amount of fruit they
produced. Those who did not produce a set minimum could be
fined or sent to prison for a brief term.

Thanks to these measures production rose considerably after
1942, but it fell sharply when the ordinance was repealed in 1947.
The Director of HCB accordingly tried to stimulate village
production by raising the price from eleven to twenty francs for
a load of fifty kilos of palm fruit. But at this period the Lele still
thought of francs as a means of paying taxes and fines, so were

[3] Ord. Leg. 68, AIMO, 10.3.42.

not tempted to earn more money than they needed for these purposes. Instead of responding positively, in 1949, after prices had been increased for a year, output fell below what it had been in 1942—a clear case of a backward turning supply curve.

One reason why the Lele were not interested in higher prices was that in 1949 opportunities for spending money were few. The scattered shops offered cloth, oil-lamps, cooking-pots, etc. at very high prices. But even in the villages close to these shops the drop in production[4] was no less marked. The Lele were pronounced lazy, apathetic, not interested in their own advancement. By 1953, Sedec, a subsidiary company of Unilevers exclusively concerned with retail trading, reorganized its trade in the territory, establishing many more shops, supervising their salesmen and watching demand and prices closely. Then trading activity went up by leaps and bounds. But other processes of change had been at work at the same time.

It was not entirely lack of opportunity to spend which had caused Lele to resist the blandishments of money. So long as the old men could require cult dues and marriage fees to be paid in kind they held the keys to social advancement within Lele society. Their position eventually was undermined not by money itself, but by an attack on a much more vulnerable front. Those who were least privileged by the standards of the old society soon found that the mission could guarantee to them the very things traditionally withheld from them. Thus it was the mission which in the long run most helped the HCB to recruit the Lele.

[4] *Table 15*

Comparison of palm-fruit production for five representative villages for three peak months of July, Aug., Sept. in kilos

Village	1943 (after 1 yr. coercive legisl.)	1947 (at end of coercive legisl. and before rise in price)	1949 (1 yr. after rise in price)
Ngoie	60,240	51,550	51,700
Yamba	63,770	70,300	56,250
Domaie	63,315	84,800	53,100
Yunda*	33,635	15,900	12,100
S. Homba	16,380	18,250	12,550

* Lack of opportunity for spending the money earned cannot be the main cause, since the greatest drop in earning was recorded for Yunda, the only village in this list which had a shop.

Missions

The first attempt to found a mission at Brabanta, by the Scheutists, failed. They opened a primary school and hospital in 1925, but were soon afterwards withdrawn. The priests who succeeded them in 1939 were determined that their work should not be restricted to the foreign labourers working for HCB. It was a propitious time for drawing the Lele into the Christian orbit. The road system was built and peace established. The Lele were still wary of wage-labour but by 1942 they would all be forced into adopting it in one form or another.

At first the mission attracted very few converts. Lele told me that they resorted to capturing village children by force, threatening their protesting parents with prison if they stopped them. The mission fathers told me that this may have been substantially true as they had no other way to start the ball rolling. All their communication, even in 1950, was through a crude form of ki-kongo,[5] which the Lele themselves learnt in the mission school in order to be able to understand the fathers. Older Lele never learnt more than a few words, and so their relations with the missionaries were apt to be blurred by misunderstandings. Once the initial stage of coercion was over, the ball began indeed to roll along of itself. The young Lele became keen, intelligent pupils, and sincere Christians of whom their pastors were justly proud.

By 1949 the mission story had become a record of expansion and success, with large numbers of baptisms and confirmations, new catechist schools being set up in the villages, built by voluntary local labour, vast congregations at Brabanta at the four big feasts of the year. A secondary school and technical school for boys started to make Lele into clerical and skilled workers to challenge the Luba near-monopoly of better paid work.

---

[5] Ki-kongo is about as far removed from Lele language as modern Greek from English, but only a very simple uninflected form was required, which they learnt easily. For conversation with the administration they had to use ci-luba, and for the staff of HCB it had to be lingala, as the region was at the boundary of the three main commercial languages, a boundary drawn differently by different European agencies.

The mission sisters

The mission convent of nuns (the Sisters of St. Vincent de Paul) similarly expanded their work with Lele girls. They ran a large primary school for catechumens, and after my last visit had opened a secondary school as well. For their work in the hospital (financed by HCB) and particularly in the maternity ward opened in 1949 they were justly renowned. They ran clinics in Brabanta and in certain favoured villages nearby where they were almost mobbed by enthusiastic patients. Fertility medicine, which included treatment at confinement and the difficult rearing of small infants, was the pride of Lele ritual. Consequently when the sisters made a name as midwives, they established European superiority in the one field which really impressed their converts. The four sisters had to exert every ounce of authority they could muster to control their large classes of girls (over 500 in 1951) learning the three R's and religious doctrine, and working in plantations from which they fed themselves and helped to supply the religious community. The nuns were enclosed by the rule of their order; their travel was restricted. Nor did they, like priests, hear confessions, order penances or give or withhold sacraments. Their kindness and devotion were obvious to all, so that even in sticky situations when their efforts to save a mother's or child's life failed Lele never showed any serious mistrust.

The mission fathers

The mission fathers had a different vocation. Their task was to create a Christian society and to create it quickly. They wanted to free the Lele from their unhappy superstitions and change their bestial habits. They succeeded in getting a law against polyandry, and made full use of the coercive power of the administration for enforcing it. At first sight their tremendous success with the Lele poses a problem. In ten years they had succeeded in smashing the framework of the pagan society, age-sets, polyandry, ordeals and the rest, so well that the ethnographer's task was already one of reconstruction rather than of straight observation. The young men and women under thirty were largely Christian, and the children, all enrolled in village catechist's schools, were fully expected to proceed to baptism.

The Lele were not, as we have seen, early attracted by the

chance of entering the European market economy—quite the contrary. So it cannot be argued that they adopted Christianity as a means of acquiring European skills and trade goods.

Nor did they enjoy the time spent as catechumens at Brabanta. They invariably described that two-year period as one of hardship and hunger. They worked both to grow their own food and to supply the mission station with its needs. The fathers' belief that they would have done as much manual work in their own villages was more likely to be true of the girls than of the young men, as we have seen. For the two years at the mission they worked for no reward, they might be abused, struck or whipped for some, to them, obscure misdemeanour. Why they endured it needs some explaining.

It was not because of sheer *force majeure* for they could not be compelled to come to the mission. The head of the mission averred that they were deeply attracted by the very idea of force as exerted by the Europeans. He once praised to me Father Tempel's book on Luba religion, *Filosofie Bantoe*, for its insisting that force was the mode which the black man's mind best understood—a revealing misinterpretation of the book's theme. In the same conversation he emphasized the necessity of using force in relations with the blacks. He did not usually employ physical violence himself, but deputed the whipping of culprits to their own comrades. On the grounds that the natives were at the stage of social evolution at which we in Europe had needed public chastisement, public penances were meted out for grave sins revealed in the confessional. Thus I saw a confessed adulterer dressed in striped pyjamas loaded with two buckets of stones staggering round the mission grounds.

The mission head believed so firmly in the value of forceful behaviour that he ended our talk by playfully laying a bet that within six months I would have proved him right by striking a black myself. However, I still feel that admiration for force in itself does not account for the success of the mission to the Lele.

It might have been sheer affection for the fathers which drew them flocking to the mission, were it not for the social distance which separated priests and laiety. On their quarterly tour of the villages the priests were more approachable and told stories round the fires at night, but at Brabanta the visitor was struck by their authoritative manner and the distance they maintained.

In a sense it was the doctrine itself which attracted the Lele. In many African mission fields otherwise willing converts have found the doctrine of monogamous marriage a stumbling-block. Here the reverse was true, for the idea of monogamy most attracted converts.

Impact of Christianity

The traditional society of the Lele was a precarious structure of privileges and counter-privileges, of oppositions cancelling one another, avoidances, alternations and devious controls. It was vulnerable to outside pressures for change. The young men were socially retarded and deprived of the rewards their society prized most highly. Women were held in subjection as passive objects of men's political manœuvres and although some initiative and play still remained to them the young girls saw plenty of scope for improvement in their lot. It was just at these points that the missionaries decided to start their campaign, reasonably enough preferring to convert the younger generation.

Young men found that through baptism they could flout the old men's privileges, have and hold a wife of their own with the full European machinery of police, tribunals and prison to protect them against retaliation. Once baptized they were encouraged to choose a Lele girl of their own age, to marry and found a Christian family. The fact that there were no girls not already betrothed to pagans was no problem. The missionaries were very strict about obliging their converts to honour those ancient customs which were compatible with Christianity. Payment of marriage dues was counted as one of these honourable customs, and so was payment of compensation for breach of contract. An old pagan whose betrothed ran away to the mission to marry a young man could not put an arrow into him or capture one of his pawns as hostage. But he had some redress at the Tribunal: he could demand restitution of the marriage gifts he had already made to her parents, and compensation for loss of pawnship rights. He could not insist on payment in raffia or camwood, but was obliged to accept Congo francs. If he resorted to violence, he would be punished. So the generation-old betrothals and pawnship settlements were in process of dissolution in 1950, money was being earned by Christians to meet their debts, and was compulsorily accepted by pagans. This was undoubtedly the spearhead of change, the point at which the young saw their advantage in breaking out of the old restrictive framework. Not only the young men, but unhappy young wives, childless women, a girl beaten once too often, those who could formerly have thought of running off to be village-wives now ran away to marry Christians. One very determined push on the strategic point and the structure started to cave in. The response of the Lele to missionary endeavour is consistent with the rest of our analysis.

The change from a pagan society to one split between a rising generation of Christians and a declining generation of pagans took place too suddenly not to leave a trail of bitterness. The old religion so tinged every aspect of Lele community life that it was impossible to be a good neighbour and a good Christian. In some places the Christians formed separate communities on the outskirts of their villages, so that by refraining from Lele ritual they would not offend their kinsfolk. This solution left the older men, less successful in hunting and cultivation, on their own. But if they lived and hunted together, the meat privileges of cult initiates rankled as a bitter grievance for the Christians. It was hard to join the communal hunt, shoot the game, and then be refused a share of meat because it was reserved to Begetters. The forest would ring with angry arguments, the Christians claiming that a little antelope was adult and so not cult meat, the pagans that it was half-grown, and therefore reserved to Begetters. Then in retaliation the Christians would secretly kill and eat pangolin or other forbidden cult meats, the truth would leak out, and the village be in an uproar at the breach of cult rules. At one time in South Homba, following such a quarrel, the pagans could think of no better way of coercing the Christians than threatening to report them to the missionaries for using sorcery—a comment on the close control exercised by the mission. The Christians accordingly stopped hunting with the village, and constraint and acrimony were the order of the day. For each individual Christian these tensions mounted again when his wife conceived and loyal to his new faith he resisted attempts of her kin to do fertility rites for her.

Though so recent, these changes went so deep that it was difficult to assess their effects. I have described a society which was in process of liquidation, which could not be understood at all without interpolation of what must have been the scene a dozen years before. Age-sets and polyandrous wives were still in existence, but the system was not being renewed. Descendants of pawns were still being exchanged, but new pawnship rights were not coming into being, since the poison ordeal by whose outcome claims were established was forbidden. Village-raiding was stopped and also initiation as warriors. Old men were being exiled for sorcery instead of subjected to ordeal, and readmitted to their villages when a new cult promised an end of evil-doing.

Speculation on the new society

All this must have changed again when the Congo became independent. One can only guess at what Lele society has become since missionary work is no longer supported by the strong arm of the state. Lele are now likely to be in the painful process of working out a new society. Certain elements of pre-colonial life will no doubt be restored. Rivalry between villages will surely burst out into raiding, so travel will be dangerous; agriculture will probably be neglected, so hunger and even famine threaten. But it seems unlikely that the young men will submit again to the restrictions which bound them in the past. The desire for European trade goods has no doubt come to stay. The influence of the political parties[7] run by agents of other tribes will have affected the political system, and the aristocratic clan of Tundu is not likely to afford leadership.[8] Sorcery will be checked once more by recourse to ordeals, but the image of the sorcerer will perhaps be changed: no more an old man skilled in ritual but the ambitious, intriguing politician.

Blood compensation, pawnship, village-wives and other customs connected with marriage pose a problem. These institutions were intimately linked with the polygyny of old men, which seems unlikely to be soon restored, yet they were very dear to the Lele.

To be consistent with our general assumption that personal choices have some determining influence on the growth of institutions we should consider the possibility that the new generations of Lele, in spite of having tasted and liked their

[7] Biebuyck and Douglas, 1961.

[8] Here I may be quite wrong since it appears that Pero Mihondo, senior aristocrat of the Western Lele, was returned to the Provincial Council of the Kasai in 1960.

freedom from gerontocratic restraints, might end by restoring the system which the Europeans gave them a chance to reject. It is just on the cards that their attachment to institutions which served the hegemony of the old may lead them to reinstate it again. For village-wives, raiding, pawnship, high marriage dues, adultery damages and the rest gave means of expressing male status in terms of rights over females. Nothing has happened to make them reject the value of male dominance. Their old system had various built-in safety valves which saved male dominance from foundering on the vagaries of women, but the new society introduced by the missionaries was more vulnerable in this respect. Though the missionaries protected monogamists, they could do nothing for the Christian whose wife ran off with another man. He was trebly humiliated since he could neither retaliate nor remarry. It is conceivable that Lele adherence to deep-rooted ideas about how relations between men and men and between men and women should be conducted may swing them back into something very like their old society based on seniority and privilege rather than on authority. Only new field-work can settle the question.

The lack of authority in the old social system has been the central theme of this study. By understanding it we can approach more closely to the problem of economic backwardness than we could by merely considering the environment and the use Lele made of it. I have tried throughout to regard the economy and the society as one. At the outset I focused on Lele poverty relative to the standards of the Bushong, and explained it later as the outcome of their distribution of power. The comparison with the Bushong is implicit throughout. The latter drew power into the hands of their royal dynasty and with security, competition and commerce their wealth grew. On the Lele side of the Kasai there was the anarchy of warring villages to contrast with the orderly devolution of control on the Bushong side. The Lele might have been drawn into the orbit of the Bushong empire if the river had not separated them. As it was, they had to cut their cloak according to their cloth and their side of the river was less fertile. They could never, with the best will, have made of their society a small-scale Bushong. Restrictions breed poverty, but the reverse is as true. Their idea of the good society included certain aims which on the more favoured bank could be achieved without restriction. On the less favoured bank of the river these aims, particularly that of securing dignity for men in old age, would have been sacrificed but for protective regulation which incidentally had the effect of restricting economic expansion.

APPENDIX A

Documentation of South Homba

Changes in residence between 1949 and 1953. (See Map VIII, Sketch Map of South Homba.)

1. Right-hand top, and right-hand side of square:
   (*a*) Lubelo 1 had died and his widow gone away charged with sorcery.
   (*b*) Bienge, young man had gone to join his clansmen.
   (*c*) Roadmenders gone away.
   (*d*) Ndong 3 had stopped counting himself as a house-husband of Buwondo 1, a village-wife; her hut had been moved to the other side of the village, where she kept house for new arrival Bwenga 1. Ndong 3 had built a new house in its place for a young wife who came in 1953.
   (*e*) Between the huts of Ndong 3 and Lubelo 2 Bwenga 12 had placed two huts (vacated by roadmenders and Lumbunji 3) for his two wives.

2. Bottom of square:
   (*a*) Ngondu 6 vacated hut and Bulomani 4 moved into it, with Mahenge 2. Ngondu 6 built on to the hut of Lubelo 8, to accommodate both his wives in one compound.
   (*b*) Ket 4's wife had died, and he had remarried the daughter of Ndong 3, and moved his hut into this side of the village.
   (*c*) Two of the unmarried boys had married and built in the village.
   (*d*) Ngondu 7 and his wife were permanently at Clinic in Brabanta.
   (*e*) Hanja 1 living with the catechist temporarily left the village.

3. Left side of square:
   (*a*) Bwenga 4 had been left by both his wives; one a widow complaining of his neglect, the other to be village-wife in Mikope.
   (*b*) Bwekamba 1 had died and his wife run away to the mission.
   (*c*) Bwenga 9, his wife had run away to be village-wife in M. Homba following expulsion of her mother, Hanja 2.
   (*d*) Lumbunji 3, village-wife with three house-husbands, left village after scandal with Lubelo 6, to be village-wife elsewhere.

4. Top of square:
   (*a*) Lubelo 11 and Bulomani 2, close friends and age-mates, moved their huts to share a single compound.
   (*b*) Lubelo 7 moved out of Lubelo 6's compound, her hut carried for her to the bottom side of the square.

Appendix A

Men of South Homba

In age-set order, numbered according to age in clan section
as shown in genealogies on pp. 276–9.

Age-sets	Name	Clan	Village Born	Diviner	Begetter	Pangolin	Twin
Manya-mangele	Ngapici X	Lubelo 1	Hanga	—	—		
	Njoku	Ngondu 1	S. Homba	—	—		
	Kombe	Lubelo 2	M. Homba	—	—		
	Pung	Lubelo 3	M. Homba	—	—		—
	Njondu	Lubelo 4	Bushongo	—	—		
	Ngomabulu	Lubelo 5	Mbombe	—	—		—
Yulu	Llungu	Ndong 1	Bushongo	—	—		—
	Bwato @	Bwenga 1	Mbombe	—	—		
	Makaka	Lubelo 6	S. Homba	—	—		
Tamananji	Buhinda	Bwenga 3	N. Homba	—	—		
	Pero	Bwenga 5	N. Homba	—	—		
	Kabenda @	Bwenga 7	Tundu				—
	Ngwe	Ngondu 3	Bushongo	—	—		
	Pongo	Bwenga 4	N. Homba	—			
	Ngomabulu	Ndong 3	S. Homba	—	—	—	—
	Badiangu	Ket 2	S. Homba	—	—		
	Kumaking	Bwenga 9	Mbombe	—	—		
	Minambo X SV	Mbwekamba 1	S. Homba				—
Luang	Bikwak @	Bwenga 12	S. Homba				—
	Mabonje @	Ndong 4	Bushongo				—
	Lukondo	Bulomani 2	Bwene	—	—		
	Ngambu	Lubelo 11	Bushongo				—
	Njondu @	Hanja 1	S. Homba				
	Mukwa	Ket 3	M. Homba				—
	Makum	Ngondu 6	Njembe	—	—		—
Christians	Ihaku Joseph	Ket 4 (married)	M. Homba				
	François	Ndong 5 (married)	S. Homba				
	Jerome	Ngondu 7 (married)	S. Homba				
	Oscar θ	Ngondu 8 (married)	Bushongo				
	Denis	Bulomani 4 (married)	Bushongo				
	Clement θ	Lubelo 12	S. Homba				
	Paul	Lubelo 13	S. Homba				
	Pius	Lubelo 14	S. Homba				
	Modest	Lubelo 17 (married)	S. Homba				
	Mapepe θ	Bwenga 16	S. Homba				
	Polidor SV	Bwenga 13	S. Homba				
	Donatio SV	Lubelo 20	S. Homba				

X dead between 1949 and 1953
θ left village between 1949 and 1953 (besides the three marked, two others who had
no other clansmen in the village left in 1949)
@ came after 1949
SV son of village

Women of South Homba

Numbered according to age in clan section, see genealogies on pp. 276–9

Clan	Name	Village Born	Nearest Village in which Clan was a Founding Clan
Lubelo	7 Mandong	Hanga Ekangu	S. Homba
	8 Mihondo @	Bushongo	
	9 Mbonje	S. Homba	
	10 Kinda Kumu	Tundu	
	15 Biong	N. Homba	
	16 Mamboyu VW	Bushongo Bwanjambi	
	19 Mwendela DV	S. Homba	
Bwenga	2 Mikic VW	Bushongo	S. Homba
	6 Pembe	N. Homba	
	8 Biong Bikara	Bushongo	
	10 Hangidi	Bushongo	
	11 Lubwani	S. Homba	
	14 Manda	S. Homba	
	15 Biong	Bushongo	
	17 Ihowa	S. Homba	
Ndong	2 Idiamaha	Bushongo	S. Homba and Mikope
Bulomani	1 Ihek	Bwene	S. Homba and N. Homba
	3 Hombo VW	Hanga	
Ngondu	2 Yembaha	S. Homba	Bushongo
	4 Pahimba	Bushongo	
	5 Niabwani VW	Bushongo	
Ket	1 Butuku VW	Bamba	Bamba and Mbombe
	5 Ihowa θ	M. Homba	
Hanja	2 Biong θ	Domaie	H. Homba
	3 Kinda θ	S. Homba	
Pata	1 Mawoha DV	S. Homba	Hanga and Bushongo
	2 Ihowa	S. Homba	
	3 Mihondo @	Bushongo	
Bulong	1 Butuku θ	N. Homba	N. Homba
	2 Lubwani θ	S. Homba	
Kamba	1 Niakala	N. Homba	N. Homba
	2 Ihek	S. Homba	
Njembe	1 Himbu DV	Kenge	Bushongo
	2 Biong X	S. Homba	
Luta	1 Piciambom	Ilebo	Bushongo
	2 Ihaku	S. Homba	
	3 Kanjamba	N. Homba	
Buwondo	1 Kinda VW	Bushongo	Bushongo
Mbwekamba	2 Pembe DV	S. Homba	Mbombe
Bucwa	1 Mapici	M. Homba	M. Homba
	2 Mbembe VW	Ilebo	
Lumbunji	1 Mbonje	Bamba	M. Homba
	2 Seraphine	M. Homba	
	3 Mahamimbendi θ VW	Mbombe	
Yong	1 Whahela VW	Yunda	Yunda
Mahenge	1 Kinda	Mbombe	Mbombe
	2 Christine DV	S. Homba	

X dead between 1949 and 1953   @ came after 1949
θ left between 1949 and 1953   VW village-wife
            DV daughter of the village

19

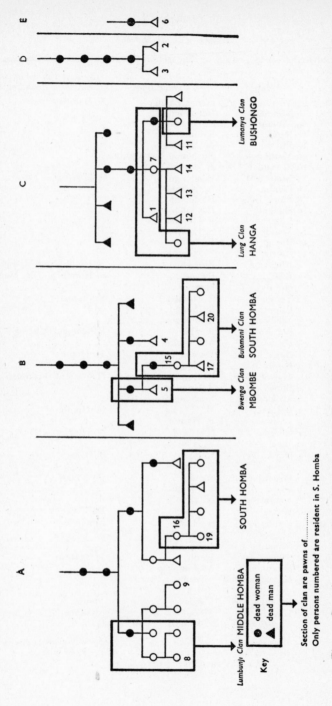

Fig. 12. Genealogy of members of Lubelo clan in South Homba: pawnship obligations. This clan was divided among six lords

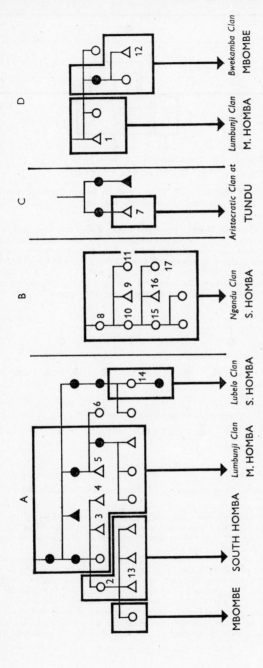

Fig. 13. Genealogy of members of Bwenga clan in South Homba: pawnship obligations. (For key see Fig. 12)
The marriages of the Bwenga pawns of the Ngondu clan illustrate how the lord's rights are exercised. Numbers 8 and 15 were married to Bushongo men; 10 and 11 were married in Bushongo where the Ngondu clan was strongest; the youngest, 17, was given by her lord to his own lord's clan.

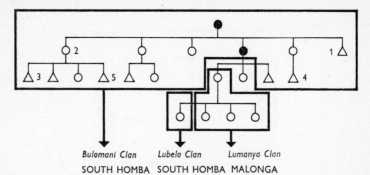

Fig. 14. Genealogy of members of Ndong clan in South Homba: pawnship obligations. (For key see Fig. 12)

The Ndong clan in South Homba belonged to the Bulomani. Only one woman was free in this descent line, the sister's daughter of 1 who had been released by the Bulomani in recognition of some debt they had incurred towards the Ndong. Not shown on the diagram are his three wives; one was his pawn (of the Kamba clan). She had six children. The eldest daughter, baptized a Christian, he allotted as wife to another Christian, the younger of the two Ket brothers who attached themselves to the Bulomani clan when they arrived.

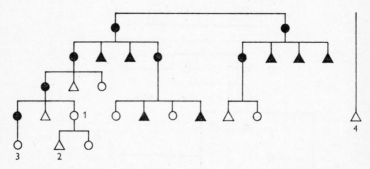

Fig. 15. Genealogy of members of Bulomani clan in South Homba

The senior members of this clan section had died or gone away, leaving 2, Lukondo, as eldest male. His continued presence in the village, after the death of one mother's brother and departure of the other, needs no explaining; pawns in six clans counted him as lord.

This is a clear case of how pawnship rights, which in the first generation are treated as a matter primarily concerning the lord in whom they originated, in the next generation may enter the common stock of heritable rights of the local clan section. Lukondo's mother's mother's mother's sister's son was the lord-begetter of Badiangu of the Ket clan; his mother's mother's sister's son begot the children of Biong of the Lubelo clan. When they died or left the village, Lukondo became to all intents and purposes the sole lord. Later Denis, 4, came to the village, and if Lukondo left or died, Denis would probably control the Bulomani pawns.

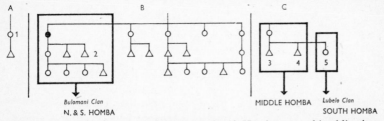

Fig. 16. Genealogy of members of Ket clan in South Homba: pawnship obligation

The Ket clan in S. Homba. Badiangu, 2, elected to remain in the village of his birth, partly because his father was a member of the Bulomani clan section there. He kept in close touch with his immediate clansmen in Kenge and Mbombe, villages to the south, went to their funerals and was called in to help settle disputes. The genealogy shows the tendency for fellow-clansmen to spread: he was the only one of the many descendants of his mother's mother to stay on in the vicinity of Middle Homba. He could trace no relationship to the other members of his clan-section.

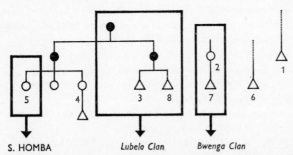

Fig. 17. Genealogy of Ngondu clan in South Homba: pawnship obligations

I have described already how, in spite of their disparate origin, the members of the Ngondu clan in South Homba behaved as a single unit in the village. Their pawnship status was as follows: the mother's mother of 3, Ngwe, had originally been paid as pawn to the Lubelo clan, but subsequently the Lubelo incurred a blood debt with the Ngondu, and released to them Ngwe's sister. Ngwe and Oscar were therefore always pawns of the Lubelo clan, but their classificatory sisters were free. In recognition of their good relations, the Ngondu gave one to the Lubelo in marriage, as a free woman. The other two were married in Bushongo, where most of their clansmen lived. Later in pursuance of revenge, South Homba village captured one, 5, and made her their pawn and village-wife. The Lubelo were good lords to Ngwe and Oscar; the latter got one of their other pawns for wife (Modestine of the Ket clan; see Case 3); Ngwe took a Lubelo girl who was daughter of a village-wife.

APPENDIX B

BIBLIOGRAPHIC REFERENCES

Biebuyck, D., and Douglas, M., *Congo Tribes and Parties*, 1961.

Bohannan, P., 'Some Principles of Exchange and Investment among the Tiv', *American Anthropologist*, 57, 1, 1955, pp. 60–70.

Brausch, G., 'Polyandrie et "Mariage Classique" chez les Bashi Lele', *Problèmes d'Afrique Centrale*, 4, 12, 1951.

Brown, H. D., 'The Nkumu of the Tumba', *Africa*, 1944.

Bryan, M. A., *The Bantu Languages of Africa*, 1959.

Bultot, F., *Saisons et Périodes Sèches et Pluvieuses au Congo Belge*, Brussels, 1954.

Burridge, K., *Mambu*, 1960.

Colson, E., *Marriage and the Family among the Plateau Tonga*, 1958.

Danks, Benjamin, 'On the Shell Money of New Britain', *Journal of the Anthropological Institute*, XVII, 1888.

De Beaucorps, R., *Les Bayansi de Bas-Kwilu*, 1933.

De Heusch, L., *La Symbolisme de l'inceste royale*, 1959.

De Jonghe, E., 'Formation récentes de sociétés secrètes au Congo Belge', *Africa*, IX, 1, 1936.

De Sousberghe, L., 'Etuis péniens ou Gaines de Chasteté chez le Bapende', *Africa*, XXIV, 3, 1954.

Douglas, M. M., 'Elicited Responses in Lele Language', *Kongo-Overzee*, XVI, 4, 1950, pp. 224–7.

—— 'A Form of Polyandry among the Lele of the Kasai', *Africa*, XXI, 1, 1951, pp. 1–12.

—— 'Alternate Generations among the Lele of the Kasai', *Africa*, XXII, 1, 1952, pp. 59–65.

—— 'Native Treatment of Leprosy in the Belgian Congo', *The Medical Press*, 17 March, 1954.

—— 'The Lele of the Kasai', ch. in *African Worlds*, edit. D. Forde, 1954.

—— 'Social and Religious Symbolism of the Lele of the Kasai', *Zaïre*, IX, 4, 1955, pp. 385–402.

—— 'The Environment of the Lele', *Zaïre*, IX, 8, 1955, pp. 802–23.

—— 'Animals in Lele Religious Symbolism', *Africa*, XXVII, 1, 1957, pp. 46–58.

—— 'The Pattern of Residence among the Lele', *Zaïre*, XI, 8, 1957, pp. 819–43.

—— 'Raffia Cloth Distribution in the Lele Economy', *Africa*, XXVIII, 2, 1958, pp. 109–22.

Douglas, M. M., 'Age-status among the Lele', *Zaïre*, XIII, 4, 1959, pp. 386–413.
—— 'The Lele' in *The Church and The Nations*, edit. A. Hastings, Sheed & Ward, 1959.
—— 'Blood Debts among the Lele', *Journal of Royal Anthropological Institute*, 90, 1, 1960.

In course of publication:
—— 'Lele Economy compared with the Bushon', for *Trade & Markets Symposium*, edit. J. Bohannan, Nat. Acad. Sci., Washington.
—— 'Techniques of Sorcery Control in C. Africa', for symposium on *Witchcraft*, edit. J. Middleton, Routledge.
Dubois, C., 'The Wealth Factor as an Integrative Factor in Tolowa-Tututui culture', *Essays presented to Kroeber*, 1936.
Eisenstadt, S. N., *From Generation to Generation*, 1956.
Gourou, P., *Atlas Générale du Congo Belge*, 1953.
—— *La Densité de la Population Rurale au Congo Belge*, 1955.
Hart, H., and Pilling, *The Tiwi of North Australia*, 1960.
Haveaux, G. L., 'La Tradition historique des Bapende Orientaux', *I.R.C.B.*, 1954.
Hoyt, E., *Primitive Trade*, 1924.
Marwick, M. G., 'Another Modern Anti-witchcraft Movement in East Central Africa', *Africa*, XX, 2, 1950.
—— 'Social Context of Cewa Witch Beliefs', *Africa*, XXII, 3, 1952.
Mayer, Philip, *Witches*. Inaugural Lecture at Rhodes University, 1954.
Menger, K., 'On the Origin of Money', *Economic Journal*, ii, 1892, pp. 239–477.
Mitchell, J. C., *The Yao Village*, 1957.
Nicolai, H., 'Problèmes du Kwango', *Bulletin de la Societé Belge*, Etudes Géographiques, 1956, 25, II.
Nicolai H. et Jacques, J., *La Transformation du Paysage Congolais par le Chemin de Fer* (BCK), 1954.
Oliver, D. L., *A Solomon Island Society*.
Pieraerts, 'Contribution à l'Etude de Deux Espèces de Raphia du Congo Belge', *La Revue Congolaise*, 1912.
Richards, A. I., *Land, Labour and Diet in Northern Rhodesia*, 1937.
—— 'A Modern Movement of Witchfinders', *Africa*, VIII, 4, 1935.
Simpson, H., *Land and Peoples of the Kasai*, 1911.
Soret, M., *Les Kongo Nord-Occidentaux*, 1959.
Southall, A., *Alur Society*, 1956.
Struyf, J., 'Migrations des Bapende et des Bambunda', *Congo*, i, 5, 1931.
—— 'Le Lukoshi', *Revue Missionnaire*, 7, 1933.

Struyf, J., 'Kahemba, Envahisseurs Badjok et Conquérants Balunda', *Zaïre*, 2, 1948.

Tempels, P., *Bantoe-Filosofie*, 1946.

Tew, M., 'Elicited Responses in Lele Language', *Kongo-Overzee*, 16, 4, 1950.

Torday, E., *On the Trail of the Bushongo*, 1925.

Torday, E. and Joyce, T. A., *Notes Ethnographiques sur les Peuples communément appelés Bakuba, Bushongo*, 1910.

Turner, V. W., *Schism and Continuity in an African Society*, 1957.

—— 'Spatial Separation of the Generations in Ndembu Village Structure', *Africa*, XXV, 2, 1955.

Unwin, A. H., *West African Forests and Forestry*.

Vandenplas, A., 'La Pluie au Congo Belge', *Bulletin Agricole du Congo Belge*, XXXIV, 1943.

—— *La Température au Congo Belge*, 1947.

—— 'La Radiation, l'Insolation et la Nébulosité au Congo Belge', *Bulletin Agric. du Congo Belge*, 1948.

Vansina, J., 'Les Valeurs Culturelles des Bushong', *Zaïre*, 9, 1954.

—— 'Initiation Rituals of the Bushong', *Africa*, XXV, 2, 1955.

—— 'L'Etat Kuba dans le Cadre des Institutions Politiques Africaines', *Zaïre*, 11, 5, 1957.

—— 'Migrations dans la Province du Kasai', *Zaïre*, 1959.

—— 'Miko mi Yool: une Association Religieuse Kuba', *Aequatoria*, 22, 2 and 3, 1959.

Van Wing, J., *Etudes Bakongo*, 2nd edit., 1959.

Verhulpen, *Baluba et Balubaïsés*.

Von Wissman, H., *My Second Journey through the Equatorial Africa*, 1886–7, 1891.

Weekx, G., 'Ambundu', *Congo*, 1, 4, 1937.

White, C. M. N., 'Factors in the Social Organisation of the Luvale', *African Studies*, 14, 3, 1955.

INDEX

Printed by Ebenezer Baylis and Son, Ltd.
The Trinity Press, Worcester
and London